NICAEA:
A BYZANTINE CAPITAL AND ITS PRAISES

Nicaea:
A Byzantine Capital and Its Praises

With the Speeches of

Theodore Laskaris
In Praise of the Great City of Nicaea

and

Theodore Metochites
Nicene Oration

by

CLIVE FOSS

with the collaboration of
JACOB TULCHIN

Archbishop Iakovos Library of
Ecclesiastical and Historical Sources Number 21

Hellenic College Press
Brookline, Massachusetts

© Hellenic College Press 1996
Published by Hellenic College Press
50 Goddard Avenue
Brookline, MA 02146

All rights reserved. No part of this publication may be reproduced, stored in a retrieval system, or transmitted in any form by any means—electronic, mechanical, photocopy, recording, or any other—without the written permission of the publisher, the only exception being brief quotations that appear in printed reviews.

Library of Congress Cataloging–in–Publication Data

Foss, Clive.
Nicaea: a Byzantine capital and its praises: with speeches of Theodore Laskaris, In praise of the great city of Nicaea, and, Theodore Metochites, Nicene oration / by Clive Foss, with the collaboration of Jacob Tulchin.
p. cm. — (Archbishop Iakovos library of ecclesiastical and historical sources; no. 21)
Includes bibliographical references and index.
ISBN 0-917653-48-3 (pbk.)
1. Byzantine Empire—Civilization. 2. Iznik (Turkey)—Antiquities, Byzantine. 3. Byzantine Empire—Capital and capitol—History. I. Tulchin, Jacob. II. Theodore II Laskaris, Emperor of Nicaea, 1222-1258. Enkomion eis ten megalopolin Nikaian. English & Greek. III. Metochites, Theodoros, d. 1332. Nikaeus. English & Greek. IV. Title. V. Series.
DF626.F67 1996
949.5—dc20

96-31951
CIP

Contents

	Preface	vii
	Introduction	1
1.	Late Antiquity	5
2.	The Dark Ages	17
3.	Recovery and Prosperity: Ninth-Eleventh Centuries	29
4.	The First Turkish Period	41
5.	The First Crusade	45
6.	The Age of the Komnenoi	51
7.	Nicaea as Capital: The Reign of Theodore Laskaris	57
8.	Nicaea under John Vatatzes and Theodore II: The Church and the Revival of Learning	65
9.	The Return to Constantinople and the Last Byzantine Phase: 1258-1331	75
10.	The Walls of the City	89
11.	The Churches and Other Buildings	97
12.	Introduction to the Speeches	123

Θεοδώρου Δούκα τοῦ Λάσκαρι
ἐγκώμιον εἰς τὴν μεγαλόπολιν Νίκαιαν   132
Theodore Doukas Laskaris:
In Praise of the Great City of Nicaea   133
Commentary on Laskaris   155

Θεοδόρου Μετοχίτου: Νικαεὺς   164
Theodore Metochites:
Nicene Oration   165
Commentary on Metochites   197

Appendix: The Seljuk "Palace"   204
Bibliography
   Sources   207
   Modern Works   211
Index   217
Figures

Preface

Nicaea was already large, important and over five hundred years old when Constantine chose it for the general meeting of the bishops of the Church in 325. The Council of Nicaea, the first of the ecumenical councils, brought eternal renown to the city which was its host, though few, perhaps, who recite the Nicene Creed composed there associate it with a real place, with a long history and many surviving buildings.

The age between Constantine and the invasions of the seventh century which marked the end of Antiquity was a flourishing time for Nicaea as it was for most cities of the eastern Empire. The following chaos of the Dark Ages brought an inevitable decline, but the powerful walls erected against a previous time of turmoil provided an impregnable bulwark and made the city a major base of army and administration in the Middle Ages. After two centuries of peaceful prosperity, it slipped into the hands of the Turks, only to be regained for Christendom by the First Crusade in a long and famous siege, the only time in its history that Nicaea succumbed to direct assault.

The next moment of glory, and the one which forms the main subject of this work, arrived with the catastrophe of 1204 when another crusade conquered Constantinople and drove the Empire into exile. Emperor and Church took refuge in Nicaea, which remained the center of a flourishing state for over half a century. This was an active time with much building in the city and region as the foundations were laid for a state powerful enough to recapture the lost capital in 1261. After fulfilling its role as protector and nourisher of the Empire, Nicaea gradually faded until the Ottoman Turks brought it into a new age in 1330.

Like most large cities, Nicaea had been the subject of formal praises in written and spoken works. Most are now fragments, but sufficient to show that the local piety represented by the Council was greatly stressed along with the normal subjects of encomia. It remained for the thirteenth century to produce two long speeches of praise which describe all the glories of the city, physical and spiritual, at a time when it was the focus of State and Church, or when those days were still a living memory. As the longest surviving documents about the city, they deserve more attention than they have received; hence the present volume, which includes their texts with a translation, commentary, and historical introduction. Actually, what was intended as an introduction has turned into a history of the city from the third to the fourteenth century, and is now far longer than the speeches.

The difficult language of these texts has kept them from being better known, for they are written in an exceptionally ornate style rendered more complex by the great learning of the authors. The first is the work of an imperial prince, Theodore Laskaris, who was himself born in the city he praises, on the day his father, John Vatatzes, became emperor, in 1222, and there received his education. His skills in science and philosophy and his zeal for eloquence produced a style which favors the abstract and expresses it in high-flown rhetoric. His words nevertheless create an impression of the city, and notably of its intellectual life, during the reign of Vatatzes, before whom the speech was delivered.

Theodore Metochites composed the other speech when he was only twenty, as an address to another emperor, Andronikos II, in 1290. It was an instant success; the young orator was taken into imperial service and soon rose to become the leading statesman of his day, and a man of immense erudition. This speech, which abounds in description and concrete detail, gives a vivid image of the city and country in a language somewhat less florid than that of Laskaris.

This work was originally intended to put the difficult Greek of these speeches into a comprehensible English, to make them available for use as an historical source. To accomplish that, I turned to my old friend Jacob Tulchin whose knowledge of classical Greek is perhaps superior to that of the authors at hand, and who is familiar with all things Byzantine. He willingly agreed to help cut through the seemingly impenetrable jungle of this rhetoric and produced a draft translation of both speeches. Together, we spent innumerable hours revising, trying to capture the meaning of the most elusive phrase, and to produce a result which would make sense. The translations, therefore, are a collaboration, with the main burden borne by Mr. Tulchin. The rest is my responsibility alone.

The speeches could not have been translated at all without a reliable text. We are, therefore, especially grateful to Dr. Sophia Georgiopoulou for allowing us to reproduce her text of the speech of Laskaris. She will publish it with full critical apparatus in her study of the prince and his works

The language posed a problem which took an exceptionally long time to solve. It was compounded by the fame of the city itself, for a horde of late antique and Byzantine writers had occasion to mention Nicaea, if only *en passant,* in reference to the Council. A great deal of material, therefore, had to be sifted before a coherent history could be written. This work was greatly expedited by Dr. Friedrich Hild of the Tabula Imperii Byzantini in Vienna, who generously sent copies of their rich file of references. These provided the basis for the narrative; others, mainly relating to the buildings, were added as the work progressed.

Preface

Most Greek names have been strictly transliterated, but a few – the latinized "Nicaea" most prominent among them – have been left in forms which are most familiar to the English-speaking reader.

In the course of composition, I have naturally incurred many obligations, a pleasure to recall and acknowledge. Father Nomikos Vaporis long since expressed interest in the project and kindly accepted it for publication. Professor Cyril Mango willingly read large sections of the manuscript and saved it from many omissions and errors. Professor Ihor Sevcenko made some valuable suggestions when this project was first conceived. Eugenia Petrides worked through the translations with great care, suggesting numerous improvements. Helene Roberts of the Fogg Art Museum provided rare photos of the Church of the Dormition from the A. Kingsley Porter Collection. Humaira Ahmad of All Souls College, Oxford, cheerfully typed the difficult manuscript of the translations and Peter Fraser of the same institution helpfully recommended an efficient assistant, Lindsay Gee. Professor Robert Renehan patiently answered inquiries and provided helpful references, and Eva Chou read the penultimate version of the text with careful attention to matters editorial and idiomatic. My sincere thanks to all.

Clive Foss
Cambridge, Mass.

Introduction

Tradition maintained that the founders of Nicaea were the Greek gods Dionysos and Herakles, a suitably august beginning for a great city; but history more prosaically records that Antigonos first established it and that Lysimachos refounded it around 300 B.C., giving it the name of his wife, which it has borne ever since. Not long after, around 281 B.C., it became subject to the kings of Bithynia, who ruled it until the last of their line bequeathed his kingdom to Rome in 74 B.C. Little is recorded of the city's history in the Hellenistic period.

Nicaea grew and flourished under the Romans because of the abundant resources of its large and fertile territory, which stretched east to the Sangarios, and of the lake which came up to its walls; and especially from its strategic location on the natural route which became the main Roman highway across Asia Minor. The prosperity thus achieved is reflected in the abundant and diverse coinage which the city struck in great quantity through the middle of the third century. In the time of Augustus, according to Strabo, Nicaea was a fine city, rectangular in shape and surrounded by walls 16 stadia (2 miles) long; it had such a regular plan that it was possible to see the four gates from a stone set in the middle of the Gymnasium. To this day, Nicaea possesses two main streets which meet at a right angle in the centre of the city, a place no longer marked by a gymnasium, but by the Church of Hagia Sophia, converted into a mosque by the first Ottoman conquerors of the city.

Roman emperors noticed Nicaea, and adorned it: Augustus allowed its citizens to build a temple to worship him together with the goddess Rome; Vespasian erected two triumphal arches where city gates still stand; and Hadrian contributed to a major rebuilding after a devastating earthquake in 120, a recurrent danger from which the city has constantly suffered. Some curious details come from the letters of the younger Pliny who was governor of Bithynia in 110-112. He revealed that prisoners condemned to a swift death in the arena or a slow one in the mines, were allowed in Nicaea to become public slaves instead, an example of remarkable local lenience. He also had to deal with an extreme case of local fiscal irresponsibility. The Nicaeans, it seems, had spent more than ten million sesterces on a theatre, still unfinished, which they had built in such an unsuitable location that it had begun to sink into the ground and its fabric had cracked. Pliny enquired whether the project should be abandoned or demolished, noting that many citizens had promised lavish additions to it. At the same time, the city had rebuilt its gymnasium, which had been destroyed by fire, but (according to a rival architect) it was so badly planned that its walls, though massive, would not be able to support the weight of a roof. Trajan left the decision in these cases to Pliny, urging him to get the buildings finished, for the Greeks were extremely fond of gymnasia.

The correspondence between Trajan and Pliny is famous for its mention of the Christians, whose community was thriving in Bithynia. Although these letters make no specific reference to Nicaea, an apocryphal tradition traces the origins of the local church back to the first century. The apostle Andrew himself is reputed to have been its founder and to have spent time in the city, working miracles, making converts, and ordaining the first local bishop. Although no authentic record of Antiquity associates the Apostle with the city, the tradition can be traced back to the fourth century, and may be much earlier. Since it developed into a circumstantial narrative in the eighth century, it will be discussed below in the context of the Dark Ages. Evidence of a more substantial kind also exists, however, to witness the presence of the early church. A group of local tombstones contains Christian language which has been interpreted as indicating the late third century. These inscriptions, which thus antedate the conversion of Constantine and provide the first direct record of the Christian community, also reveal the close integration of the Christians into the larger pagan society.

In general, the first three centuries of Roman rule passed in a peace so profound that history has few events to record. The city, like most others of any size, celebrated games and festivals, and was adorned with imposing public buildings. Sources mention the theatre and gymnasium, as well as the walls, the temple of Augustus and Rome, and a temple of Apollo outside the walls; many others, of course, would have existed. The city was normally administered by a council and municipal officials, with the people possessing only nominal power. As in many places, there was a good deal of factional strife, but the details are unknown. Another kind of quarrel, however, was renowned: the incessant rivalry between Nicaea and Nicomedia, the two greatest cities of the province. Bitter feelings were expressed in a constant strife over titles and rank. Nicomedia, as the metropolis of the province and seat of an imperial temple, had qualifications to which Nicaea could not aspire, but each could claim to be 'first city' of the province, and encourage the strong feelings of their citizens toward the rival. At the end of the first century, Dio Chrysostom, a noted orator and native of the region, gave a surviving speech to reconcile the two, but his efforts were in vain, and the rivalry long continued.

In spite of its size and wealth, Roman Nicaea has left few remains. Parts of the theatre survive, and the triumphal arches of Vespasian, rebuilt by Hadrian, still stand on the main roads to the city. Recent excavations have revealed a good deal about the construction and decor of the theatre, but the great cracks which Pliny mentioned are nowhere evident in the surviving remains. The ancient walls and other public buildings, however, have all disappeared, leaving only scattered traces within and outside the city. Most prominent among them is a tall obelisk in the necropolis north of the city, the funerary monument of a Roman of the second century.[1]

NOTES

[1] Eyice (1988) presents a general history. For the ancient city, see the detailed survey of Ruge (1936) with full references, and, for the monuments, Schneider (1943). Excavations of the theatre are reported in Yalman (1981, 1991); see also the summary in *AS* 35 (1985) 197f., most useful for the Roman remains. For the Christian inscriptions, see Johnson (1984) 15-58, 139f, and for the territory of Nicaea, with its settlements and topography, the excellent survey of S. Sahin in *INikaia* 2.1.3.-44. For the rivalry with Nicomedia, see Robert (1977).

1. Late Antiquity

After centuries of peaceful prosperity, Nicaea brusquely entered a new age in the late third century, when changed circumstances caused the city to be surrounded by a powerful ring of walls and to assume an appearance which would characterise it through all subsequent history. During the chaotic reign of Emperor Valerian (253-260), an army of Goths from southern Russia descended on the peaceful and unprotected cities of northwest Asia Minor and spread devastation throughout the country. The inhabitants of Nicaea and Nicomedia fled on their approach, leaving a huge booty to the pleasantly surprised barbarians, who, after they had failed to advance much farther, revisited the two great cities and burned them before returning home to plan further attacks.[1]

This devastation, no doubt accompanied by anticipation of more of the same, provoked the construction of a formidable defensive rampart. The new walls, the earliest and finest of late antique Asia Minor, became a major feature of the city which they protected for over a thousand years. Later writers about Nicaea rarely fail to mention them, and they became, as shall be seen, the subject of especial praise in the thirteenth century and before. The walls had the signal honour of being figured on the coins of Gallienus (253-268), who began their construction, and of the usurpers Macrianus II and Quietus (260-261). Surviving inscriptions show that they were finished by Claudius Gothicus (268-270), much of whose work still stands amid the changes of a millennium of constant use. In their original state, the walls were five kilometres long and stood about nine meters high; they had about eighty towers which rose to thirteen meters, and were surrounded by a moat. The curtain was built of rubble reinforced by bands of brick, while the towers were faced entirely in brick. Its survival into modern times shows that the circuit was built with great strength and skill; it served as a model for later fortifications (those of Constantinople doubtless reflect its influence) and were still powerful enough to impress the Crusaders eight hundred years after they were built.[2]

The new age also brought a serious attempt to impose a religious conformity in which the official cults would triumph over the growing Christian church. The Great Persecution, launched by Diocletian and continued by his successors of the early fourth century, raged violently at Nicomedia, but was felt less severely at Nicaea. Nevertheless, the local church saw the martyrdom of several saints who were long to be of importance to the city. The accounts of their lives, though often lacking in substantive information, are of considerable interest as reflections of local conditions and of the mentality of the time.

The earliest of the local saints, Tryphon, is supposed to have been a victim of the persecutions of Decius (249-251). According to the rather fabulous account of his life, the young Tryphon was herding geese near his native village when he was discovered by imperial troops. They had been sent to scour the empire for him, for he alone was reputed to have the power of curing the emperor's daughter, who was possessed by a demon. After succeeding in this task, Tryphon returned in peace to his home until the persecutions of Decius broke out. He was then brought before the governor in Nicaea, refused to abjure Christianity, and was finally executed after terrible tortures. Such a narrative might seem a mere fable, but the life, though containing elements copied from lives of less obscure saints, manifests much authentic language of Late Antiquity, and the cult of Tryphon is early and spread far. A monastery was dedicated to him in the capital in the late fifth century, then other churches, one of them built by Emperor Justinian. The saint even gave his name to a peninsula on the Gulf of Nicomedia.

Tryphon's fame derived from his powers and a miracle. He could clear fields, vineyards, and orchards infested by reptiles or insects when a special service was celebrated and oil from his lamp was sprinkled on the land. A famous miracle took place every year in Nicaea at the saint's main church. The lilies kept by the lamp which lit the martyr's image blossomed in midwinter, and, when they were cut, they bloomed again out of season. The miracle is described in the encomium on the saint written by the emperor Theodore Laskaris (1254-1258), who had witnessed it. He stressed that it took place in public, in the church, not in some hidden place. Since Theodore ruled a state whose patriarch resided at Nicaea, it was especially apt that he should praise the local saint, who in his day was the patron saint of the city, but he was not the first, for Leo the Wise (886-912) had also written an encomium.[3] The importance of the cult will be considered again in the context of the thirteenth century.

The other local saints are far more shadowy. Neophytos, who is supposed to have been the first holy man to frequent the Bithynian Olympos, returned to Nicaea during the Great Persecution. There, as punishment for his unassailable Christianity, he was baked in an oven for three days, then (when that failed to have the desired effect) thrown to wild beasts who would have nothing to do with him, and finally despatched by the troops. His body was recovered, and a church built in his honor. His life contains some early praises of Nicaea, to which this account will return.[4] The fate of his contemporary, the clothes-dealer Eustathios, was similar. After refusing to recant, and suffering horrible tortures as a result, he was executed outside the city. In his final prayer, he invoked a blessing on the fisherman he saw in the lake, an authentic local touch.[5] The pious doctor, Diomedes, on the other hand, died peacefully before the imperial troops could arrest him; he later became the patron saint of Nicomedia.[6] Less fortunate were the lady saints, Theodote, who was burned alive with her sons, and Antonia, who resisted roasting on a grill only to be thrown into the lake in a sack.[7] Bassos, who appears to have fallen victim to the same persecution, is equally obscure, but had sufficient fame to become the subject of a homily by John Chrysostom.[8] Whatever the merits of their biographies, all these saints found a place in the calendar of the Orthodox Church, and in the later life of the city.

The church triumphed over its persecutors to rise to supremacy under the patronage of Constantine. Success brought many problems into the open, notably those of heresy, and the teachings of Arius caused such widespread disturbance that Constantine resolved to settle the doctrinal questions by a synod of bishops, the First Ecumenical Council. He called the fathers to meet in Nicaea in 325, thereby granting the city an immortal fame. The Council had originally been summoned to meet at Ankyra, but Constantine changed the venue so that he could himself easily attend, for Nicaea was close to his residence at Nicomedia. Other reasons for the change have also been suggested: a real or threatened rebellion in support of the deposed emperor Licinius which obliged Constantine to stay near his capital; and a desire to thwart the ambitions of the bishop of Nicomedia, Eusebios, who was a leader of the Arians. It is evident that Constantine could have chosen Nicomedia had his own convenience been the prime concern. The decision to meet in Nicaea, therefore, can be seen both as a rebuke to Eusebios, and as another stage in the perennial rivalry between the two great cities.[9]

The doctrinal issues which occupied the Council and their resolution are known to practically everyone familiar with Christianity: orthodoxy was established and the creed still recited was drafted. These matters will not be repeated here. Unfortunately, no detailed account of the proceedings of the Council has survived, but the biography of Constantine by Eusebios provides a few glimpses of the events. When Constantine summoned the bishops, he allowed them to use the imperial post, so that as many as possible could attend; according to a tradition which cannot be verified, 318 bishops were present. Whatever their number, they could meet in a single 'house of prayer' within the imperial palace.

On the last day of Council, when the disputed questions had been settled, the bishops all assembled in the central and largest room of the palace, where benches were disposed along the sides. The Emperor advanced to the head of the room, sat on a golden throne, and nodded to the bishops to be seated. He then gave a speech and commenced the discussions which led to unanimity on the new definition of the faith and of the means of calculating Easter. It was

25 August 325; the Council had completed its business in exactly three months. The end of the Council coincided with the twentieth anniversary of Constantine's accession to power, an occasion for festivities and a great banquet in the palace. The celebrations were not open to the public; troops with drawn swords guarded the entrance as the bishops filed into the inner chamber where the emperor was reclining at dinner.[10]

The description of the Council gives a faint impression of the splendor of the occasion and the magnificence of the palace which stood in Nicaea. But the impression alone must suffice, for no remains are standing, nor has the location of the palace or its 'house of prayer' ever been established. In later ages, Nicaea contained a church which was known as the site of the Council; it will be considered below.

The triumphant orthodoxy of the council was somewhat marred by the activities of Theognis, bishop of Nicaea, a city which later took great pride in its role in establishing the orthodox faith. As an adherent of Arius, he refused to accept the Nicene creed, and was accordingly sent into exile. Three years later, he recanted and was restored to his see, but his conversion was superficial, for he proceeded to become a leader of the Arian party against Athanasios. After the death of Constantine, he became a major supporter of the effort to restore Arianism which was led by his neighbor Eusebios of Nicomedia, but he soon vanished from history.[11] Equally disturbing to the dignity of the city were the actions of the patron of the Council, for Constantine did not hesitate to despoil Nicaea of statues to adorn the hippodrome of his new capital.[12]

Orthodoxy, here as elsewhere, had rivals in many sects beside the Arians. An undated late antique inscription adorned the tomb of a certain 'divine-minded' Gerontion, who was buried together with his wife and three associates. It proclaimed him as the 'father of the church of the Pious' and its language suggests that the others were fellow sectaries. Arrogation of such a name for a church indicates heterodoxy and suggests the presence of the Novatians, a puritanical sect for whom such a title would be natural. Their activities are well attested in the region.[13]

The fame of the local church did not stop Nicaea from being a centre of pagan learning during these years. When the great sophist Libanios was driven from Constantinople by his rivals in 342, Nicaea, the 'city of Dionysos,' as he called it, received him gladly, after extending an invitation by means of honorary decrees. Libanios stayed there and taught for some time until called to Nicomedia by the governor, who offered him an official position.[14] Libanios cherished the memory of the city which, as he later wrote, had received him in her embrace, and long remained in contact with friends there. Most notable among them was Aristainetos, a leading member of the local aristocracy, who had studied in Athens, learned his Plato well, and retained an interest in letters. He sent, or promised to send, books to Libanios. His distinction caused imperial ministers to offer him high posts, but he was so fond of his native city that he would not consider leaving. Finally, he was persuaded to accept the governorship of the diocese Pietas, recently named after the wife of Constantine II, and there soon met his death, as he was caught in the dreadful earthquake which ruined Nicomedia in 358. Like many intellectuals of the time, he was a pagan.

Correspondence between Libanios and Aristainetos was sometimes forwarded by Klematios, a close friend of the sophist, who held the useful office of *agens in rebus,* or imperial courier. This enabled him to travel frequently; on one occasion, he stayed in Nicaea on his way from Rome to the Persian frontier, and was doubtless a frequent visitor to the city. After the death of Aristainetos, his relative Entrechios took over responsibility for his family. He, also, had studied in Athens and was a correspondent of Libanios. At an early age, he became successively governor of Palestine and Pisidia, but retired from public service on the death of Julian, whom he had known personally. In 388, he was living as a private citizen in Nicaea.[15] These are the only individuals who appear in the history of late Antique Nicaea. They give the impression of a cultivated pagan aristocracy, such as would have been found in any of the great cities of the Empire. The sources, however, do not allow its size or fortunes to be traced.

In the middle of the fourth century, Nicaea was a splendid city, deserving of formal praises, the first of a long series which reflects admiration of its nature and buildings through the end of the Byzantine period. An anonymous work, the *Expositio totius orbis et gentium,* written in about 350, thus described the city:

> Et Nicaeae quidem civitatis dispositionem difficile est alibi invenire; regulam autem putat aliquis impositam esse omni civitati propter aequalitatem et formositatem, ita ut omnia aedificiorum culmina aequali decorata libramine splendidum intuentibus praebere videantur adspectum; et est in omnibus ornata et constans.
>
> It is difficult to find elsewhere a city plan like that of Nicaea; one would think it a model set for all cities on account of its regularity and beauty, which are such that the tops of all its buildings, adorned with an equal symmetry, appear to offer a splendid view to the beholder. It is decorated and harmonious in every respect.[16]

The regularity here praised no doubt reflected the street pattern as well as the height and arrangement of the buildings. Hellenistic and Roman Nicaea had been laid out with two main streets intersecting at the centre, where they were probably crowned by a double triumphal arch. A late antique inscription mentions a stone tetrapylon, that is, a four-sided arch of the kind usually erected at the junction of main streets. Such structures were especially congenial to the regular planning of Late Antiquity, and frequently served to mark the centre of a city. This was probably the case at Nicaea, although the location of the arch is not specified. Here, as elsewhere, the arch, a prominent landmark, apparently gave its name to a district of the city.[17]

At this time, Nicaea almost became the site of another council of the church. When a synod was called to meet in Nicomedia in 358, that city was destroyed by a devastating earthquake and the bishops assembled instead at Nicaea. This was done on the advice of Saint Basil, who thought that the questions in dispute should be settled in the city where they had first been raised. The Emperor, however, decided otherwise because of the recent earthquake in the province, and the synod eventually met in Seleucia in Cilicia.[18]

Such fears were justified all too soon. In 363, the greater part of Nicaea was destroyed by an earthquake, and another disaster, apparently on a larger scale, struck five years later.[19] At that time, large numbers of people, including most government officials, were killed, and the beauty of the city destroyed, according to Gregory the Theologian. His brother, Kaisarios, a successful doctor who had risen high in the imperial administration, was one of those fortunate to survive the quake, though he died of disease soon after.[20] It is likely that these blows had a severe affect on the city, perhaps analogous to the devastation of 358, from which Nicomedia never really recovered. In both cities, decline would have been accentuated by the foundation of Constantinople, which drew away much of the resources and population of the area. Nicaea nevertheless continued as an important city as long as it was part of a Christian state.

Kaisarios, who barely survived the quake of 368, filled offices which reveal another aspect of the city's importance. He was the chief imperial tax collector in Bithynia, and was in charge of the local treasury. This establishment, one of a series set up in the provinces by Diocletian, was the repository for the bullion, coins and other goods collected as taxes. It in turn provided the precious metals which were struck into coins at the local or nearby mint. In this case, the mint was in Nicomedia. Distribution of mint and treasury between the two cities may be yet another reflection of their ancient rivalry. In any case, location of the treasury at Nicaea clearly shows that the city played a significant role in the imperial administrative structure.[21]

Because of its location on the main highway to the east, Nicaea became the seat of major events. The emperor Julian passed through it in 362 on the way to his ill-fated Persian expedition, and two years later the army returned and stopped there after the sudden death of Jovian, in order to select a new Emperor. The civil and military authorities, after some discussion, chose

Valentinian, who was summoned from Ankyra. On 25 February 364, he arrived and addressed the whole army assembled in its camp, probably outside the walls. After a speech filled with encouragement and promises, he was escorted to the royal palace in the city.[22]

Valentinian soon appointed his brother Valens to rule the east, but he was barely installed when he had to face the revolt of Julian's relative Prokopios, who achieved rapid success in and around the capital in 365. His forces, advancing from Helenopolis on the gulf, swiftly and unexpectedly seized Nicaea and drove off the emperor's attempt to recapture it. In fact, the garrison of Nicaea almost succeeded in capturing Valens as he was besieging Chalcedon, but he managed to escape to the east and regroup his forces. Later, when Prokopios gained control of Kyzikos, he sent its commander Serenianus, count of the domestic troops, to Nicaea to be imprisoned. In the following year, when Prokopios was defeated and executed, his relative Marcellus, the commander at Nicaea, executed Serenianus, who had been held in the palace. According to another account, Prokopios took refuge in Nicaea after his defeat, and was there betrayed by Florentius, whom he had put in charge of the city.[23] In any case, it is apparent that Nicaea was an important fortress and base of operations for Prokopios, as it was to be for many others.

The reign of Valens saw a revival of Arianism and conflict within the Church. One of the greatest champions of orthodoxy was Saint Basil, whose accomplishments, according to a late and perhaps legendary tradition, included a miracle at Nicaea. The story relates that Valens had been met at Nicaea by a delegation of Arians who had persuaded him to turn the local cathedral over to them. Basil heard the protests of the orthodox as he passed through the city, then persuaded the emperor to allow him to judge the case. The church was sealed and both parties retired to pray; according to agreement, the church was to belong to whichever of them could cause its doors to open. While the Arians prayed in vain, Basil and the orthodox retired outside the city to the Church of Saint Diomedes, where they spent the night in prayer. In the morning, both parties entered the narthex of the cathedral. After the Arians failed to budge the door, Basil made the sign of the cross on it and prayed; the door opened if its own accord, and the church reverted to the orthodox. Valens, the writer adds, was not cured of heresy, but was burned in Thrace (at the battle of Adrianople) before entering a more permanent fire.[24]

Whatever the merits of this apocryphal account, it does record the existence of a Church of Saint Diomedes outside the walls, and the events it describes were long celebrated by the Orthodox Church every 19 January. Another incidental association of Saint Basil with the city is more authentic. In 375, he confided a letter which he had written to the bishop of Samosata to the care of the *peraequator* of Nicaea. The letter thus attests the existence of such a local official, responsible for the revision of the census on which taxes were based.[25]

Like a few other places on the main highway, Nicaea gained a transitory importance in the late fourth and early fifth century when the imperial court was in the habit of forsaking the heat and humidity of the capital for the fresher upland plains of Ankyra during the summer. The city was one of the favored stopping points, probably because of its excellent location and imperial palace. Laws issued from there in 398 and 405 attest the imperial passage.[26]

The history of the city in the fifth century is relatively obscure, with an occasional mention revealing something of the church and of the continuing military role. The pious patriarch Attikos (406-425) sent 300 gold solidi to Kalliopios, a priest of Nicaea. He wrote that he had heard of 10,000 people in the city who needed charity (not a precise amount, as he noted, but indicative of a multitude), and asked the priest to distribute the money not only to beggars who lived on charity, but to those who were ashamed to beg, and make no distinction of religion – all, whether they followed or opposed the Patriarch, were to benefit.[27] This brief hint of a local situation suggests that the city had a large population (perhaps swollen by immigration from the countryside) which put a strain on its resources, and that among them were a number of heretics or pagans. The sum which the Patriarch sent at first seems small for a myriad of poor, but it was actually quite substantial, for one gold piece would pay a worker for a month or more; three hundred of them could therefore relieve the distress of a large number.[28]

In the middle of the century, Nicaea barely missed becoming the site of another ecumenical council. The emperor Marcian called one to meet there, but then moved it to Chalcedon, so that he could conveniently be present.[29] At that Council, the ancient rivalry between Nicaea and Nicomedia flared up and consumed a whole day of the proceedings. Debate was opened by Eunomios of Nicomedia. He claimed that Anastasios of Nicaea had excommunicated priests of Basilinopolis who were subject to the jurisdiction of Nicomedia. Anastasios replied that when Julian "or someone before him" had raised Basilinopolis to municipal status, he had taken councillors from Nicaea and provided that new ones were to be enrolled from the same source, if their numbers ever fell below the norm. Basilinopolis, he therefore maintained, should be subject to Nicaea. He cited a letter of John Chrysostom (it is known from no other source) in support of his claim. The discussion soon became heated, with the bishops calling each other liars. When the Council investigated, they found that Valens and Valentinian had granted Nicaea the rank of Metropolis (an honor formerly reserved to Nicomedia, the capital of the civil province), but also that Valentinian had specifically ordered that the promotion of Nicaea should not damage the rights of Nicomedia. Nicaea had thus become a metropolis of second, and purely honorary rank. The Council concluded in favor of Nicomedia, saying that it was the older and true metropolis, and that Nicaea should have the rank of metropolis, but be above other bishoprics in honor only.[30] In these debates, Antiquity was still alive in a Christian setting, for the intense rivalry between the two cities was ancient, and destined long to endure.

The city appears in the history of the late fifth century because of its association with a series of revolts. In 476, during the brief rise of Basiliskos to supreme power, he sent his nephew and chief general, Armatos, against the legitimate emperor, Zeno. When they met at Nicaea, Zeno bribed his opponent with gifts and the rank of Caesar for his son. Armatos thereupon changed sides, and Zeno was restored to power; but the general's treachery was rewarded with execution, and his son was made a priest.[31] Five years later, the Isaurian general Illos put down the revolt of Marcian, who believed he had a claim to the throne. Then, fearing the hostility of the population of the capital toward his semibarbarous troops, he withdrew to spend the winter in Nicaea.[32] Finally, in 498, Longinos the Isaurian led an unsuccessful revolt against Anastasios. When he failed and the emperor's victory ended the period of Isaurian supremacy, he was tortured and executed in Nicaea.[33] Although these events seem not to have effected the city directly, they clearly show its importance as the greatest fortress in the vicinity of the capital.

In the sixth century, the great highway across Anatolia guaranteed a continuing importance to Nicaea. This was the place where ambassadors from the king of Persia were met and entertained, probably in the royal palace which had stood since the time of Constantine.[34] Likewise, couriers of the imperial post passed through so often that they had their own residence and bath in the city, which was an important centre of communications.[35] By the time of Justinian, however, Nicaea was partially in decay, the result, no doubt, of the frequent earthquakes, as well as a natural consequence of the general diminution of municipal resources, and of the growth of Constantinople. The aqueduct, the palace, and the establishments of the post – essential elements of the urban landscape – had all fallen into ruin, a situation which implies a serious decline in civic life. Justinian, who was especially concerned with maintaining the post and road system, restored all these buildings, and also built a long and substantial bridge west of the city over a stream which had carried away the earlier, smaller structure.[36] Unfortunately, another quake struck in 557 and caused considerable destruction, but no later repairs are attested.[37]

Justinian also built churches and monasteries on the city, none of which has certainly survived, but the two most important churches which lasted into modern times, the Dormition and Hagia Sophia, may have been monuments of this period. Neither is securely dated, but the former has been attributed to the late sixth century on convincing grounds, while Hagia Sophia is generally agreed to date from the fifth-sixth centuries. Both will be discussed in some detail below.

The archaeological record of Late Antiquity is scattered. It contains, of course, the massive fortifications, among the finest of their day anywhere in the Empire, as well as the churches just mentioned. It also includes a notable monument of the first period of official Christianity, a subterranean vaulted tomb discovered in the necropolis three miles northeast of the city. This structure of brick and rubble contained a rectangular burial chamber whose two graves had been looted. Its most striking feature was the brightly colored and well-preserved covering of frescoes which adorned the walls and ceiling. In addition to geometric designs, they portrayed scenes of Paradise, with flowers, peacocks and a Christogram. The style of the frescoes, which are an outstanding example of their kind, indicates the mid-fourth century.[38] Beside these few monuments, the material record is virtually silent, with no trace of civic buildings or residences.

The archaeology may be supplemented to some extent by evidence from epigraphy, consisting of several tombstones found in and around the city. The most valuable, already mentioned, reveal the existence of a triumphal arch and a religious sect. Others illustrate both ecclesiastical and civic life. They include verses which proclaim the piety of a nun, thus confirming the existence of the nunnery which Justinian built or restored; the tomb of a *dekanos* or undertaker; and celebrate the cleaning of a baptistery (or perhaps a tomb). They indicate two common occupations, a baker and a gardener; mention foreigners (an Egyptian, and a family of Italians); and reflect the role of the military in a city on a main highway. The army is represented in tombs of an ex-*protector*, member of the corps from which commanders were drawn, of a *primicerius,* who was probably an official of this corps, and of a German, Walter, whose bilingual epitaph no doubt attests the presence of barbarians recruited into the imperial forces. The inscriptions also give the names of some villages of the surrounding countryside and provide the earliest evidence for the local Jewish community and, as already considered, for the earliest Christians.[39]

The scattered sources for the period do not allow a detailed image of the city to be reconstructed, but they offer indications of its nature, society and role in the empire. The city was evidently large and well-built: its regular street plan featured two boulevards which crossed in the centre where they were covered by an elaborate arch, and its buildings were closely arrayed along them. It was adorned by an imperial palace, the site of the first Council and still in use in the sixth century, by several churches, and by establishments for the imperial post. Although severely damaged by earthquake in 363, it was extensively restored by Justinian.

The imperial government and army were much in evidence in such a city because of its location on the main highway through Anatolia, its powerful walls, and its economic function as the seat of the regional treasury. The church was no less prominent, since Nicaea was the seat of a bishop and had the glory of hosting the Council. Its Christian population included heretics, Arians and Novatians; they all shared the city with Jews, apparently few in number, and pagans. In the fourth century, the pagan aristocracy was still rich and prominent; by the fifth, it disappears from the public scene at a time when the poor are first in evidence. It is likely that the city had a large and varied population, that its buildings filled much of the area within the walls (which were presumably built to include the inhabited area), and that it prospered for most of the period.

Nicaea appears at the end of Antiquity, in 602, when Saint Theodore of Sykeon visited Nicomedia. There, a local Jew encountered him, seeking a blessing on himself and on a Jewish child whom he had brought from Nicaea.[40] This event, which confirms the presence of Jewish communities in both cities, took place during the last period of peace the country was to know for centuries. Troubles began with the revolt of Phokas in the same year. When the usurper gained control of the capital, the emperor Maurice fled to Bithynia, sending his son Theodosios with the imperial signet ring to seek help from Chosroes of Persia. Some reported that Theodosios got as far as Nicaea, when he was called back by his father, others that the troops of Phokas had caught him there and brought him back. According to these versions, he was executed with the rest of the imperial family. Another account, however, maintained that Theodosios succeeded in escaping to Persia.[41] In any case, Chosroes did avenge his old friend and ally, Maurice, by moving against his murderer, and beginning a long and devastating war which left Asia Minor in ruins and introduced a new and harsher age.

NOTES

[1] Zosimos I. 35.

[2] For the walls, see the basic work of Schneider (1936) with the additional comments of Foss and Winfield (1985) 79-120.

[3] *Vita* of Saint Tryphon, related texts and full discussion are in *AASS Nov.* 4. 318-383.

[4] Ioannou, *Mnemeia* 239-251.

[5] Halkin (1975).

[6] Westerink (1966).

[7] Theodote: Delehaye (1937); Antonina: *PG* 117.333f; *AASS Mai* I.744-746. There is some confusion about her fate; one account has her thrown into the lake in a sack *(sakkos)*; the other roasted in an oven *(lakkos)*.

[8] Delehaye (1932). I have omitted some saints whose connection with Nicaea was only incidental.

[9] For the reasons for choosing Nicaea, see Barnes (1981) 214 and Johnson (1984) 128f.

[10] Eusebios, *Vit. Con.* 3.6-15; cf. Socrates I.8. Hefele-Leclercq (1908) I. 386-652 have a full discussion of the events; for the site of the meetings, see 408 n.2. For the sources about the First Council and their problems, see Batiffol (1925) and, for the Council in general, the series of articles in that issue of *EO* (vol. 24, part 4) devoted to it. The great room of the palace where the Council was held was still standing in the eighth century: see Mango (1994) 356f.

[11] Socrates I.8,14,23,27,35; II.2.

[12] *Scr. orig. CP.* 189, a work of very doubtful reliability: see Dagron (1984) 128-132.

[13] *I Nikaia* 1.577, with the restorations and interpretation of J. and L. Robert in *BE* 1980.517. For the Novatians in Bithynia, see Foss (1987).

[14] Libanios, *Or* 1.48.

[15] Aristainetos: Seeck (1906) 85-87; Klematios: 110f., Entrechios: 12f.

[16] *Expositio*, cap. 49.

[17] *I Nikaia* 1.173, the epitaph of a baker οἰκῶν ἐν λιθίνῳ τετραπύλῳ, for which I suppose a district named for the monument, though the inscription could be taken literally to indicate a bakery actually installed in the arch. For parts of cities named for buildings see the example of Side: Mansel (1963) 24f.

[18] Sozomen 4.16.

[19] 363: Amm.Marc. 22.13.5; 368: *Chron. Pasch.* 557; cf. Socrates 4.11.

[20] Greg. Naz. *Or.* 7.xv, xx (*PG* 35.773f.).

[21] For the treasuries, see Jones (1964) 428f., and Hendy (1985) 383ff.

[22] Julian: Amm.Marc. 22.9.5; Valentinian: *ibid* 26.1.3-5; 26.2

[23] Amm.Marc. 26.8, 10; cf. Zosimos 4.6.4, 4.8.3-4 and Philostorgios 9.5 (117f), with a somewhat different version of the events.

[24] Amphilochios 206-211 (Latin in *PG* 29. cccxi f.); *SynaxCP* 405.

[25] Basil., *ep. 198*.

[26] 398: *CodTh* 8.1.14; 405: *CJust* 5.4.19; 2.33.4.

[27] Socrates 7.25.

[28] See Ostrogorsky (1932).

[29] Theod. Lector 1.3.4 (*PG* 86.168).

[30] *ACO* 2.1.3.417-421. The site of the disputed place, Basilinopolis, which must have stood in the border region between Nicaea and Nicomedia, has not been determined. Most recently, S. Sahin in *INikaia* 2.3f. has shown reasons for rejecting the normally accepted location at Orhangazi at the west end of the lake, and proposed a site in the pass, on the modern road between Nicaea and the Gulf of Nicomedia, in the vicinity of Yalakdere. So far, proof is lacking, and inspection of the region did not reveal any suitable sites in the hilly country of the neighborhood.

[31] Evagrios 3.24

[32] Malchos, *fr.* 20 = Suidas, s.v. Pamprepius.

[33] Marcellinus Comes, *s.a.* 498.

[34] Con. Porph., *de Ceremoniis* 400. The passage is undated, but the mention of Dara and Nisibis as frontier cities indicates a date after the foundation of the former in 505.

[35] See the folowing note.

[36] Procopius, *de Aedificiis* 5.iii.

[37] *Vita Symeon Styl.*, cap.106.

[38] The tomb and its frescoes are fully described and illustrated in Fıratlı (1974).

[39] For these, see *I Nikaia* 550 (nun), 531 (decanus), 570 (baptistery), 553 (baker), 554 (gardener), 551 (Egyptian), 557 (Italians, ex-protector; see Johnson [1984] 23f.), 558 (primicerius), 574 (Galterius or Walter), 615 (Jews).

[40] *Vita Theod. Syc.*, cap. 156a.

[41] Theophylaktos Simokattes 301, 304; cf. Kedrenos I.709.

2. The Dark Ages

Darkness descends on Nicaea in the early seventh century, and lasts through the tumultuous age of invasion and urban decline which followed; the city is not mentioned in the narrative sources for a century after 602. During this period, Nicaea, like most other cities, doubtless fell into decay, but it always retained its role as a great fortress, and as such became the capital of one of the most important provinces of the Empire. Late in the eighth century, its ecclesiastical glory was greatly increased when it became the seat of a second Ecumenical Council.

Nicaea reappears in history in a context characteristic of the new age, on the occasion of the Arab onslaught on Constantinople which began in 715. While preparations for the attack were being made, Byzantium was in chaos. Artemios, who had only occupied the throne for two years, was faced with a revolt of the fleet; he withdrew from the capital and took refuge behind the walls of Nicaea. His rival Theodosios eventually captured Constantinople, and sent the patriarch and high officials to Nicaea to negotiate with Artemios. After receiving assurance of his safety, he surrendered and abdicated.[1] He had evidently placed his trust in Nicaea because it was easy to defend (especially against an enemy whose main strength lay in his fleet), was well situated for receiving reinforcements, and yet was close enough to the capital to keep abreast of the situation.

The ephemeral Theodosios lasted only a few months before yielding in his turn to Leo the Isaurian. Meanwhile, the Arab army, after advancing across Anatolia, arrived at the walls of the capital, and began a long blockade. They suffered from the harsh winter of 716-7, from the deadly Greek fire of the Byzantines, and from an attack by the Bulgars. In a late stage of their campaign, they sent out an army to ravage the region of Nicaea and Nicomedia, but they were driven back by imperial forces hidden in the neighboring mountains.[2] After this, the remnants of the Arab armies withdrew ignominiously. Although their main object was not achieved, there is no doubt that the Arab campaign inflicted considerable damage on the region.

A decade after this war, in 726, Leo III issued his famous decree against icon veneration and began a century of internal strife. The initial decree, which provoked a riot when imperial troops tore down the image of Christ on the gate of the imperial palace at Constantinople, was followed by an imperial council in 730. This adopted iconoclasm as the official doctrine of the Church, and began a period of active persecution. Few victims, however, are attested and many of them (especially from the reign of Leo, when the persecution seems to have been mild) are shadowy. Among them is Saint Theophilos, a native of Tiberiopolis, who was brought to the court in Nicaea when the persecution broke out, and tortured, but finally allowed to return to his native monastery.[3]

The city enjoyed only a brief respite from attack after the siege of Constantinople. In the summer of 727, two Arab armies advanced with Nicaea as their goal. A force of 15,000 light-armed troops under Amr established a blockade, while the main army under Muawiya, containing 85,000 men according to the exaggerated estimate of the chronicler, followed with heavy equipment. The siege began, and part of the walls were knocked down in the vicinity of the Church of the Fathers but the prayers of the faithful kept the Arabs from the precinct of the church. At that time, the church was adorned with images of the holy fathers of the Council; according to Theophanes, they were still adored in his day, the early ninth century. The army which defended Nicaea was commanded by a staunch iconoclast, Artavasdos. One of his likeminded soldiers, seeing an icon of the Virgin, threw a stone at it, brought it down, and trod it beneath his feet. That night the Virgin appeared to him reproachfully in a dream, and the next day, when he was fighting from the walls, a stone from an enemy catapult decapitated him, a fitting payment, wrote the chronicler, for his sacrilege. After failing to capture the city, the Arabs finally withdrew with a great booty of prisoners and goods.[4]

Although the city remained intact, its walls were severely damaged. The sections around the north and southwest gates, where the fighting had apparently been heaviest, were repaired with an elegant facing of reused marble, which thickened and raised the walls and towers. The work was commemorated in an inscription which still survives.[5] The walls were rebuilt at the expense of one the most important buildings of the ancient city, the theatre. After vast quantities of stone were taken from all parts of the building, it lay in ruins and became a site for burial and dumping, of which more will be heard below.[6] The ruin of such a structure, essential to the life of the city through the sixth century, gives clear evidence of the transformation commonly observed at other sites but is virtually invisible at Nicaea because of the lack of excavation. Here, too, it would appear that the urban fabric was rent, and that medieval city, plundering its glorious but now useless past for practical and immediate needs, lived among the gradiose ruins of a different age. Whatever the condition of the city, it is not difficult to imagine the devastation wrought by two major attacks within a decade, with the land ravaged, peasants, livestock and foodstuffs carried off, and the basis of urban life seriously shaken.

Just after the Arab attack, in 728 or 729, the first of a long series of Western travelers reached and described Nicaea. Willibald, the Bishop of Eichstätt in southwestern Germany, spent two years in Constantinople on his way back from a pilgrimage to the Holy Land. During this time, he made an excursion to Nicaea to see the church where the Ecumenical Council had been held. He found that it was adorned with images of the fathers who had attended the Council, and strongly resembled the church on the Mount of Olives whence Christ had ascended to heaven. His brief description deals only with the church; he does not mention the city as a whole or the condition in which he found it.[7]

Nature, as often, compounded the damage wrought by man when another earthquake, this especially destructive, struck in 740. Its effects were widespread, with much of the capital and surrounding region flattened, but Nicaea seems to have suffered worse than any, for only one of its churches was left standing. The quake was followed by aftershocks which lasted a year.[8] The destruction, in fact, may not have been so severe as portrayed, for the walls survived, and the place was suitable to play a role in the revolt of Artavasdos in 743. The general, formerly Count of the Opsikian theme, briefly assumed supreme power on the death of Leo III. He had great initial success, seizing the capital and surrounding country, and being proclaimed emperor; but within a year Constantine V, son of Leo, had gathered support, defeated opposing armies, and regained the capital. Artavasdos took refuge in Nicaea, but soon had to withdraw to a nearby castle where he was finally captured. His activities in Nicaea, where he claimed to have come to raise troops, and his success in putting together a force there, once more reveal the importance of the city as a military base.[9]

The new Emperor was an ardent iconoclast; he showed his conviction by summoning a general council in 754 which approved the doctrine once again, and by carrying on active persecution. Among its victims was a high-ranking imperial secretary of noble family, Theodore. After being denounced, interrogated, and exiled to a remote fortress, he was recalled in the hope that he had learned his lesson. When he persevered in his orthodoxy, he was tortured and exiled to Nicaea, where he spent six miserable years before his death in about 767.[10] Details of his life are known from the biography of his son Nikephoros, who later became Patriarch and a noted chronicler.

The next appearance of Nicaea in history is covered with glory, as she became the seat of another, and the last, Ecumenical Council. This Seventh Council, which restored orthodoxy after the long interlude of iconoclasm, was an event which was long to redound to the praise of the city. The Council, originally convened in Constantinople in August 786, had a bad start when troops loyal to iconoclasm broke into the church and disrupted the proceedings. The Empress Irene, anxious to restore orthodoxy, disbanded the troops on a pretext and moved the assembly to Nicaea, a place convenient to the capital and court, with appropriate associations, and not, it seems, a centre of heresy. The first session was duly convoked on 24 September 787 when the

Patriarch, representatives of the Pope and of the eastern patriarchs, and 253 bishops assembled before the ambo of the "holy great church which is called Sophia." The Empress was represented by the count of the Opsikion, and civilian dignitaries. Ironically, one of the first items of business involved the bishop of Nicaea, Hypatios, in an unfavorable light. With five colleagues, he had been instrumental in frustrating the first attempted council, and had held a meeting designed to ensure the continuance of iconoclasm. All however, repented, and were restored to full grace and office.

During the seven sessions held in Nicaea through 13 October, and attended by varying numbers of bishops and monks (the fourth had the greatest crowd, with 335 bishops and 132 abbots), image worship was discussed in detail, iconoclasm refuted, and its adherents repented or were condemned. Many technical questions were treated, and a set of canons issued. The final session, at which the Empress was present, was held in Constantinople. It was probably here that the wordy speech of Epiphanios of Catana, appended to the acts of the Council after the canons, was delivered. Although much of it is longwinded rhetoric which congratulates the Church of its deliverance from error, it contains the first formal encomium which celebrates the role of the city as a bastion of orthodoxy. This is worth citing in full, for comparison with later praises:

> χαίροις δὲ καὶ σὺ Νικαέων περίκλυτον ἄστυ, τὸ ἐν μητροπόλεσι περίπυστον ὄνομα, τῆς Βιθυνῶν ἐπαρχίας τὸ εὐκλεέστατον ἀκροθίνιον· ἡ πρότερον μὲν ταῖς τῶν ἁγίων ὀκτωκαίδεκα καὶ τριακοσίων θεοφόρων πατέρων ἴχνεσιν ἁγιασθεῖσα, νῦν δὲ τοῖς τούτων διαδόχοις τριῶν ἑκατοντάδων σὺν πέντε δέκασιν ἀριθμῶν ἐκπληροῦσιν· εὐλαβῶν τε μοναχῶν οὐκ εὐαριθμήτων πλήθει, ταῖς αὐταῖς τῶν εὐλογιῶν περιχυκλουμένη χάρισιν. Ἔν σοι γὰρ τῆς ὀρθοδόξου πίστεως ὁ θεμέλιος ὑπό τινος σατανικῆς δυστροπίας σεισθεῖναι κινδυνεύων ἑδραίωσιν ἀκλόνητον εἴληφεν. Ἔν σοι τὸν ἄγριον ἐκεῖνον καὶ ἀτίθασον θῆρα Ἄγριον ὁ θεῖος ἐκεῖνος τῶν πατέρων χορὸς τὰ ἱερὰ τῶν Γραφῶν ἐφαπλώσαντες λινὰ ἐζώγρησαν, καὶ τοῖς φοβεροῖς κατηχόντισαν ἀναθέμασι· κἀντεῦθεν τὸν υἱὸν τοῦ Θεοῦ καὶ πατρὸς ὁμοούσιον τῷ γεγενηκότι πᾶσα φύσις ἀνθρώπων θεολογεῖν ἐκμεμάθηκεν. Διά τοι τοῦτο καὶ τὸ παρὸν ἱερώτατον σύνταγμα τῆς ἰσαρίθμου ταύτης χορείας δυὰς εὐσεβῶν βασιλέων ἕν σοι συγκροτηθῆναι τεθέσπικεν, Εἰρήνη νέα Ἑλένη σὺν υἱῷ γνησίῳ νέῳ Κωνσταντίνῳ, οὓς ἡ ἔν σοι τοῦ πνεύματος χάρις τοῖς τότε καὶ νῦν ἁγίοις ἐπιλάμψασα πατράσι, φυλάξοι δαψιλέσι χρόνοις ἀτάραχον αὐτοῖς τὸ κράτος δωρουμένη, καὶ τῶν ἐχθρῶν τὰ φῦλα πρὸ ποδῶν καταστρῶσι· ὡς ἂν ἡμῖν ἡ τῶν ἀγαθῶν μὴ διαλίποι χορηγία· χαίροις τοίνυν ὦ μητροπολέων περίδοξον κάλλος, ἐν τούτοις, ὅτι ἕν σοι τὸ πρῶτον ἡμῖν τῶν ἀγαθῶν ἀνέφυ, ἕν σοι δὴ ἦν τὸ τέλος,

The Dark Ages   21

οὐχ ὡς πρὸς ἀξίαν πρὸς ἀριθμὸν δὲ ἥτις ἐστὶ τῶν σεπτοτάτων εἰκόνων τῆς καθολικῆς ἡμῶν ἐκκλησίας ἡ ἀρχαία παράδοσις, ἐν τοῖς ἰδίοις ἀποκατασταθεῖσα ὅροις.

> Hail to you also, famed citadel of Nicaea, a name renowned among the metropoles, glorious crown of the province of Bithynia; previously hallowed by the presence of the 318 holy, godly fathers, now by their successors to the number of 350, and by the crowds, hard to number, of the reverend monks; you are surrounded by the favours of their blessings. For in you the foundation of the orthodox faith, when in danger of being overturned by a certain Satanic perversity, received its unshakable establishment. In you, that divine assembly of the fathers captured the wild and savage beast Arius by spreading out the holy net of the Scriptures, and shot him down with fearful curses; and thence we – the whole of mankind – have learned the doctrine that the Son of God the Father is of the same nature as His Begetter. Therefore, the duality of the pious emperors has ordered the present holy assembly of this company, equal in number to that one, to be brought together in you – Irene the new Helen with her son, the true new Constantine. May the grace of the spirit which shines in you from the holy fathers of that time and now, preserve them for plentiful years, granting them undisturbed rule. May it throw the hosts of enemies down at their feet, just as the abundant supply of good things may not be lacking for us. Hail, therefore, famed beauty of the metropoles, for this, that in you the first of our blessing arose, and in you the final one also, not in importance but in number: the restoration of the ancient tradition of the holy icons of our catholic Church to its proper place.[12]

Similar, though shorter praises had already been given at the fifth session of the Council, by John, the representative of the eastern patriarchs, who spoke thus of the city:

Εὐλογητὸς ὁ Θεὸς ὁ δοξάσας τὴν φιλόχριστον Νικαέων ταύτην πόλιν ἐν ταῖς ἡμέραις Κωνσταντίνου καὶ Εἰρήνης τῶν φιλοχρίστων ἡμῶν βασιλέων. Εὐλογητὸς ὁ Θεὸς ὁ ἀναδείξας αὐτὴν διπλῆς χάριτος ἀξίαν. Τὴν πίστιν πρῶτον ὧδε Χριστὸς ἐτράνωσε, νῦν δὲ διὰ τῆς ἁγίας συνόδου ταύτης τὰ τῆς οἰκονομίας αὐτοῦ σύμβολα πᾶσιν ἐφανέρωσεν· Ἄρειος ὁ δύσφημος ἐνταῦθα καθῃρέθη· τῶν θεοστυγῶν εἰκονοκλαστῶν ἡ αἵρεσις ἐνταῦθα ἠφανίσθη. Εὐλογητὸς ὁ Θεὸς ὁ λέγων διὰ τοῦ ἁγίου ἀποστόλου Ἰωάννου· ἐγώ εἰμι τὸ

ἄλφα καὶ τὸ ὠμέγα. Εὐλογητὸς ὁ Θεὸς ὁ κατ' ἀρχὰς ἐνταῦθα
καὶ ἐν τῷ τέλει τὴν ὀρθόδοξον πίστιν κρατύνας.

> Blessed be God who glorified this Christ-loving city of Nicaea in the days of Constantine and Irene our Christ-loving emperors; blessed be God who proclaimed it worthy of a double honour. Christ first revealed the faith here, and now he has made the signs of his guidance manifest to all through this holy ecumenical council. The infamous Arius was deposed here, and the heresy of the God-hating iconoclasts has here been obliterated. Blessed be God who said through the Apostle John, 'I am the alpha and the omega.' Blessed be God who here in the beginning and the end has strengthened the orthodox faith.[13]

In the eyes of the Christians of the Middle Ages, the Church of Nicaea had the additional renown of tracing its origins back almost to the time of Christ, for a tradition which assumed definitive form in the eighth or ninth century identifies its founder as the Apostle Andrew himself. As already considered, this tradition may go back to the second century, but certain association of Nicaea with the Apostle first appears in the fifth, in the work on the miracles of Saint Andrew by Gregory of Tours. He recounts that Andrew stayed some time in Nicaea and drove away demons who dwelt in tombs by the side of the road, but provides no substantial information about the city. The anonymous narrative of the Dark Ages, on the other hand, contains details of real interest both for the antiquities of the city, and as an illustration on the medieval mentality.

According to this story, the Apostles John and Andrew travelled together to Ephesos, where the Lord appeared to Andrew and told him to go to Bithynia. He therefore departed with a band of disciples, followed a route through Phrygia and Mysia, crossed Mount Olympos, and arrived at Nicaea, then a village, not yet a city. Even its lake was then very small. The place, however, was later walled and adorned by the Emperor Trajan. Although only a village, Nicaea was populous, with many Jews who had a large synagogue, and pagans who worshipped Apollo at his oracle; there were also many who were sick or possessed by demons.

Near the village, at a distance of 67½ stadia (about 8½ miles) stood a bare rough rock called Lochous. It was an especially dangerous place since a dragon shared it with eight murderous bandits, two of them possessed by demons. Saint Andrew, taking his iron staff with a cross and two disciples, made short work of them: he slew the dragon, baptised the bandits, and as a result made many converts. Another roadside rock, Katzapos, was equally noxious, for it contained a temple of Artemis and many unclean spirits whose activities kept the road closed for much of the day. Andrew tore down the temple, set up a church, and cleansed the site. In a nearby dark and wooded village, Daukomis, he killed another dragon, and purified the site of a temple of Aphrodite. His activities were so inspiring that he managed to convert and heal great numbers of pagans, but the Jews resisted him. Finally, therefore, he converted their synagogue into a church dedicated to the Theotokos, ordained the first bishop of the city, Drakontios, who was later martyred, and departed for Nicomedia and parts north.[14]

Much of this account, of course, is fabulous, in spite of some attempts to give it an air of ancient authenticity. Nicaea for example, was never a village, nor is there any reason to believe that the lake grew like the city in historical times. Trajan, as will be noted in connection with the speech of Metochites, did play a role locally, but not the one described here. The first Bishop of Nicaea, the martyr Drakontios, is absent from the calendars of the Orthodox Church. None of the temples can be identified, nor can the place names, but the latter are no doubt genuine (for this is one aspect of the story with which locals would be well acquainted), and the mention of a large rock by the road a few miles from the city shows familiarity with the country, for the south shore of the lake is in fact dominated by just such a rock, Karacakaya, which rises steeply above the road some ten kilometres from Nicaea.

The destroyed temples may reflect the abundant presence of ancient ruins in the neighborhood. Such remains were generally considered to be the abode of demons; hence the infestations which the apostle could cure. Pagan tombs were dangerous for the same reason; they were usually situated along roads, as in this account. Yet the real infestation of roads, so prominent here, probably came less from dragons and demons than from the other element which briefly appears, from bandits, whose activities are certainly attested in a later and better known period. Most interesting (and authentic) is the presence of Jews, who are attested in Late Antiquity and the Middle Ages. Their activities attracted the attention of another saint, as will be seen in the following chapter. No record of the synagogue, however, exists, nor is there any church which appears to have been converted from it; such an act was perhaps wishful thinking on the part of the pious citizens of the Dark Ages.

Ecclesiastical renown was not the only which the city had, for by this time (and perhaps long before), Nicaea had become one of the great administrative centres of the Empire, the capital of the Opsikian theme, or military province, which embraced most of northwest Anatolia. As such, it was well known to the Arabs, who learned the organisation and highways of the Empire through war and trade, and it was one of their authors, Ibn Khordadbeh, who in the mid-ninth century provides the first account of the administrative system and of the city within it. According to him, "Nikia" was eight miles from the sea on a lake of fresh water which was twelve miles long and contained three mountains. A gate led from the city to the lake so that the inhabitants, in times of danger, could send their women and children to the safety of the mountains in the lake.[15] Although some of this is confused and no doubt represents the exaggerated accounts of travellers – Nicaea is really about twenty miles from the sea, and the lake contains no mountains, although hills on its steep southern shore might have provided suitable refuges – it is clear that the city was known abroad as a powerful fortress with an unusual means of defence. The main Byzantine description of the themes, written by the emperor Constantine Porphyrogenitos in about 930, similarly lists Nicaea as the first city and metropolis of the province.[16]

As the capital of a theme, Nicaea was the seat of a general (who in this case bore the title of *komes,* or count), a substantial garrison, and a civil administration. A few seals which have survived from letters of local officials give an impression of the complex administrative system. They name Nicholas, eparch, or head of the municipal government; Strategios, *paraphylax,* or commander of the garrison; Gregory the *protokentarchos,* a military officer; and a number of *kommerkiarioi* of the local *apotheke.*[17] The latter were officials charged with the levying of taxes on trade and the storage of goods paid in as taxes.[18] The *apotheke* was evidently the successor of the regional treasury attested in the fourth century, but whether it was the same establishment under a different name cannot be determined. In any case, its existence attests to the continuing economic importance of Nicaea. The seal of the *kommerkiarios is* of 695; the other officials are dated to the eight through the early tenth centuries. They reflect both the civil and military life of the city, which was not only a major fortress (the role in which it usually appears in history) but a centre of trade and administration.

The city was probably also the abode of an aristocracy of local landowners, the kind of people who frequently held high office. One of them appears in the life of Saint Peter of Atroa, who was active in the early ninth century. He was based in a monastery at the foot of the Bithynian Olympos, where he received the visit and prayers of a lady of senatorial rank who owned an estate in the vicinity. He cured her son of rickets and the lady returned home to Nicaea. Her husband then set out to see the saint himself, but fell ill on his estate, and was obliged to request Saint Peter's help through a messenger. The saint soon came and provided him with a respite of ninety days for repentance. During that time, the grateful patient took care of widows and orphans, distributed his goods to the poor, freed his slaves, and forgave his debtors.[19] The landowner is never named, but was evidently a man of considerable wealth, the possessor of estates and slaves. He was of senatorial rank and lived in the city, thus a member of a provincial aristocracy rarely recorded in sources of this period.

When Saint Peter met the landowner, he was constantly moving to avoid the agents of the iconoclastic government, for in spite of the work of Seventh Council, a new dynasty had reestablished iconoclasm in 815, and persecution was again active. As before, the doctrine met bitter opposition, whose leaders included the bishop of Nicaea, Peter. He is best known from his correspondence with the leader of the iconophiles, Theodore of Studios, who referred to him as a champion against the iconoclasts famed in East and West, and urged him to persevere in his faith despite persecution. Peter needed little encouragement, and proceeded to build churches (probably at Nicaea) and carry out works of charity.[20] On his death in 826, Theodore wrote a letter of consolation to Joseph, who had been appointed abbot by Peter. He presided over the Monastery "of the Potters," probably so named because it stood in the potters' quarter of the city.[21] The opposition was not as powerful as the government, however, and the see of Nicaea was next held by an iconoclast, Inger. He was urged to repent by the famous monk, later a saint, Ioannikios of Mount Olympos, who warned him of his impending demise. Inger ignored the advice, and collapsed while sitting on the episcopal throne.[22]

Inger was apparently succeeded by Ignatios, who held office under the iconoclast Theophilos (829-842). Formerly *skeuophylax,* a high official of Hagia Sophia in the capital, he is best known for his biographies of the Patriarchs Nikephoros and Tarasios. He was also the author of a collection of letters which provide some details about his see. One of them expresses concern over the slow collection of taxes from church property in the diocese, and another complains of the quality of the fish in the local lake, all too mediocre to send as a gift to his correspondent.[23] Ignatios was deposed when the iconoclasts returned to power and spent the rest of his life in exile, writing his numerous works.

After the restoration of orthodoxy, Nicaea received a suitable bishop, Theophanes, one of the most famous victims of the iconoclastic persecution. Theophanes, who had been a monk in Palestine, was arrested, beaten, and exiled before being brought to Constantinople to be confronted by the emperor Theophilos himself. When he and his brother Theodore refused to repent, they had insulting verses tattooed on their foreheads and were henceforth known as the brothers *graptoi.* Theodore eventually died in exile, but Theophanes survived to gain his reward in the form of the see of Nicaea.[24]

Such a center of religion, wealth, and power needed adequate defence, for the massive walls which surrounded it were now almost 500 years old. During the ninth century, the Arabs made spectacular advances against the Empire, culminating in the capture of Ankyra and Amorion in 838. The importance of Nicaea was once again manifested during this campaign, when it served as the basis for organising imperial resistance and defence.[25] It would soon prove valuable as a base for moving against the enemy in the successful age which to was follow. Preparatory to the great Byzantine successes of the ninth and tenth centuries, Michael III (842-867) devoted considerable attention to the fortresses of Anatolia, and made particularly impressive changes at Nicaea. The walls were extensively rebuilt and raised to a new height, and many towers were added to the circuit. His work is especially evident on the southwest, adjacent to a section repaired by Leo III, where the new wall uses a decorative masonry with bands of brick, and on the southeast and east where new towers were added to each of the old ones to double the defensive strength of the wall. These rebuildings, executed in 858, represent the greatest modification of the walls before the Laskarid period.[26] The city was again the object of hostile attention in 872 when the Paulician heretics of the eastern frontier passed through it on the spectacular raid which took them as far as Ephesos.[27] Thereafter, an age of peace began, as the frontier was pushed to the east, and Anatolia was no longer subject to attack.

NOTES

[1]Theophanes 385f.
[2]Theophanes 397.
[3]*SynaxCP* 125ff.
[4]Theophanes 406.
[5]Inscription: Schneider (1938) 49 no. 29; walls: *ibid.*, 33 and Foss and Winfield (1985) 100.
[6]See Yalman (1981); see below, 90f.
[7]Willibald, *Hodoeporicon* 272, cf. *Itin.* 293f. For the church, see 113f discussed below.
[8]Theophanes 412.
[9]Nikephoros 62; the details about Nicaea are from the otherwise fuller account of Theophanes.
[10]*Vita Nicephori* 143; cf. *SynaxCP* 723.
[11]For the Council, see Mansi 12.951-1154, 13.1-820 and Hefele-Leclercq (1910) 3(2).741-98. Opening: Mansi 12.991-1000; Hypatios: *ibid,* 1016-56 *passim.*
[12]Mansi 13.455.
[13]Mansi 12.301.
[14]See *Acta Andreae* with the discussions of Dvornik (1958) 173-5 and Johnson (1984) 68-74.
[15]*BGA* 6.106. The same author, ibid., 102 refers to Nicaea as the place from which vegetables were shipped to Constantinople and locates it opposite Hisn al-Ghabra, a place on the main highway from the interior to Constantinople. He seems in this case to have confused Nicaea with some other place, perhaps the port of Pylae.
[16]Con. Porph., *de Thematibus* 69. Unfortunately, this list of *poleis episemoi* like much of the work, gives every appearance of being abstracted from an earlier source, probably of Late Antiquity.
[17]Zacos and Veglery (1972) 3156, 2400, 1968, 194.
[18]For the *apotheke,* see the long and novel discussion of Hendy (1985) 626-634, 654-662, which, however, does not adress the question of continuity.
[19]*Vita Petri Atr.,* caps. 51-53.

[20] Theod. Stud., *epp.* 1191, 1203, 1355, 1410, 1611.
[21] *Ibid.*, 1633-36; for the church, see Darrouzès (1975) 114.
[22] *Vita Ioannicii* 360A, 406C. On Inger, who curiously bears a Scandinavian name, see Mango (1973) 18f.
[23] For Ignatios, see Mango (1981). Published editions of Ignatios' letters are not available to me, but a new edition by Professor Mango is in preparation.
[24] *Vita Theophanis et Theodori* 219f.; cf. the later but no more specific text edited by Featherstone (1980) 147.
[25] Genesios 69.
[26] See below, chap. 10.
[27] Genesios 121.

3. Recovery and Prosperity: Ninth-Eleventh Centuries

A new age began with the reign of Basil I (867-886), a time when Nicaea was the scene of the activities of Saint Constantine, the subject of a biography which provides some details of local conditions and of the importance of the city. According to this account, which was composed in the early tenth century, Constantine was a Jew from the Phrygian city of Synnada, who had been converted to Christianity by a miracle which showed the power of the Cross. He eventually came to Nicaea, where he settled in a village so high in the mountains that it was frequently covered by clouds. One day, a voice which issued from the cloud directed him to the Monastery of Phlouboute, where he was baptised, and took his new name. From there, he travelled to Cyprus, where he acquired the hand of a certain Saint Palamon. He then returned to Nicaea, to the Monastery of Hyacinth, which was renowned for the holiness of its monks, and there deposited the hand, in the Church of the Virgin.

At this time, Nicaea was famed as a center of trade, and had a settlement of Jews devoted to commerce and to their religion. Since they regarded Constantine as a renegade, they plotted to kill him, but he miraculously escaped. While in Nicaea, he performed many miracles, producing huge catches of fish and crops of grapes. His local fame was great, as were his powers of persuasion when he convinced two monks not to leave the monastery, as they had planned. To seek more peace for his devotions, Constantine finally withdrew to Mount Olympos, where he established himself in a monastery and continued to work miracles.[1] This account not only gives some insight into the lives of the urban and rural population but shows, as few others do, the continuing importance of the city as a civilian centre and reveals the existence of the local Jewish community. These Jews were apparently the object of the attentions of Bishop Gregory, who may have lived in the tenth century. He wrote a treatise about the baptism of Jews, giving a list of questions to be asked of them.[2]

During the tenth century, when the sources devote more attention to civil affairs, Nicaea had several distinguished bishops. The most noted was perhaps Alexander, whose skill in rhetoric brought him a high position in the capital where he became a professor and leading churchman. In about 945, however, he fell into disgrace and was exiled. His letters from exile tell more of the man than of his see, but they do reveal that the Patriarch sent a commission of enquiry to Nicaea where, it appears, the bishop had been involved in misadministration of church property. Among his complaints, alleging the good works he had done, he mentioned the decoration of the Church of Roufinaous, which may have been in Nicaea.[3] Theodore, who presided over the church in the mid-tenth century, also rose to great influence in the capital, where he became involved in intrigues against the patriarch. His numerous letters, though, tell nothing of his see, for, like most churchmen of ambition, his interests lay in Constantinople.[4] In some correspondence, Nicaea appears in an unflattering context. The Patriarch Nicholas Mystikos (901-903, 912-925) received news from an unnamed correspondent that he was going to live in Nicaea, in the company of its treacherous inhabitants; he asked protection against their wiles from his friend Nicholas.[5] The same patriarch had occasion to write a stern letter to the Count of the Opsikion because priests had come to him from Nicaea, complaining that clergymen were being drafted into the army. Nicholas wrote to express his horror, and to point out that the church of Nicaea had ancient privileges because it had been site of the two Councils, and that these were not to be violated.[6] In about 960, Theodore, Bishop of Cyprus, was exiled to a small house in Nicaea, whence he wrote letters seeking deliverance.[7] Few of these letters provide details about the city, nor is it clear whether the reference to local treachery reflects the well-known disdain of Byzantine worthies for life in the provinces, or some contemporary reality. In any case, the strength of the walls and the presence of a large garrison would have made the place suitable for exile.

The city was honored in 959 by a visit from the emperor Constantine Porphyrogennetos, on his way to Mount Olympos and its holy monks, to seek their prayers for success against the Arabs. The chronicler of the event describes the city as one of ancient wealth and a large population.[8] It was also one of some charity, for it possessed a *xenodocheion,* or hospice for travellers, an establishment which often provided for the poor and infirm; it is known from a seal of its director, who held the high rank of *protospatharios.*[9] Naturally, the hospice also reflects the importance of the highway.

The long period of peace was rarely interrupted. When Attaliates, writing a century later of the reign of Nikephoros Phokas, described the state as being in such a bad way that the Arabs were advancing as far as Nicaea, he was probably exaggerating, but the city did suffer severely from a civil war on one occasion.[10] In 978, Bardas Skleros, whose revolt against Basil II had caused tremendous disturbance in Asia Minor, moved against Nicaea, defended for the emperor by Manuel Erotikos. After ravaging the surrounding villages, Skleros brought up his siege machinery and began to bombard the walls. Since the defenders resisted fiercely, destroying his ladders and machines with Greek fire, Skleros abandoned hope of making a successful assault, and determined to blockade the city. As the siege dragged on, the garrison started to go hungry, for no supplies could be brought in. The commander, therefore, began to look for a stratagem which might avert certain defeat. Erotikos ordered sacks to be filled with sand covered by a thin layer of grain. These were shown to captured prisoners who were released with the message for Skleros that the city, which could not be taken by force, feared no famine either, since it had food for two years. He did, however, request Skleros to allow him and his men to withdraw peacefully. When this was granted, the garrison and much of the population departed for the capital with their possessions.

Skleros was in a rage when he discovered the trick, but he had learned from experience the value of the fortress, installed a strong garrison of his own, and used Nicaea as his main base. From there, he moved to defeat Bardas Phokas, the new imperial commander, before finally being subdued.[11] Although the assault had failed, it did inflict damage. The siege machinery included *helepoleis* or moving towers, which battered down parts of the walls, and caused one large tower at the southernmost angle of the circuit, a particularly vulnerable point, to collapse partially, so that it seemed to have sunk to its knees. This tower was to be the scene of considerable fighting in a much more famous assault a century later, that of the First Crusade. It was singled out for mention by Anna Komnena because the commander Erotikos was an ancestor of the Komnenos dynasty, and her own great-grandfather.[12] This narrative is the first of several accounts of attacks in the city; it reveals both the strength and weakness of the walls: they were so powerful that no force could hope to overcome them when they were properly defended, but there was no defence against the famine which could result from blockade, especially if a sizable population had to be fed.

In normal times, the rich land around the city provided abundant resources in crops and animals, while the lake was filled with innumerable fish. Some of these fish are mentioned in contexts while illustrate the life of the city and its surrounding region. Leo, bishop of Synnada, who was famed for his embassy to Rome and France in 997/8, refers to one kind of fish in a letter addressed to his colleague, Gregory of Nicaea. In it, he jocularly swore by the numerous small and ill-omened *kordakia* of the lake. By that, he meant the bleak, a fish which swims in schools just below the surface and frequently jumps above it to catch flies, thus seeming to imitate the movements of a notorious erotic dance, the *kordax*.[13] There were perhaps of more interest as a sight than a dish, for they are generally considered too small to be worth eating. Such seems to have been the view of the ninth-century Bishop Ignatios (though he does not mention the fish by name). More recent attitudes, however, have been different: in the early sixteenth century, bleak of Iznik were such a common item in the markets of Bursa that they were the subject of regulation, and in modern times they have been caught in great quantities and salted for shipment to Constantinople.[14]

•

Another fish was plainly of more consequence, as the life of Saint Neophytos of Nicaea, which is preserved in a manuscript of the eleventh century, reveals:

> Ποταμὸς δέ ἐστιν ὁ Φαρμούτιος· οὗτος βορράθεν Νικαίας περὶ τοὺς πρόποδας τῶν Ἀστακηνῶν ὀρῶν ἀναβλύζων, καὶ χῶρον ὅτι πλεῖστον ὕπτιον καὶ πολύδενδρον τοῖς ἑλιγμοῖς παραμείβων, καὶ τοῖς μετὰ τὴν Τραϊανοῦ γέφυραν λειμῶσί τε καὶ κήποις, Νεῖλος ἄλλος γιγνόμενος, τῇ Ἀσκανίᾳ ἐπισμίγνυται λίμνῃ. Τούτου τὸ ὕδωρ κάλλιστον, ὡς καὶ τοὺς ἀπὸ τῆς λίμνης ἰχθύας ἐν καιρῷ τοῦ ἔαρος τὸν ὁλκὸν ἀνατρέχειν, καὶ ἀγρευομένους, ἥδιστον ὄψον οὐ Νικαεῦσι μόνοις, καὶ ἀστυγείτοσι γινομένους, ἀλλὰ δὴ καὶ ὑπερορίοις, καὶ πλέον τοῖς ἀβροδιαίτοις τῶν Βυζαντίων. Φύσις γὰρ τοῖς ἰχθύσι τοιαύτη, ὡς νεαλεῖς πυρὶ ὀπτωμένους, ἀδιαφθόρους ἐπὶ πολὺ διαρκεῖν.

> There is a river called the Pharmoutios which gushes forth in the foothills of the Astakene mountains north of Nicaea and, as it winds, passes by a very flat and well-wooded region. In the meadows and gardens after the bridge of Trajan, it becomes another Nile, and mingles with the Askanian lake. Its water is excellent, so that the fish from the lake swim up its channel in the springtime. As they are caught, they become a pleasing dish, not only for the Nicenes and their neighbors, but also for foreigners and especially for the gourmets of Byzantium. For the nature of this fish is such that if it is cooked on the fire when it is freshly caught, it will last a long time without perishing.[15]

These unnamed fish evidently had a place in the local economy, since they were worth shipping to Constantinople, where they were considered a delicacy; they appear to have been the silurus or sheatfish.[16] The Arab geographer Idrisi, who wrote at the court of Roger of Sicily, in the mid-twelfth century, mentioned a third kind of fish which had a different value. His account also reveals other products of the lake:

> In the lake of Nicaea there is a small fish, a span [about six inches] long and of greenish color, with fine bones. When it is cooked with pennyroyal and eaten by someone with a fever he is immediately relieved of it. There are small crayfish in the lake. When these are cooked with their residue and the liquor is squeezed out and drunk once, it is useful for chronic coughs. There are also small hollow pumice stones in the lake and on its banks. When one of these is hung from the thigh of a woman

who wishes to give birth, the birth is speeded without delay; this has been clearly demonstrated. This stone is called 'Nicene' or 'stone of Nicaea.' The wise men mention it in their books and describe its characteristics.[17]

The unnamed fish is evidently the chub, which is noted as greenish or blue, full of small bones, and valueless as food.[18] The account of Idrisi, which has some appearance of a description of wonders in a far-off country, also reveals another kind of resource of more than local importance, the medicines which could be made from the products of the lake and sold abroad.

The city as a whole earned the praise of the biographer of Saint Neophytos, who included a formal but brief encomium in his narrative:

> Οὐ πολλὰ μόνον, ἀλλὰ καὶ τερπνὰ τῆς κατὰ Βιθυνίαν Νικαίας τὰ καλλωπίσματα. Καὶ τίνα ταῦτα; Θέσεως ἐπιτηδειότης, ὡρῶν εὐκρασία, ἀροσίμη γῆ καὶ πολύφορος πέριξ, ἄμπελοι εὐκληματοῦσαι, ἐλαῖαι κατάκαρποι, ὀχετοὶ ναμάτων ἀμφιρρύτων, μύλωνας στοιχηδόν, λειμῶνάς τε καὶ παραδείσους καὶ λουτρὰ καταρδεύοντες, τειχῶν ἐρυμνότης, ναῶν κάλλη, οἰκητόρων λαμπρότης, καὶ χρειῶν ἀφθονία τῶν τε ἄλλων καὶ δὴ καὶ τῶν ἀπὸ τῆς γείτονος λίμνης ἀπολαύει, πρὸς τούτοις καὶ τῶν ἐκ θαλάσσης καλῶν, ἡμερησίας οὐδὲ ὅλως ὁδὸν ταύτης ἀφεστηκυίας. Ἔχει τι καὶ ἄλλο τῶν πόλεων καὶ βασιλίδος αὐτῆς ὑπερφυὲς καὶ ἐξαίρετον, ἐφ' ᾧ καὶ μᾶλλον σεμνυνομένη, καὶ ὡς ὀφθαλμός τις εὔκυκλος καλὸν ἀπολάμπων, οὐ Βιθυνίαν μόνον, ἀλλὰ καὶ πᾶσαν τὴν ὑφήλιον καταυγάζει. Καὶ δικαίως· θεῖον γὰρ κατ' εὐδοκίαν τοῦ κρείττονος. Ὁποῖον δὲ ἄρα τοῦτο; Τὸ τῆς ὁμοουσίου καὶ ζωαρχικῆς Τριάδος μυστήριον, ἐν αὐτῇ τρανῶς κηρυχθέν, καὶ συλλαβαῖς ἁγίων ὀκτωκαίδεκα καὶ τριακοσίων πατέρων, πρὸς δὲ καὶ βασιλέως μεγάλου καὶ τῶν πώποτε φιλοχρίστου βεβαιωθέν, εἰς δόξαν μὲν καὶ φωτισμὸν τῶν ἀληθῶς ὀρθοδόξων, αἰσχύνην δὲ καὶ ἀναθεματισμὸν τοῦ μανιώδους Ἀρείου, καὶ τῶν ἀμφὶ αὐτὸν δυσωνύμων.

> The adornments of Nicaea in Bithynia are not only many but delightful. And what are they? The convenience of the location, the mildness of the climate, the arable and fertile land round about, the luxuriant vineyards and fruitful olives, the streams flowing round in their channels, supplying water to the rows of mills, fields, gardens, and baths; the strength of the walls, the beauty of the churches, the splendor of the inhabitants, and the abundance of all other necessities, especially those which it en-

joys from the neighboring lake and, in addition to all these, the goods from the sea which is not a whole day's journey away.

It has something else, more special and outstanding than other cities and even the capital itself, by which it is renowned and, shining brightly like a well-round eye, illuminates not only Bithynia but everything under the sun. And justly so, for it is something divine. What sort of thing could that be? It is the mystery of the consubstantial and life-giving Trinity, clearly proclaimed there, and confirmed by the writings of the holy 318 fathers in the presence of the great Christ-loving king for the glory and enlightenment of the truly orthodox and for the shame and anathema of the raving Arius and the accursed ones around him.[19]

In a few words, the anonymous author praises the site, the climate, the wealth of the land and the lake, the buildings and inhabitants and – in most detail since the context is religious – the glory which came from the First Council of the Church.

John the Geometer, a famed poet of the tenth century, had something similar to say in a few words addressed to Nicaea:

Ἡ τῶν Ἀθηνῶν ταῖς ἐλαίοις μὴ φρόνει
Νίκαια ταύταις καὶ περὶ τούτων ἀμπέλοις
λειμῶσι, κήποις, δένδρεσι, ζώοις, λίμνῃ,
νικῶσα πᾶσι, καὶ κέκληται προσφόρως

Let Athens not boast of her olives, for Nicaea is victorious in all these and, in addition, in vineyards, meadows, gardens, trees, animals and its lake; she is suitably named.[20]

The significance of these passagers will become evident when they are placed in the context of the praises of Laskaris and Metochites.

In these centuries, when the power of Byzantium was at its height, Nicaea prospered from the natural wealth of its situation. Peace ensured success, but as in previous ages, it was frequently interrupted, most seriously in the late eleventh century. Thereafter, troubles were almost constant, and the tranquillity of these years did not return until the city was for a moment capital of the empire in the thirteenth century.

The negligence and anti-military policy of the successors of Basil II rendered Byzantium, which seemed overwhelmingly powerful, surprisingly weak and open to attack from a new and more deadly enemy, the Turk. The military party which wished to strengthen the defences eventually saw no alternative to revolt. Its leader, Isaak Komnenos, therefore advanced from his native Paphlagonia toward Nicaea in the summer of 1057. Cheered by the enthusiasm he found on his way, he made the city his goal because of its strategic value: it could serve as a base for advance on the capital, or, if his efforts were unsuccessful, it could provide a strong refuge in defeat. Komnenos took the city at the first assault (he evidently met little resistance), deposited his treasures and baggage within the walls, installed a garrison, and pitched his camp twelve stades, or half a mile, to the north at a place called Polemon. The imperial forces were camped nearby, and there was frequent contact between the two armies, but since neither could persuade the other to change sides, the loyalist force moved off to Petroa, an elevated location fifteen stades from its enemies. The two armies eventually fought at a place curiously named Hades. At first Komnenos was defeated and withdrew to the north, but his commander Kekaumenos inspired the army by pushing into the enemy camp, and victory soon followed. Control of Nicaea was decisive: Komnenos soon moved on to take Nicomedia and then to be received in the capital.[21]

Komnenos' success was brief, for he abdicated within two years, leaving the throne to Constantine Doukas, under whom the Turkish threat became far more ominous. The next blow to Nicaea, however, came not from them but from an unexpected yet not unusual quarter. In 1065, a devastating earthquake levelled much of the city; the cathedral Church of Hagia Sophia and the Church of the Fathers were shaken and came crashing down. In addition, large parts of the city walls along with many public buildings collapsed, and the city, according to the chronicler, barely escaped total destruction.[22]

Life nevertheless went on normally for most of this period, but the sources offer only rare glimpses into the activities of peaceful prosperity. As always, landowners complained about their taxes and had problems collecting debts. One of them, an unnamed Nicaean who owned an estate called Dekte, appealed for assistance to his friend Michael Psellos, then a great power at court. Psellos obliged by writing to the judge of the Opsikion, asking relief for his friend; the results are unknown.[23]

Real problems, however, were near at hand. In 1071, Romanos IV was crushingly defeated by the Turks at Manzikert, civil war followed, and Asia Minor was so rapidly overrun that within a few years Turkish bands were freely swarming everywhere in the chaos and collapse of the imperial defences. Although the sequence of events is difficult to reconstruct, it is clear that Nicaea held out against the flood and was still Byzantine in February 1078 when Nikephoros Botaniates revolted against the feeble regime of Michael VII Doukas (who was advised by Psellos).

The emperor, in an effort to save the situation, called on the Turkish tribesmen led by Suleyman, son of Kutlumush, who obliged by marching against the rebel. Botaniates, meanwhile, had attracted the allegiance of other Turks, including the mercenaries who served as the imperial garrison at Nicaea. They left to join him at Kotyaion, and together all marched westward across the

Sangarios and thence toward Nicaea. Before Botaniates reached the city, the forces of Suleyman caught up with him, but he managed to beat back the advance party and draw near to the walls. Here, to his dismay, he found an imperial army arrayed against his tiny force (he was said to have only 300 men), but they swiftly acclaimed him and he was able to enter the city without opposition. Once established in Nicaea, Botaniates received the homage of former enemies, Suleyman and Mansur, the sons of Kutlumush, and they prepared to join his offensive against the capital.[24]

The revolt now had new strength and an essential base. The rebel army, augmented by the Turks, rapidly occupied Bithynia. The commander of Nicomedia came to Nicaea to join Botaniates and the important naval bases of the Gulf, Pylai and Prainetos, willingly opened their gates. Chalcedon was soon occupied and the rebel army camped opposite the capital by the beginning of March. The revolt was received with favor and enthusiasm throughout the region, for much of Bithynia had been devastated by the Turks since 1071 to become desolate and unapproachable; the population was overjoyed to see these strategic and rich lands once again under Byzantine control.[25]

The final triumph of Botaniates was not long in coming. At the end of March, Michael abdicated in his favor, and a delegation of notables set out from the capital to greet the new emperor. They sailed to Prainetos, then continued on foot to Nicaea, having no fear of the Turks who were overrunning the intervening country like flocks, for when the Turks heard that the ambassadors were going to their ally Botaniates, they willingly let them pass. After receiving the welcome news of his proclamation, Botaniates hastened to Prainetos and sailed to the capital where he assumed supreme power.[26]

Possession of the throne in itself did nothing to relieve the pressure from the Turks. Botaniates therefore sent an army to Nicaea, which was to be the base for campaigns into Anatolia, but the troops refused to move on to the East because of lack of supplies. Another force, the so-called "immortals" who were skilled in archery, were then shipped across to Chrysopolis to join and strengthen the first, with the aim of freeing Asia Minor from the Turks. They in their turn supported a revolt by Constantine Doukas and, though this was soon suppressed, the troops were recalled and the Turks left free to make further advances.[27]

The power of Botaniates outside the capital was severely restricted by a series of revolts which broke out when his rule proved no more competent than that of his predecessor. One of the most serious was led by Nikephoros Melissenos, who was proclaimed emperor in Asia. He gained the support of the Turkish chiefs, no doubt including the sons of Kutlumush, and went round the cities of Asia to receive their allegiance. They willingly opened their gates to him as emperor; he in turn entrusted them to his Turkish forces, who were installed in the cities of Asia, Phrygia, and Galatia without a fight. Since he now had a large army, Melissenos managed to capture Nicaea, and used it as a base for his further ambition.[28]

Botaniates, who had no illusions about the seriousness of this threat, attempted to send his young and successful general, Alexios Komnenos, against Melissenos. When he refused, the campaign was entrusted to the eunuch John, the *protovestiarios,* who was accompanied by George Palaiologos, a member of the high nobility.[29] The army marched through Bithynia and camped at Basileia, forty stades or five miles from Nicaea. At the urging of Palaiologos, they captured the strategic Fort Saint George on the north shore of the lake; then against his advice, planned to attack Nicaea. Palaiologos explained that the enterprise would be filled with risk, for the city was strongly defended from its ramparts and there was a real danger that the Turks of the countryside might march against the attacking force and trap it between their men and the city walls. The eunuch refused to listen, led his forces up to the walls, and endured the insults of the defenders in vain, for as foretold, the Turkish auxiliaries appeared, and the imperial force was obliged to withdraw.

The army returned to Basileia which contained a large fortified enclosure with few entrances. As the troops tried to rush in, they were harassed by the Turks and John was barely saved by Palaiologos. The army soon withdrew to Helenopolis on the coast and thence to the capital, leaving Melissenos in full charge in Anatolia. His forces now advanced to the Bosporos and there made contact with Alexios Komnenos who had in the meantime also revolted. The two rebels arrived at an accommodation by which Melissenos should receive the title of Caesar; Komnenos then easily occupied the capital and became emperor in April 1081.

The immediate preoccupation of the new regime was with the West, where the Normans were preparing to cross to Durazzo and march on Constantinople. Alexios had therefore to call on all available reserves, including the commanders of Anatolia who were ordered to come with as many men as they could, leaving only necessary garrisons behind. Among them was the Caesar, who fought beside Alexios against the Normans in Thessaly. During this period of confusion, when the Byzantine possessions in Asia were virtually stripped of their defence, Nicaea slipped from imperial rule for the first time in its history and became the centre of a Turkish state under circumstances which the sources do not describe. It is most probable that Suleyman, who headed the Turkish troops in the region in support of Melissenos, gained complete freedom of action when his former patron was sent to the west, and by refusing to recognise the new emperor Alexios, established his own independence.

The sources, which provide an unusually detailed narrative for parts of this period, reveal little of the internal condition of the city. For that, the archaeological evidence is once again of value. It shows that the walls and churches were extensively repaired after the earthquake of 1065, and that the Roman theatre, the site of the sole excavation, remained in a state of desolation. Much pottery of the ninth and tenth centuries has been found in association with oyster shells and scattered burials. It would appear that the area was used as a dump, perhaps for neighbouring houses, which may have been built in and over the ruins of the ancient structure (though no trace of them has yet been reported). In other words, even during this period of prosperity, the area within the walls was evidently not entirely built up or put to productive use, but resources were available for the repair of buildings essential for the physical or spiritual welfare of the city.[30]

NOTES

[1] *Vita Constantini*, passim.
[2] Dmitrievskii (1901) 1027f.; cf. Darrouzès (1949) 64, with reference to an edition not available to me. The date of Gregory is unknown, but the MS containing his works was written in 1027.
[3] Darrouzès (1960) 27-32 (life and works), 83-86, 88 (letters).
[4] *Ibid.*, 49-57 (life), 261-316 (letters).
[5] *Ibid.*, 137.
[6] Nicholas Patriarch, *ep.* 150, p.466; probably written 915/18.
[7] Darrouzès (1970) 335.
[8] Theophanes Continuatus 464.
[9] Zakos (1984) 263, dated to the late ninth or early tenth century.
[10] Attaliates 223.
[11] Skylitzes 323.
[12] Anna Komnena XI.I.
[13] Leo of Synnada, *ep*, 27, p.44; see the long and fascinating commentary of Robert (1961) 102-115. The recent editor, M. Vinson, curiously seems to question Robert's interpretation in her commentary, p. 117, on the irrelevant grounds that he had not seen the passage of Idrisi.
[14] Ignatios: above, 29; Bursa: Beldiceanu (1973) 224; shipment to Constantinople: Devedjian (1926) 227f.
[15] *Vita Neophyti* 246f.; cf. Robert (1961) 106.
[16] Robert (1961) 109.
[17] Idrisi 807; my translation.
[18] According to Devedjian (1926) 229f., the common fish of the lake were the carp, silurus, chub, bream, and bullhead, along with eels and crayfish. Of these, the chub best suits Idrisi's description; its medical value seems otherwise unknown.
[19] *Vita Neophyti* 239f.; cf. Robert (1961) 157f.
[20] Text in Cramer, *Anecdota graeca*, 315. In another verse, *ibid.*, he mentions Nicaea as one of the three cities best endowed with olives, along with Athens and 'Prainestos.' The latter has usually been taken as Praeneste in Italy, but that is not a noted centre of olive production. Most probably, the name of Prainetos on the gulf of Nicomedia, a place especially rich in olives and no doubt well known to an inhabitant of Constantinople, should be read.
[21] Attaliates 91; cf. Skylitzes Cont. 657f.

[22] Attaliates 91; cf. Skylitzes Cont. 657f.
[23] Psellos, *epp.* 117, 120.
[24] Bryennios 239-242; Attaliates 265ff.
[25] Attaliates 267f.
[26] Attaliates 269, 272.
[27] Attaliates 306-310.
[28] Bryennios 301; for these events in the context of the Turkish conquest of Anatolia, see Cahen (1948). Nicaea appears to have been the mint for Melissenos' coinage: Hendy (1985) 428f.
[29] For what follows, see Bryennios 303-11.
[30] See Yalman (1981, 1983, 1984).

4. The First Turkish Period

In 1081 Nicaea gained the distinction of becoming the capital of the first Turkish state established on the soil of what was eventually to become Turkey. This first period of Turkish rule is known almost exclusively from the pages of Anna Komnena, for there are no Turkish sources, and oriental writers who deal with the early history and conquests of the Seljuks were familiar only with events which took place further east. Anna's narrative, fortunately, is more than adequate to show the importance of the state and its capital, as well as the threat which it posed to Byzantium; but it deals far more with the state than the city, about which it gives few details.[1]

No sooner had Alexios Komnenos gained supreme power than he had to deal with Suleyman ibn Kutlumush who had seized much of Anatolia and made Nicaea his capital. This choice no doubt reflected previous experience of the area first as a raider then as the ally of various pretenders; it showed that he clearly appreciated the strategic value and strength of the place, and that his ambitions were directed westward, for Nicaea, as he could have learned from his former patrons, was the ideal base for operations against Constantinople. The city thus became capital of a state which controlled Bithynia, the northern routes across Anatolia, and much of the central plateau.

Alexios came to the throne at a time of grave danger from the West, but before he could deal with the Normans he had to face the Turks whose attacks were more immediate, for Suleyman's raiding parties were plundering everything as far as the Bosphoros. The inhabitants of the capital could see the Turkish camps across the straits, while the people of the local cities were afraid to leave the safety of their walls. Alexios therefore sent a force of heavy-armed troops who descended on the coastlands at night, ambushed the Turks, and gradually took control of the coast. In this way, the region opposite Constantinople, along with the territory of Nicomedia, returned to imperial control, and a treaty was concluded which fixed the Drakon River as the boundary between the two powers.[2] The immediate need to secure this vital coastland illustrates the danger which the state at Nicaea could pose.

Suleyman's career, though glorious, was short. He claimed the exalted title Sultan (which was not officially his), and began to behave like the ruler of a major state. In 1084, he set out for the East in the hope of further conquests, urged on by the Armenian Philaretos, who had established a small state in Cilicia and had come in person to Nicaea for support. After impressive initial successes, Suleyman met with defeat and death at the hands of the Seljuk

Sultan Malik Shah in 1086. Suleyman had left a certain Abul Qasim as supreme commander in Nicaea. When his patron was killed and Anatolia fell into chaos, Abul Qasim claimed the title of Sultan and succeeded to most of Suleyman's domains, though turning Cappadocia over to his own brother.[3] Malik Shah, who wanted to restore order in Anatolia, now proposed a marriage alliance to Alexios by which he would return the coastal lands to the Byzantines. Alexios seduced the messenger into becoming a Christian and used him to gain control of Sinope on the Black Sea, but refused the alliance.

This malentente between the great powers left Abul Qasim free to expand. He continued to harass the coast, provoking Alexios to send out small forces, then, when these proved ineffective, a substantial army strengthened by western knights, directly against Nicaea. The Byzantine general Tatikios led the force up to the walls without encountering any resistance until a body of Turks suddenly emerged from the gates. The Franks repelled them with great losses, but when nobody came forth to fight the next day, Tatikios withdrew to a camp north of the city. Rumors now arrived of a large Turkish army on its way from the east; Tatikios, knowing he would be no match for that, planned to withdraw to Nicomedia, then to the capital. Abul Qasim, watching from a tower of the walls, saw the Byzantine retreat, and set out in pursuit. He caught up with them near Prainetos, but was worsted in the subsequent fight, leaving the imperial force free to withdraw.[4]

This defeat must have been relatively minor, for Abul Qasim soon seized Kios on the Sea of Marmara and began to build a navy. Alexios in alarm sent the imperial fleet and an army, again under Tatikios, who burned the Turkish ships before they could sail and, after two weeks of skirmishing, drove the enemy back to Nicaea.[5] The sequence of these events is far from clear, as is the nature of victory or defeat in this context for, shortly after, Abul Qasim was able to gain control of Nicomedia, the main bulwark of the highway to Constantinople.

Both sides, however, were soon distracted by a new threat, as Malik Shah had sent a large army under Bursuk to reduce Nicaea. Abul Qasim thereupon made a truce with Alexios who decided that Bursuk represented the more serious threat and, in an effort to keep his enemies divided and the stronger power at a distance, supported his erstwhile foe. Abul Qasim soon needed Byzantine aid, for Bursuk indeed brought a huge army and laid Nicaea under a siege which lasted three months. Alexios once again sent Tatikios, who took Fort Saint George on the north shore of the lake. The imperial troops manned its battlements against Bursuk and made such a noise that the besiegers were terrified into withdrawing, thinking that the emperor had arrived in person. The Byzantine auxiliaries were of no further avail, however, for when they realised that they were hopelessly outnumbered, they withdrew to the capital.[6]

The walls of Nicaea protected Abul Qasim so well that the attacking force finally withdrew, and the Sultanate of Nicaea, left in peace, prospered for the next few years. During this time, Alexios continued to be preoccupied with troubles in the Balkans and the growing menace posed by the fleet of Chaka, the Emir of Smyrna. Malik Shah, meanwhile, had not abandoned his plans for taking Nicaea, and again proposed a marriage alliance, with cession of territory, to Alexios. The proposal was brought by Buzan, along with a large army. Despite several attempts, the walls of the city and the aid of the emperor, who disdained the marriage, once again provided a sufficient defence and Buzan withdrew to the East. Abul Qasim now hoped to secure his position by gaining recognition from the Sultan, and set out for Persia with a large supply of gold. This proved of no avail as the Sultan referred him to Buzan who had him killed.[7]

Buzan now held authority over Nicaea, but still had not entered it, for Poulchas, the brother of Abul Qasim, had come from Cappadocia and installed himself in the city. Alexios began to treat with him, promising a great bribe if he would surrender Nicaea, thus hoping to gain by diplomacy what he had been unable to accomplish by arms. Poulchas expressed interest but kept waiting for news of his brother. The death of Abul Qasim might have made a difference to the fortunes of the city, but it was soon followed by that of Malik Shah in November 1092. This was the signal for considerable confusion and fighting, during which Buzan went east and was killed in battle. Prior to this, the Sultan had received the two sons of Suleyman. On his death, they escaped to Nicaea, where the citizens received them with enthusiasm. Poulchas voluntarily turned control over to them as the rightful rulers, and the elder, Kilich Arslan, was chosen as Sultan. He installed the families of the occupying force in the city and made it his capital. He then deposed Poulchas from his command, put Mahomet in charge of all the troops and of Nicaea and himself left for the East.[8]

The new Sultan desired good relations with Alexios, even to the extent of collaborating with him against his own father-in-law, Chaka of Smyrna, whom he treacherously had killed. As a result, the rulers of Constantinople and Nicaea made a treaty which ensured peace in the coastal regions. The terms, which have not been preserved, were no doubt favorable to the Sultan who had rendered such valuable service to the Emperor.[9] For a few years, the Turkish state of Nicaea was at peace with the Empire until an unexpected disaster – though a great triumph for the Christians – arrived in the form of the First Crusade.

The Seljuks thus maintained Nicaea as their capital for some fifteen years, a glorious moment for Turkish history since this small state was the forerunner of larger and more permanent dominions. During these years, the Turks no doubt adorned and transformed the city which would have seen the erection of its first mosques and, perhaps, of a suitable palace for the Sultan. No trace of these has survived; the former was probably obliterated and the residence adapted by the restored Byzantine government. Less imposing remains, however, are preserved and have long been visible to anyone who cared to look, though curiously they have hardly been noticed. They consist of a group of Seljuk tombstones, many of them inscribed, which were built into a tower of the south wall to repair damage inflicted by the First Crusade [Fig. 8]. I shall discuss them in another context; for the moment, they may be noted as providing the only material and epigraphic record of this Seljuk state, and the only names – none of them known to history – of its denizens.[10]

NOTES

[1] For this period, the detailed account of Cahen (1948) is indispensable, and has been extensively used here; see also the very clear summary of Melikoff (1968) 79-88.
[2] Anna Komnene 3.xi.
[3] *Ibid.* 6.ix-ix.
[4] *Ibid.* 6.x.
[5] *Ibid.* 6.x.
[6] *Ibid.* 6.xi.
[7] *Ibid.* 6.xii. In all this, I follow the narrative of Anna Komnene with some reservations, for more than once she gives the impression of recounting the same event twice in a slightly different guise. If proper criticism of the sources were possible, a different and less complicated picture might emerge, but in the lack of comparative material, there seems little possibility of checking Anna's account.
[8] *Ibid.* 6.xii.
[9] *Ibid.* 9.iii.
[10] For the palace, see the Appendix below, p.204.

5. The First Crusade

One of the best-known and dramatic events in the history of Nicaea was the attack of the First Crusade. For the soldiers of the West, it was the first fortified city they had to capture on their way to the Holy Land. It was a place whose strong walls left a lasting impression, and provided an almost insuperable challenge for their techniques of siegecraft. The importance of the event caused the chroniclers to leave a detailed account, which reveals much about the city and especially its fortifications, and is worth considering in some detail, as a uniquely vivid narrative.

The first crusading force to reach Asia Minor was the irregular, though numerous, band of Peter the Hermit.[1] After crossing the Bosporos on 6 August 1096, they proceeded to Nicomedia and arrived at Helenopolis on the south shore of the Gulf of Nicomedia (the crusaders called the place Civetot from its Greek name Kibotos). They camped in a convenient location where supplies were easy to get: merchants brought them food, drink and oil at fair prices. The Emperor warned them to stay there until they had a larger force, for he knew they were not yet equal to the power of the Sultan, whose capital was their first goal. After some weeks, however, they grew restless and sent a raiding party across the mountains to the lands of Nicaea where they captured cattle, sheep, and goats from the Greeks who were living under Turkish rule. In spite of the warnings of Peter, this success encouraged the Normans in the army to undertake a larger expedition. Seven thousand infantry and three hundred knights advanced to the walls of Nicaea, plundered its fields, and carried off hundreds of cattle. According to Anna Komnena, an unfriendly Greek source, they committed unspeakable barbarities, even roasting captured babies on spits.

When the German contingent saw this success, three thousand of them with two hundred knights set out to capture the unoccupied castle of Xerigordos, which belonged to the Sultan.[2] They gained a complete victory, capturing abundant supplies and establishing a base for raiding the fertile lands about Nicaea, but the Turks arrived with a strong army which included many skilled archers, and attacked the castle only three days after the Crusaders had taken it, on 29 September. They reduced the garrison to distress by gaining control of the well outside the walls along with the stream below them, then drove the defenders back from the ramparts by their arrows, but were unable to make much progress against the fierce defence until they managed to pile up a great quantity of wood by the gate, burn it down, and force an entrance. Except for two hundred youths who were led into slavery, the Germans were slaughtered. Worse was to come.

During the next week, the Turks sent out parties to enquire about the damage the Crusaders had done in the neighboring villages, and to cut off stray raiding parties. They placed ambushes along the road to Nicaea, then spread rumors in the crusaders' camp that the Norman contingent had captured Nicaea and were growing rich from the plunder. The mass of the crusaders, therefore, marched in force, but in disorder, up the valley of the Drakon. Here they unexpectedly met a large Turkish army in the woods and were completely routed. The dead were piled up in huge heaps by the river so that later, when the main crusade came to the site and refortified it, they used the bones to make mortar for its walls. Anna Komnena reports that the fort still stood in her day, built of stones mixed with bone. The fortress is indeed still standing, but the bones are nowhere evident. The survivors of this carnage fled precipitously downstream to Civetot; they were pursued by the Turks who killed all except the best-looking women and boys. Those they carried off in triumph to Nicaea, along with the spoils of the camp. The few survivors of Peter's army were rescued by the imperial fleet.

This disastrous beginning showed the importance of Nicaea, a great fortified base for the Sultan, a place essential to take if the crusade were to make further progress. Accordingly, when the main body of the Crusade arrived in Asia Minor the following year, Nicaea was its first goal.[3] Part of the force was ferried across to Civetot to follow the route of their unfortunate predecessors, while the main army crossed into Asia Minor and moved on to Nicomedia where its leaders stopped to plan the further advance. The Emperor established his headquarters at Pelekanon, not far to the west, in order to be near the scene of action and in the hope of contacting and suborning the population of Nicaea. At Nicomedia, the crusaders, seeing that the road to Nicaea was too small to accommodate such a great force, sent three thousand men ahead to widen the narrow passes through the high hills which lay between the two cities, and to mark the road with wooden and iron crosses. The army then followed, arriving before the walls of Nicaea on 6 May 1097.

The crusaders were overawed by the strength of the fortifications which, with their walls, towers, and even double walls, seemed insuperable. One of them accurately appraised the situation by describing the city as heavily fortified by man and nature. On one side was the lake, while the three others were protected by a moat filled from the overflow of three small streams. The walls were so high that they need fear neither the attacks of man nor the assaults of machines, and the ballistas of neighboring towers were turned to face each other in such a way that no one could approach the wall without danger, and anyone who succeeded would soon be overwhelmed by missiles cast from the battlements. Another crusader, with understandable exaggeration, thought that there were no less than three hundred towers.[4] The walls seemed all the more formidable since the Sultan had installed a large garrison and strengthened the gates.

The knights got a good view of the fortifications as they jousted in the fields outside; some, who attacked hastily, were driven back by darts and arrows from the walls. Within a few days, a regular supply of provisions was ensured, sections of the wall were assigned to each leader, and all was ready for the siege. The attack began on 14 May, as the crusaders surrounded the city. News of these events soon reached the absent Sultan, who sent a message promising immediate reinforcement. His messenger, however, was intercepted and revealed to the crusaders that the main Turkish force was nearby in the mountains. When the Sultan arrived, therefore, the Christians were ready for him, and gained a significant victory as the Turks descended into the plain and attempted to force their way to the gates. The enemy was driven back, and never attacked again. Heads of the Turks who had been killed were brought back to the camp; some were thrown over the walls to demoralise the defenders; others were sent to the Emperor as a sign of the first Christian victory.

The siege now began in earnest. The attackers built wooden siege-towers and catapults, while others prepared iron-clad battering rams, and sappers approached the walls under the cover of archers and crossbowmen. Most of these efforts were in vain, for the place was well defended, and many perished from shots fired from the ramparts. Two knights built at their own expense a so-called "fox" of oak beams, a massive machine which provided shelter for twenty sappers. Unfortunately for them, it collapsed as it was being dragged to the walls and all within were killed.

Some progress was made: one tower was badly shaken by the constant stones of the catapults, but, even though the fabric was ancient, the mortar was so hard and the stones so firm that none of them could be shaken loose. Finally, more catapults were brought to bear, cracks appeared, and some stones started to fall loose. Soldiers then crossed the ditch in a wicker-work cover and began to attack the tower with picks. Finally, such a large hole was made that two men could enter, but further progress was impossible because the Turks filled the interior of the tower with large stones, and the attack was stymied.

The crusaders realised that they could never hope for success as long as the Turks could be supplied from the lake, with which the fortifications communicated directly. They therefore took dramatic and highly practical measures: a multitude of men was dispatched to Kios, with orders to bring ships which had been supplied by the Emperor. There were silently dragged overland by night, across a high and difficult ridge, and arrived in the lake at dawn. They were manned by crusaders and men supplied by the Emperor. At first sight, the Turks thought that their supply fleet was arriving, but then realised, to their astonishment, that those ships were still anchored next to the walls. According to Anna Komnena, whose version differs in many ways from that of the crusading historians, the ships were manned and transported by the Emperor, who further helped the plan by establishing control over Fort Saint George on the north shore of the lake. In any case, the city was blockaded from all sides.

The resistance now became fiercer than ever. The Turks, seeing that the walls had been shaken and one tower seriously damaged, redoubled their efforts. They poured a burning mixture of lead, oil, and pitch down from the battlements, along with the usual arrows and stones, and used torches and oakum to ignite the wicker shelters of the attackers. One Turk in particular, though wounded and transfixed with twenty arrows according to witnesses, kept up the defence until a knight shot him down with a crossbow. After these troubles, the crusaders hesitated to make further attacks, but one brave soldier in armour moved up to continue removing stones from the tower that the Turks had blocked. He went on working despite a rain of missiles, but, to dodge the arrows, he stood close to the walls, where he was overwhelmed by stones and finally killed. To the indignation and humiliation of the attackers, his body was hoisted up, stripped, and displayed by the defenders.

Most of the fighting was concentrated around the tower of Gonatas, so named because it had been partially undermined by Bardas Skleros in 978 and seemed to be leaning on its knees *(gonata)*. It stood on the south side of the circuit, not far from the south gate which was the only one the Turks had not blocked. At this point, the crusaders were thoroughly demoralised, feeling that nothing could avail against the wisdom of the ancients who had built the wall. Nevertheless, a Lombard engineer still had hope and promised, on payment of fifteen pounds of silver, to build a device which could undermine the tower. He constructed a heavy portable shelter with a sloping roof off which the missiles of the Turks glided uselessly. When this was moved against the base of the tower, the men within were able to dig a great hole and insert heavy beams to support the tower. They filled the chamber thus excavated with a mass of sticks, dry grass, and twigs, which they then set on fire. By midnight, the flames had done their work and the tower, no longer supported, collapsed backward with a great crash, making deep cracks in the adjacent walls. On the news of this disaster, the wife and children of the Sultan attempted to escape from the city, but were captured.

While the siege was in progress, the Emperor had been negotiating with the Turks. He offered bribes and an amnesty if they would agree to surrender to him rather than to the crusaders, and warned of the suffering they would face if the Franks took the city. The Turks, realising that their situation was hopeless, willingly accepted terms which allowed them to withdraw in peace.

Arrangements were naturally made to conceal this agreement from the crusaders; the Byzantine force, therefore, joined in the final assault on the walls. Just as the combined armies were about to break into the city, however, the astonished crusaders saw the standard of the Emperor flying from the ramparts, and the imperial troops entered the city, making sure to take possession of the keys to the south gate which had remained unblocked. The crusaders perforce accepted the *fait accompli* which, in theory saw the fulfillment of their immediate goal, the capture of Nicaea.

When the final terms were arranged, the Turkish leaders were sent to Fort Saint George, where many of them received gifts and entered imperial service. Boutoumites, who had conducted the negotiations with the Turks, was made *doux,* or military governor of the city, and Christians who had been captured by the Turks were returned. Among them was a nun from the army of Peter the Hermit, who complained that she had been constantly raped by the Turks. She received absolution and was taken back into the host. Shortly afterwards, however, a message came from her Turkish captor, asking her to come back because he could not live without her, and even offering to become a Christian. The scandalised army soon saw the nun willingly return to her former tormentor, for reasons, it was said, of lust. The crusaders in their turn had captured Turks, among them a youth named Axouch, whom they presented to the Emperor. He became a Christian, took the name John, and enjoyed a phenomenal career. Under John Komnenos, he was virtually second in command of the Empire, and thus in a position to ensure the succession in 1143 of John's younger son, Manuel.[5]

After these and other settlements had been made, the crusaders were allowed to visit Nicaea in groups of ten, for the Emperor remained suspicious of their intentions and did not want any large number of them present in the city at one time. The crusading leaders received gifts from Alexios and pledged their fealty to him, but the army was not allowed to plunder the city. This order caused great resentment, for the men felt that they had expended tremendous time and effort without reward. They could only accept the imperial order but this point marked the beginning of great bitterness between Latins and Greeks. With these feelings in mind, but elated by their great victory, the army moved on. The siege of Nicaea had lasted seven weeks and three days.

NOTES

[1]The most detailed account is that of Albert of Aix I.15-22; cf. *Gesta francorum* I.2 and Anna Komnene 10.vi. Runciman (1950) 128-132 gives a clear modern narrative.

[2]Xerigordos may be identified with the castle of Coban Kalesi in the valley of the Drakon: see Foss (1996) 63-68.

[3]For what follows, the main source is Albert of Aix II.20-38, with details added from *Gesta francorum* 2.7, Anna Komnene 10.xi, 11.i-iii, Raymond of Aguilers 239f., Fulcher of Chartres 332-334, Stephen of Blois 885-7, and Baudri of Dol 26-31. See also Runciman (1950) 175-188.

[4]Raymond of Aguilers 239; Stephen of Blois 886.

6. The Age of the Komnenoi

Under the restored rule of Byzantium, now ably managed by the emperors of the Komnenos family, Nicaea enjoyed a century of uneventful peace which was only disturbed when civil war formed a prelude to the great event of 1204, the capture of Constantinople by the Fourth Crusade and the concomitant transfer of the capital to Nicaea.

By regaining Nicaea, Alexios Komnenos had reestablished imperial control in the rich and strategic lands of western Asia Minor and driven the Turks back to the central plateau, where they made Ikonion, or Konya, their capital. Yet the Turks were by no means crushed and, as their state grew in organisation and strength, their attacks continued to afflict all parts of the territories still in Byzantine hands.

In 1113, for example, Alexios was camped on the Asiatic shore of the Bosporos preparatory to meeting an expected Turkish attack when he received news from Kamytzes, governor of Nicaea, that the Turks had descended on that city. He swiftly marched to Kibotos where a more detailed report related that the huge invading force, estimated at 40,000, had divided into three parts, one of them directed against the rich plains of Mysia; this group had already devastated the region around the lake of Nicaea. Alexios ordered Kamytzes to follow them, while he himself took a short route over the mountains and eventually defeated the Turks in Phrygia.[1] It is apparent that the Turkish bands were able to penetrate every part of the country, and that the role of fortified cities, which they were unable to take, was decisive in organising resistance and maintaining imperial authority. The account also reveals the great disparity of forces: even if the number of Turks was greatly exaggerated, they were certainly superior to the five hundred men whom Kamytzes commanded in their pursuit.

The situation was not very different three years later when news of a large-scale attack once again reached the Emperor. This time, determined to strike a major blow against Ikonion, he gathered his forces at Lopadion in Mysia and advanced to Fort Saint George on the north shore of the lake, and to Nicaea. After returning to Mysia, he heard that the Turks had reached Fort Saint George and were moving westward. He responded by marching again to Nicaea, then continued to Nicomedia where he raised more troops for his major effort.[2] Here, too, the ubiquity of the Turks and the relative weakness of the Byzantines seems apparent. In the sequel, however, Alexios successfully penetrated to the outskirts of Ikonion, and concluded a treaty which might have stabilized the frontier had it not been followed almost immediately by the deaths of its two signatories, the Emperor and the Sultan.

The Turks were not the only enemies whom the new government had to face, for the Normans and other Latins of the West were equally hostile, especially in the aftermath of the Crusade. Enmity between Greeks and Latins was sharpened by the schism which had divided their churches since 1054. Consequently, there was much religious polemic, some of it written by two bishops of Nicaea.[3] The more important, Eustratios, was a distinguished theologian and philosopher who became trusted counsellor of Alexios. He engaged in public disputation with the Latin monks who visited the imperial court and wrote a book against the western heresies. Ironically, he fell himself into error and was deposed in 1117. His successor, Niketas, carried on the work by composing a treatise on the various schisms which had arisen between the eastern and western churches. Both these worthies, however, were far more active in the capital (the goal of all high ecclesiastics) than in their own churches.

The energetic policies of Alexios' son John (1118-1143), with campaigns deep into Turkish Anatolia and construction of fortresses to ensure imperial control of the rest, brought a peace to the area which was hardly disturbed until the end of the century. Only one unwelcome and unexpected interruption occurred after the death of John and accession of his son Manuel (1143-1180), at a time when relations with Turks were in a state of uncertainty. In 1147, the German and French contingents of the Second Crusade reached Byzantium on their way east. The Germans crossed into Anatolia in September hoping to gain victory by themselves before the French arrived. When the French contingent reached Constantinople, therefore, they were assailed by rumors that the Germans had captured Ikonion and won great booty. They consequently hastened on past Nicaea and were camping by the shores of the lake when suddenly some German nobles appeared with horrifying news. Instead of the reported victory, the German force had met with a crushing defeat and was rapidly falling back on Nicaea.

The Germans, as it turned out, had stopped at Nicaea, bought supplies for eight days – supposedly sufficient to see them through to Ikonion – and acquired guides to lead them through the rough mountain country to the east. They soon ran short of provisions and were ambushed by the Turks near Dorylaion. The defeat was overwhelming: they sustained considerable losses in the field but even more during the disorderly retreat which brought the remnants of their force back to Nicaea in November. Here, they complained, they sought food but had to pay exorbitant prices: the Greeks demanded their weapons and armor, effectively stripping them. The French king advised his German colleague to buy supplies in Nicaea and meet him at Lopadion. The Crusade then went on to face further problems and ultimate disintegration

The Age of the Komnenoi

while still in Asia Minor, far from its goal.[4] This account once again emphasises the strategic importance of Nicaea; it was the natural base for an army moving eastward, not only from its convenient location, but because its rich lands made it an excellent source of supplies. As the Germans found when they arrived unexpectedly, though, local wealth had its limits and a sudden increase in demand could drive prices to extremely high levels.

Frequent traffic between East and West gave Nicaea an international reputation as a great fortress and a place of intrinsic interest. The Arab geographer Idrisi mentioned the city several times in the work which he wrote in 1154. Most of the passages, however, are abstracted from Ibn Khordadbeh, a writer of the ninth century, with some embellishment. Among the additions are statements that the city was so old that the name of its founder was unknown, that it was a large and beautiful place, and, in the passage quoted above, that its lake was full of wonders.[5]

A contemporary writer at the other end of the Mediterranean, William of Tyre, wrote a long history of the Crusades during the second half of the twelfth century. Most of his account of the First Crusade is derived from earlier sources, but one passage which does not have a known source is worth quoting here as another example of a formal encomium of the city, and the only one in Latin.

> Est autem civitas situm habens commodissimum, in planitie constituta, non longe tamen a montibus, quos pene ex omni parte habet in circuitu; agrum optimum, glebam uberem, sylvarumque et nemorum nihilominus multas habens commoditates. Sed et lacus multae latitudinis et longitudinis maximae, juxta praedictam urbem positus, in occidentalem porrigitur plagam, per quem navigio ex diversis partibus civitati maximum praestans munimen, ipsis moenibus, ventis intumescens, illiditur. Ex reliquis autem partibus circa murum, vallum erat in circuitu, ex influxione fontium et rivulorum restagnans; quod plurimum accedere volentibus ad urbem, impugnandi causa, ministrare poterat impedimentum. Erat autem praetera bellicoso referta populo; muris et turribus sublimibus et valde densis, opere solido compactis, insignis admodum et munita: ita ut accedentes nostri et urbis mirarentur munimen et operis soliditatem.

> Nicaea has a very favorable site. It lies in the plain, yet is not far from the mountains by which it is surrounded on almost every side. It has excellent land, rich soil, and in addition, the many advantages afforded by woods and forests. Next to the city, and extending to the west, is a very wide lake of great length which, when swelled by the waves, washes the very walls. Across this lake ships from various parts bring provisions, and this is the

best defence the city could have. A moat surrounds the walls on the other sides, and this is always filled to overflowing by the influx of springs and rivulets. This of itself would prove a serious obstacle to anyone approaching the city with hostile intent. In addition, Nicaea had a very large and warlike population and was so remarkably defended by thick walls and lofty towers of solid masonry that our men as they drew near marvelled at the massive construction of the fortifications.[6]

The long period of peace came to a brusque end after the death of Manuel, when a weak and unpopular government was faced with constant plots and finally with a major revolt led by Andronikos Komnenos, cousin of the late emperor, in the Spring of 1182. As he advanced from the east, he came to "the greatest city Nicaea, which presided over Bithynia" only to find that the governor, John Doukas, resisted his blandishments, though they were reputed to be more powerful than siege engines. He therefore left the city untaken as he advanced on the capital where he was soon admitted as regent for the young Alexios II, son of Manuel.[7] In this instance, the usurper could ignore a powerful fortress on his route because he was sure of support in the capital.

Once established in power, Andronikos showed his true character by slaughtering large numbers of the aristocracy and in the process creating another occasion for coming to Nicaea. The population of the city revolted against his rule, and opened the gates to Isaak Angelos and Theodore Kantakouzenos, enemies of the emperor, in September 1183. The revolt, which soon spread to Prusa and Lopadion, provided Andronikos with an excuse for assuming the full imperial power.[8] In the Spring of 1184, therefore, he moved against the rebels and began a long siege of Nicaea, another well-documented event in the life of the city.

When the imperial forces began their blockade, the defenders rained down missiles and insults on the Emperor, who was more enraged by the words than the weapons. The garrison, swollen by recent defections from their enemies and by a contingent of Turks, barred the gates and trusted in the walls which had the reputation of being impregnable since they were built of burnt brick. For several days, Andronikos approached the walls, but could accomplish nothing as if, in the florid language of the chronicler, he were attacking Arbela or the walls of Semiramis or shooting his arrows into the air. Although he brought up siege towers, catapults, and battering rams, as well as using a force of sappers to undermine the walls, he made no progress, for the city was well equipped with artillery of its own and his machines were demolished by stones projected from the ramparts or burned by parties who issued forth from posterns.

Finally, Andronikos adopted a typical gruesome tactic by bringing the mother of Angelos and tying her to a battering ram which he set in motion.

Although the defenders were naturally horrified, they directed their missiles with such skill that the old lady was unharmed and eventually, by making a sally, burned the equipment and drew her up to the battlements by a rope. After this, their insults and the emperor's rage grew tremendously.

The strength of the walls and weapons of the defenders effectively made the city invulnerable to assault, but not proof against human error. Theodore Kantakouzenos, who was the soul of the defence, one day saw Andronikos riding round the walls and rushed forth from the east gate to fell him with his lance. Instead, his horse took a fall and he was rapidly seized and decapitated. After this, the garrison lost heart and began to make plans for capitulation. Nicholas the bishop urged them to throw themselves on the mercy of the Emperor, and formed a procession of the clergy and the unarmed populace. As this issued from the gate, Andronikos could not believe his eyes, but thought he was dreaming. Nevertheless, he took swift advantage of the situation to seize the city and punish the leaders of the revolt, including the Turks who were all impaled in a circle round the walls. This colorful account of Choniates reveals yet again the strength of the walls and general superiority of defence to attack; but at the same time, it shows that those walls were of no avail by themselves, if the defenders were poorly led or demoralised.

Andronikos soon came to a bad end – he was torn to pieces by a mob – but his successors had no fewer problems to face in Asia Minor where the Turks, profiting from Byzantine problems, were making considerable progress. Soon after the death of Manuel, they had taken Dorylaion and Kotyaion, the two great bulwarks of the frontier essential for maintaining a Byzantine foothold in the central plateau and keeping the Turks from settling in the rich coastal plains. As a result, Nicaea was more exposed to attack than it had been since the time of Alexios. By 1199, a new emperor, Alexios Angelos, was on the throne. He provoked the Turks by arresting all their merchants in the capital and forbidding the Greeks to trade with them. Fearing material retaliation as well as the possible disaffection of his people, he marched to Nicaea and Prusa to secure them against possible attack from Dorylaion, now a major Turkish base. After staying more than a month, he returned to Constantinople.[9] This is the last recorded event at Nicaea before the Fourth Crusade which brought new glory to the city as it became the seat of Emperor and Patriarch, the capital of the Byzantine state in exile.

NOTES

[1] Anna Komnene 14.v.
[2] *Ibid.* 15.ii.iii.
[3] For the careers and writings of these bishops, see the convenient summary of Beck (1959) 618f.
[4] Odo of Deuil 91, 97.
[5] Idrisi 805, 807 (tr. Jaubert 302, 304; cf 199, 305, 312).
[6] William of Tyre, 3.1, tr. Babcock and Krey 152f., with some modifications.
[7] Choniates 244, 246.
[8] Choniates 269; for what follows, see *ibid.* 280-86.
[9] *Ibid.* 496.

7. Nicaea as Capital: The Reign of Theodore Laskaris

The capture of Constantinople by the Fourth Crusade in April 1204 was the greatest disaster the Empire had known. The significance of losing a city which had remained inviolate for nine hundred years as the great centre of civilization in the Christian world was bitterly appreciated by all. In the aftermath, the Empire seemed to disintegrate, with pretenders springing up in East and West, while the new Latin rulers of Constantinople moved aggressively into Anatolia and the Turks seemed poised for new conquests. Yet during this chaos the surviving Byzantine state had an emperor and he and his more famous brother found a suitable headquarters in Nicaea where the Empire first took refuge, then built its strength, and finally issued forth to recapture the lost capital. For more than fifty years, Nicaea was the capital of the reduced, exiled empire and as such has given its name to the state, "the Empire of Nicaea." For some of that time, it was the political and military centre, for all of it the seat of the Byzantine Patriarchate and throughout the period flourished as a centre for refugees who brought a learning and culture which soon took on a life of its own.[1]

When the crusaders were at the gates of Constantinople and Alexios V ignominiously fled the city, a party of notables chose a new Emperor, Constantine Laskaris, in the cathedral Church of Hagia Sophia. Since there was no hope of maintaining resistance in the capital, he led his followers, and with them the whole imperial tradition, across the Bosporos to Asia Minor. Although the brief career of this Constantine is poorly known, it is overwhelmingly likely that he settled on Nicaea as his base of operations and that it was from there that he and his brother Theodore led the defence against the initial attacks of the Latins who had rapidly seized northwest Asia Minor, from Abydos to Nicomedia. Their emperor, Baldwin, in fact, had hardly gained power when he announced that Nicaea and Prusa were his special goals.[2] Although the Latins soon had to withdraw their garrisons to face the growing Bulgar menace, the fledgling Byzantine state still ran the great risk of being squeezed between two hostile powers, the Latins and the Turks. Constantine, however, managed to secure a settlement with the new sultan, Ghiyath ed-Din Kaykhosraw, who apparently feared that an increase of Latin strength would ultimately present a serious threat. This was virtually the last act of Constantine, who seems to have perished in or shortly after the battle of Adramyttion in March 1205, when the Latins gained a major victory.³

Theodore Laskaris succeeded his brother, taking the title of Despot, rather than Emperor, in the Summer of 1205. At first, his situation was precarious. The Byzantines of Anatolia were divided, with each following an independent policy.⁴ The inhabitants of Nicaea, for example, refused to admit Theodore as their ruler and it was only with great difficulty that he persuaded them to take his wife into care. He then went to Prusa and the surrounding region where he gained support and was recognised as ruler in place of the former emperor Alexios Angelos, who was still alive.⁵ Within a year, Theodore had made treaties with Latins and Turks and united the Byzantine resistance. By March 1206, he was definitively established in Nicaea which thereafter became his capital and main military base.⁶ As such, it was soon put to use, in the Autumn of 1206, as the point of departure for operations against David of Paphlagonia who had entered into an alliance with the Latins and was posing an immediate threat to the city and region.⁷ Similarly, in April 1207, it was from Nicaea that Laskaris attempted unsuccessfully to dislodge the Latins from Nicomedia.⁸

During this period of confusion, many of the political and intellectual leaders of the Empire became refugees and sought the convenient sanctuary of Nicaea. Notable among them was the historian and former minister, Niketas Choniates, whose work provides the basis for much of the present narrative. He left Constantinople four days after its capture, when it seemed evident that he and his family would not be able to escape the Latin marauders, and took up residence in Selymbria. When the increasing menace of the Bulgars made that place unsafe, he returned to the capital, but, unable to endure life under the Latins, left once again at the end of 1206, this time for Nicaea "girded about with the highest rank of all the Eastern cities under the Romans and renowned for the strength of its walls." He settled and remained there until his death in about 1215. The period was not a happy one for Choniates, who had risen to high positions under the previous government. Although he gave several speeches before the Emperor – a clear indication that his rhetorical talents were still appreciated – and managed to continue work on his lengthy history, he never gained any political influence and frequently complained of the cold reception he had from the inhabitants, among whom he lived "like a prisoner."⁹ The reasons for his misery are unknown: lack of political success was perhaps due to poor relations with the Laskarids or their followers (his failure to emigrate with them might suggest this), but allowance must be made, as always, for the Byzantine rhetorical convention of speaking ill of life in the provinces compared with that of Constantinople.

The refugees included a figure who came to dominate the intellectual life of the age, Nikephoros Blemmydes, who left the capital as a child in 1205.

After staying four years in Prusa and receiving primary education, he moved to Nicaea and there studied poetics, based on the works of Homer and other ancient poets, and rhetoric, from the antique but universally employed texts of Hermogenes and Aphthonios. He also began the study of logic, but in 1213 moved to Smyrna to pursue higher studies.[10] More will be heard of him.

Members of the aristocracy and leaders of the church also fled the capital for Nicaea, among them two future patriarchs, Maximos (1216) and Germanos II (1222-1240). These groups in particular felt the lack of an Emperor and looked for ways to have Laskaris crowned, for he had been generally recognised as despot and was winning substantial victories. For their purposes, they needed the authority of a high churchman, such as the Patriarch, John Kamateros. He, however, had taken refuge in Didymoteichon in Thrace and refused to leave. Theodore and the Nicene leaders, therefore, convened a synod which elected a new Patriarch, Michael Autorianos, a man of high education, skilled in Greek and foreign languages, on 20 March 1208. A few days later, he crowned and anointed Laskaris who was thus in a position to deal with the developing rival Greek power of Epiros.[11]

The coronation attracted many dignitaries, among them Nicholas Mesarites, a cleric of Hagia Sophia who was active in negotiations for union between the Greek and Roman Churches. As a leader of the metropolitan clergy, he conveyed a message from them to Laskaris expressing their disquiet at having no patriarch and returned with the despot's sympathetic reply summoning the clerics to attend a meeting in Nicaea in March 1208 to choose a new patriarch. When the time came, Mesarites attended the synod, but by now, like many others, he despaired of the situation under the Latins, and settled in Nicaea without ever returning home. The patriarch made him *referendarios* (the official charged with communications between Emperor and Patriarch) in gratitude for his services in the cause of union, and installed him in the Church of Christ *tou Bolenou*, a dependency of the Monastery of Ano Lakkous within the walls. Mesarites stayed there until about 1212, when he became bishop of Ephesos. After settling in Nicaea, he wrote an account of his journeys to the inmates of the Monastery of Euergetes in Constantinople. These colorful descriptions provide a striking image of local conditions in the kind of detail rarely found.[12]

In his first journey, Mesarites crossed in a skiff to Chalcedon, then continued on foot to the monastery of Rufinianai where he spent the night. The next morning, he made his way to a nearby harbor and embarked on a ship loaded with amphoras of wine which brought him to Neakomis on the south shore of the Gulf of Nicomedia. He found this place burnt and in ruins, barely preserving the appearance of a town and noted, with the typical viewpoint of the city-dweller, that it was filled with houses of twigs and mud instead of stone and mortar. After a breakfast of millet bread and heavy muddy fish which resembled tuna, Mesarites joined a mule train loaded with pickled fish in baskets and made the all-night journey across the mountains. The drivers kept themselves awake by singing and the priest was glad of their company and protection. When, however, he attempted to join them by singing hymns, they rebuked him, saying that the mountains were full of highwaymen and bandits and that his song should therefore be rough and barbarous, and that he should ride quickly and show no fear. He followed this advice and was relieved to arrive at the lake shore at dawn, and to see the towers of Nicaea in the distance.

For the second journey, Mesarites and his party sailed on a ship full of soldiers and archers which transported them to the port of Pylai on the Gulf, "the beginning of Asia and the entrance to our eastern paradise." They debarked at night and slept on the beach, where a group of merchants, who were seeking passengers to Nicaea in order not to return without a load and to gain some extra pay, found them. A price was agreed, and the clerics set out. The first stage of the journey was miserable: hail and snow fell (it was March) and the branches of overhanging trees whipped them as they passed along the winding roads. They finally arrived at dusk at Fort Saint George, where they found a place to sleep and some bread, wine, meat and salted fish to eat. Their room, however, was full of smoke which kept them awake and combined with the frost to make them all catch cold. They were happy to remount in the morning and leave as quickly as possible for Nicaea whose battlements and towers soon came into view, gleaming white as snow.

Such accounts will sound familiar to anyone who has read travellers of the last century or visited remote parts of Turkey, but they offer more than entertainment, for they serve to set the city in a landscape and to illustrate its relations with Constantinople. Roads between the two cities were rough and dangerous – and these were not obscure paths or back roads, for on both journeys Mesarites followed the main highways. A traveller would not normally want to journey alone or even in a small party on foot, yet he would apparently have no trouble finding transport with one of the mule trains which carried goods between Nicaea, the Gulf, and Constantinople. The Latin occupation seems not to have affected trade or communication – Mesarites makes no mention of frontiers or obstacles even though the whole region of Nicomedia was in the hands of the Latins – and the mule trains seem to have passed freely between the two states. Life would appear to have continued normally at that level, even though the Greeks and Latins were frequently at war. With their homely detail, the letters of Mesarites give an unusual glimpse into the setting of the city whose gleaming walls were a delight for those who had taken the trouble to approach them.

Theodore Laskaris soon brought strength and security to his new state. In 1211, the former Emperor Alexios III left Epiros, where he had been staying, and sailed to the hospitality of Ghiyath ed-Din of Konya, who was prepared to support his claims to the Empire. The Sultan's embassy to this effect reached Laskaris in Nicaea and caused considerable consternation until the Emperor was assured of full support. He then marched forth from the capital to Antioch on the Maeander where he won a resounding victory which ensured peace on the eastern frontier for the next half century. During the battle, Laskaris captured Alexios whom he stripped of his royal insignia and confined in the Monastery of Hyacinth at Nicaea. He eventually died and was buried there.[13]

Struggle with the Turks was followed by less successful encounters with the Latins, who gained much territory in the northwest. The fighting led to a treaty in 1212 which defined and stabilized the frontier. After this, the Latin rulers allowed Greeks to leave Constantinople, and many priests and monks came to Laskaris and were settled in the churches and monasteries of Nicaea. By this time, perhaps because of the growth of Latin power in the north, Laskaris began to spend part of the year in his southern realm, around Smyrna and Nymphaion. Consequently, he transferred the imperial mint, which had been striking silver, bronze and perhaps gold at Nicaea, to Magnesia.[14] Laskaris was still often in Nicaea, however: one of the final acts of the reign, in 1222, was the reception of a Latin embassy in Nicaea and the conclusion of another treaty with an exchange of prisoners.[15] Later in the same year, after establishing a viable state and laying the foundations for further progress, Laskaris died in Nicaea, and was buried in the monastery of Hyacinth.[16]

During the reign of Laskaris, Nicaea was not only the centre of political, diplomatic, and military activity, but was the seat of the Patriarch and of the Orthodox Church in exile. As such, it was the place where synods were held, and where the representatives of foreign churches were received.[17] In 1209, for example, a council was held in the patriarchate to regulate the affairs of the Church of Cyprus, then under Latin domination.[18] Five years later, a long-standing dispute came to a head and threatened to cause serious dissension in Nicaea as it had much earlier in Constantinople. Discussion revolved around the question of whether the Father was greater than the Son, and of the nature of the holy sacraments. Problems, which verged on heresy, were stirred up by learned clerics who had emigrated from Constantinople and brought the disputations of the former capital with them. The Emperor responded energetically to a matter which could severely disrupt the stability of the state if it were allowed to spread by laying aside his wars against Turks and Latins in order to lead the fight against possible heresy.[19] Such an issue gives a brief glimpse of what must have been a major problem in the city: the reception and accommodation of large numbers of refugees, many of them used to high civil or ecclesiastical rank. Room had to be found both physically and socially for new arrivals, and it is unlikely that their relations with the long-established local population were easy.

Embassies and synods continued to be a feature of local ecclesiastical life.

Most important among them, perhaps, was the mission sent by the papal legate in Constantinople in 1214. Once again, the circumstances are preserved in a colorful account of Mesarites, which reveals local conditions of another kind.[20] By this time, Mesarites had been given the high rank of Bishop of Ephesos, and as such he answered the imperial summons to choose a new patriarch when Michael Autorianos died in August 1214. He found the Emperor at Sardis, freshly returned from compaigning against the Turks. They proceeded together to Nicaea, where Laskaris settled the dogmatic disputes among the clergy, installed Theodore Eirenikos as the new patriarch, and swiftly left the capital for Paphlagonia on receiving the news that Alexios of Trebizond had been defeated by the Turks. A few days later, the legates of Rome arrived to initiate discussions about reunion of the churches. When he heard of this, Laskaris returned from the east, carried on talks with the legates and decided to send an embassy to Constantinople for further discussions. He chose Mesarites as its head.

The bishop and his party set out for Nicomedia and arrived at the southern shore of the Gulf where they waited a day and a night, apparently unable to cross to the opposite shore because it was in the hands of the Latins. In the morning, they almost met with disaster when a ship appeared; it turned out to be full of pirates, and they barely managed to escape to the hills with the loss of only one servant. They would have suffered worse had not the legate opportunely sent a ship which drove off the pirates and brought them safely to Constantinople. After ten days of inconclusive but not hostile discussions, Mesarites and his men returned to Nicaea with representatives of Cardinal Pelagius, crossing directly to Pylai and arriving the next day. When they learned that the Emperor had left for the east, they followed him to Pontic Herakleia with considerable misgiving, for the Turks were reported to be overrunning the Sangarios valley. Thanks to a military escort, they arrived safely. Here, after long disputations, the Roman legates returned directly by sea to Constantinople, while Mesarites made his way back to Nicaea overland, through the snow and ice which had now set in. The rough journey was good preparation for the reception he received; he was expelled from the house he had occupied and forced to live in discomfort suitable to a prisoner, for the new patriarch had little sympathy for dealing with the Latins and made Mesarites the victim of his indignation at being addressed by the Cardinal merely as "Archbishop of the Greeks." Mesarites stayed on at Nicaea until the emperor arrived, and there attended the celebration of his marriage with an Armenian princess. After that, he returned to Ephesos and apparently never revisited Nicaea.

Once again, Mesarites appears as a remarkable source for activities which took place in the city – reception of embassies, synods, royal weddings – and for hinting at the kind of disputes which could cause serious disturbance. He also gives another view of conditions in the surrounding area, this time the danger of travel in the sea of Marmara, infested by pirates, or perhaps simply Latins ready to attack the Greek shore.

The new Patriarch Theodore occupied his throne for only a short time. When he died in January 1216, the Emperor was campaigning in the Thrakesian theme and had no desire to interrupt his activities. At the same time, he recognised that the Church needed a head and called on Mesarites to hold local synods (apparently in Ephesos) to decide whether the Emperor had the right to propose a new patriarch while he was away from the capital. The assembled bishops agreed that he could indeed so act, and Laskaris chose his confessor, Maximos, a man, it seems, of little learning but skilled in the ways of the court and *gynaikeion*. The new patriarch was crowned in Nicaea in June 1216, when the Emperor returned.[21]

The final synod of the reign took place in 1220 when Laskaris called the bishops together to consider whether negotiations for union with the Roman Church should be pressed further: the subject was dropped after encountering the opposition of both Latins and Greeks.[22]

Nicaea contained its share of odd characters in the time of Laskaris, as appears from an anecdote inserted into the history of Akropolites. A certain simple man used to walk along the streets of the capital saying to all he met, "The good king will soon arrive." When news of this reached the court, Laskaris summoned him and asked, "What about me? Do you not think that I am a good king?" and heard in reply, "What have you given me that I should consider you good?" Laskaris pointed out that he spent much effort fighting for his people, to which the simpleton answered that the sun also did much good, but by nature, and got no thanks for it, and that the Emperor was similarly just doing his duty. Laskaris then asked if he would be considered good if he gave a present, and getting a very positive reply, made him a gift of clothing and money. Thereafter, his new-found friend began cursing anyone seeking another good king, for this one, he maintained, had all the virtues.[23]

Such a homely story was no doubt intended to show the close relations between Laskaris and the people of his capital, which seem in general to have been good. One cryptic source, however, claims that the Patriarch Maximos, to whom ecclesiastical writers seem to have been hostile, stirred the Emperor up against the people of Nicaea. If this has reference to the kind of factional sedition which frequently disturbed cities at this time, or to disputes between refugees and residents, it might not be surprising, but no substantiating details are recorded.[24] In any case, Laskaris' claim to struggle constantly for the Nicenes was justified by his incessant campaigns which brought security and stability to the state, and more immediately, by his work of construction in the city where, as will be seen below, he extensively rebuilt the fortifications and created a more powerful bulwark than had previously existed.

NOTES

[1] It is not purpose here to retell the history of the Nicene empire, but to concentrate on the city. For the general background, see the works of Meliarakes (1898), Gardner (1912) and Angold (1975).

[2] Choniates 612.

[3] For Constantine, see the excellent study of Sinogowitz (1952), who had the merit of discovering not only an unexploited source of great value, but far more remarkable, a new Byzantine emperor.

[4] Choniates, *Or.* 14. 134.

[5] Acropolites 10f.

[6] For these events, see Choniates *Or.* 14 with the important discussions of Sinogowitz (1952) and van Dieten (1971) 143-155; cf. Choniates 638.

[7] Choniates 640; cf. van Dieten (1971) 150f.

[8] Villehardouin 120f.

[9] Choniates 635, 645; for details of his life in this period, see van Dieten (1971) 46-51.

[10] Blemmydes, 2, 55.

[11] Akropolites 11; cf. Angold (1975) 43f; patriarchs: Nicephoros Kallistos 465.

[12] Mesarites, *Reisebericht*, in two parts: 35-43 give the main account of the journey to attend the synod of 1208, while the first journey is recorded only in a fragmentary account, 43-46. See Heisenberg's introduction, 5-12.

[13] Acropolites 15-17. According to one version, Skoutariotes 457 (*ap.* Acropolites 278) the former emperor was blinded because of his treachery in joining the Turks.

[14] Clerics: Akropolites 30; mint: Hendy (1985) 443-5.

[15] Dölger, *Regesten* 1706.

[16] Akropolites 32.

[17] For the activities of the patriarchate in this period, see Laurent, *Régestes* 1203-1349.

[18] Laurent, *Régestes* 1210; for site of the council, see below, 111.

[19] See Laurent, *Régestes* 1212 with full discussion and references. The key text is Mesarites, *Bericht* 11-18.

[20] For what follows, see Mesarites, *Bericht* 3.8, 10f, 33, 46f., with the appended comprehensive commentary of Heisenberg.

[21] Laurent (1969) 134f.; texts in Kurtz (1906) 103-5.

[22] Angold (1975) 15.

[23] Skoutariotes 463 (*ap.* Acropolites 279f.).

[24] Nikephoros Kallistos 465.

8. Nicaea under John Vatatzes and Theodore II: The Church and the Revival of Learning

The "Empire of Nicaea" reached its height under John Vatatzes (1222-1254) whose great successes in the West and work of consolidation at home laid the foundation for the triumphs which followed his death. Yet, the Empire in exile ceased to be an "Empire of Nicaea" in this reign, for Vatatzes soon moved to the South, which became his regular base of operations – to Nymphaion where he had his palace and regularly spent the winter, and to Magnesia whose walls guarded the mint and treasury. Nicaea nevertheless retained its prominence as the seat of the Patriarch and became an important centre of education and culture.

Even though it was no longer his residence, the Emperor was frequently present in Nicaea. In 1241, his marriage with Constance, daughter of Frederick II, was celebrated in the city with great festivity and a procession of the imperial couple followed by ambassadors, the nobility, foreign troops, and the people, paraded from the church to the royal palace. Texts of the very appealing songs by Nicholas Eirenikos which accompanied the ceremonies have been preserved.[1] The German princess had in her entourage three Calabrian monks who decided to stay with her in Nicaea. The Patriarch willingly welcomed them and allowed them to enter the Monastery of Hyacinth. Subsequently, when it was discovered that they had been ordained below the canonical age, they were suspended for three years, but were later restored to office.[2] The reign of Vatatzes functionally came to an end in Nicaea in February 1254, when the Emperor, stopping on his way back from a campaign, was suddenly struck dumb as he sat on his bed. He fell back, paralyzed, and so continued for two nights and a day until he recovered sufficiently to continue to his favored Nymphaion, where he soon died.[3]

The Nicene Church continued its normal activity as the centre of the Orthodox Church in exile. Its supremacy, however, was disputed by Michael, Despot of Epiros, who claimed independence for the bishop of his capital. Consequently, a synod was held in Nicaea in 1232 to discuss restoring unity between the two branches of the Church.[4] In the same year, five Franciscan friars who had been captured by the Turks as they returned from a pilgrimage to the Holy Land escaped to Nicaea. They were received by the Patriarch Germanos with whom they began discussions about union of the churches.[5] As a result, the Patriarch sent an emissary to Rome with them and the Pope in his turn sent four representatives to enter into serious discussions. The narrative of this embassy reveals further details about the city and the Latins' perception of it.[6]

The legates left Rome in the middle of 1233. They arrived in Nicaea on 15 June 1234, escorted by representatives of the Emperor and the Patriarch as well as the clergy of the cathedral, who met them with great rejoicing far outside the gates of the city. They arrived toward evening, and asked to be taken to the cathedral to pray, but their hosts instead brought them to another church where the First Council had been held and showed them the image of the Fathers of the Council on its walls. Finally, after a long tour of the city accompanied by priests and a crowd of townsfolk, they came to the residence which the Emperor had prepared for them and found it filled with everything necessary for their comfort.

The next two days saw a preliminary interview with the Patriarch, then a meeting with the Emperor, and an inauspicious beginning to the theological discussions. After that, the Roman monks felt the need for strength through prayer and requested a church or chapel for their own use. The Patriarch assigned them a suitable church next to their residence and in it they celebrated Mass the next morning. The congregation included Latins, French, English, and various nations evidently resident at Nicaea, most of them no doubt mercenary soldiers of the Emperor.[7] At the end of the service, one Latin came to them in tears because his priest had accused him of attending the legates' Mass. They were so indignant at this interference that they protested to the Patriarch who ordered the offending priest immediately defrocked and paraded through the city as far the patriarchate; he was then forgiven at the intercession of the friars. The rest of their stay was occupied by fruitless disputations in the royal palace and the patriarchate and finally on 27 June, since the Emperor was to depart the next day, they took their leave and returned to Constantinople. The next and more colorful stages of the discussions, which culminated in a shouting match, took place in Nymphaion and fall outside the present subject.

When Germanos, the Patriarch who presided over these meetings, died in 1240, there was considerable dispute about the succession. He had himself favored the great scholar Blemmydes and commended him to the Emperor on his deathbed. Vatatzes, however, opted for a candidate whom he thought might be more amenable by supporting a local man, Methodios the abbot of the Monastery of Hyacinth, and he was duly installed. According to the contemporary historian Akropolites, the new patriarch claimed to know a good deal but actually had little understanding. In any case, he died after only three months in office, leaving a vacancy which was to endure two years before the Emperor could find a suitable incumbent.[8]

A document rounds out the picture of the Nicene Church in this reign, a chrysobull of Michael Palaiologos issued between 1268 and 1271 to define the property and privileges of Hagia Sophia in Constantinople. According to this, the Patriarchate, when it was established at Nicaea, enjoyed only the revenues of the local metropolitan church. Although these were barely adequate to meet its needs, Laskaris was unable to make any substantial additions. Vatatzes, however, gave considerable property to the church after he regained the theme of Optimaton (the region of Nicomedia) from the Latins in 1241.

At first, Vatatzes restored some properties which had belonged to the patriarchate before the Latin occupation; these consisted of villages and fields with their dependent peasants as well as an old monastery and a market whose sites remain to be identified. Later, as his kingdom expanded, he added two rich and productive areas: the territory and harbor of Herakleion on the Gulf of Nicomedia together with fields, mills and a fort; then a region on the Lake, near Fort Saint George, with fields, villages, and a share of the imperial olive grove.[9]

It appears from this that the new patriarchate of Nicaea was relatively poor for some thirty years after its establishment, dependent upon the revenues of a metropolitan bishopric which, though large and prosperous, was not on the scale of the patriarchate. The local bishopric was evidently suppressed in favour of the patriarchate, for the revenues would not have sufficed for both, and no Bishop of Nicaea is recorded during this period. Two separate sets of clergy, however, were maintained, one for Nicaea and one to represent the clergy of Hagia Sophia in the former capital.[10] The Patriarch presided over both. After the great successes of Vatatzes in northwest Asia Minor, the state was more prosperous and could afford to make considerable donations of land, among them properties which the church had lost to the Latins. The consequent increase in revenues was no doubt a major factor in the construction of buildings and growth of education notable at Nicaea in the following decades.

The flourishing of Nicaea as a centre of culture and education is already evident in the time of Vatatzes, and the plant then encouraged continued to bloom until the conquest of Constantinople, when letters, like the administration and patriarchate, were transferred back to the ancient capital.[11] The beginnings were slow. When Nikephoros Blemmydes came to Nicaea in 1209, he could learn poetics and rhetoric, the elements of an education, but had to move to Smyrna and Ephesos for higher studies. The state nevertheless took some interest in higher education, maintaining the office of "Consul of the Philosophers," who had been the head of advanced studies in Constantinople.[12] Since Theodore Eirenikos had the title before he became Patriarch in 1214, it appears that the office was reestablished soon after the transfer of empire and that education was one of the prime concerns of the state.

During the reign of Vatatzes, Demetrios Karykes was Consul of the Philosophers and also a high officer of state. His role in education involved manifold duties which brought him into contact with the Emperor, other scholars, and foreign prelates. When Blemmydes finished his studies, he was examined by Karykes in the presence of Vatatzes, who took a personal interest in education and forthwith enrolled the successful candidate in the imperial service.[13] It was Karykes who opened the disputation with the Latin delegates at Nicaea in 1234, and Blemmydes who was the major advocate there of the Greek position.[14]

Nikephoros Blemmydes, by all accounts of his contemporaries and the evidence of his numerous surviving writings, was the greatest scholar of his age, a man highly skilled in classical learning of all kinds, and a voluminous writer. Although much of his work was done at his monastery in Ephesos, he played an active role at Nicaea early in his career. In 1220, he was enrolled in the patriarchal clergy in the capital and rose from reader to deacon to logothete, all in the space of thirty days. He served the Church during the next four years, a time marred for him by the jealousy and intrigues of the Bishops of Nicomedia and Kyzikos: both of them, however, soon came to a bad end.[15] The presence of these bishops at Nicaea suggests that the Church in exile followed the example of that of Constantinople by maintaining a permanent Synod of Bishops who resided at the patriarchal court or at least were frequently in attendance. Like their predecessors of earlier centuries, they no doubt preferred life in the metropolis, where they could participate actively in the affairs and intrigues of the Church, to the more homely duties which awaited them in their sees.

In 1227, the patriarch entrusted Blemmydes with the task of investigating and extirpating the "Manichaeans" in the region of Nicaea – that is, he was to destroy the dualist Bogomil or Cathar heresy which appears to have taken root in Asia Minor. The job soon proved uncongenial for a churchman whose main interest was scholarship, since he was obliged to deal with political matters as well as injustice and corruption. His description of his service focused on the difficulties he had with an *archon,* a member of the local aristocracy. This official, whose position appears to have been in the municipal or provincial government, arrested a certain reader of the church of Nicaea in order to seize the considerable wealth he was reputed to have. It was only with great difficulty that Blemmydes was able to rescue his fellow cleric.[16] The work of Blemmydes, nevertheless, appears to have been successful, for the Patriarch next assigned him the same job in Nymphaion, where he was also to administer the church for the local bishop. This proved too great a burden, and he withdrew to Lesbos. Although he was brought back to Nicaea and received with great honor, he retired again to a monastery, this time in Mount Latros. His last and perhaps most dramatic act in Nicaea took place in 1234 when he led the discussions with the Latin delegates. On that occasion, his merits failed to appeal to the Latins, who regarded him as somewhat of a windbag, as their report indicates: "surrexit quidam philosophus, facto magno et prolixo prologo." After that, Blemmydes settled first in the Troad, then Ephesos, where his major work was accomplished in the tranquility of a monastery.[17]

Although Blemmydes spent much time in Nicaea, he could use little of it to advance the cause of learning, which was mostly in the hands of others. One of them, Theodore Hexapterygos, was the teacher of the historian Akropolites, who described the scene in 1233 when he and his fellow students were summoned before the Emperor to be assigned to the teacher, and told of their responsibilities and opportunities. Hexapterygos, it seems, was highly skilled in rhetoric and composition, but relatively deficient in mathematics. When he died, Akropolites continued his studies with Blemmydes, no doubt in Ephesos.[18]

When Vatatzes died in 1254, he was succeeded by his son Theodore II, who only reigned for four years. In that short time, though, he brought about a real advance in education at Nicaea, for he was a natural patron of learning, being well trained in philosophy and a prolific writer. He was also a great lover of the new capital, as will become evident from his speech on the city, delivered while he was still a prince, at court before his father.[19] Soon after assuming the throne, Theodore hastened to Nicaea, to supervise the election of a new patriarch, for the previous incumbent had died at about the same time as Vatatzes, and a successor was immediately necessary to crown the new Emperor and ensure the functioning of the Church. The choice of the synod called for the election fell on the new Emperor's friend and former teacher Blemmydes. At the last minute, however, he declined the honor and resisted all attempts at persuasion. Theodore wanted the matter settled promptly in order to deal with a Bulgar attack. He therefore himself chose Arsenios, a monk of Lake Apollonias, who in a week was promoted through the ranks of deacon and priest to become Patriarch. Arsenios, later notorious for his opposition to union with Rome, was described by Akropolites as skilled in speech and action, but deficient in learning, a man who had received an education in philosophy, but understood little of it.[20] The new Patriarch proceeded to crown Theodore and together with him effected a major advance in education at Nicaea.

Up to this time, young men of the aristocracy received their education from private teachers, usually in the southern cities of the Empire. Theodore now made a fundamental change by setting up an imperial school in Nicaea. He appointed two teachers, Michael Sennacherim for rhetoric and Andronikos Phrangopoulos for poetics, sending them six students with his congratulations and wishes for their success. He also made material provision for the maintenance of the the school by providing allowances for both teachers and students.[21] Sennacherim, who was known as a scholiast on Homer, later rose to great prominence, largely through his skill in the law. Under Michael Palaiologos, he became head of the imperial tribunal and *mesazon*, or main intermediary between the Emperor and his subjects. When Constantinople was recaptured in 1261, Sennacherim heard the news at Nicomedia and, alone among the Byzantines, correctly predicted that the success would prove a disaster for the Empire.[22]

The new school was established in the Church of Saint Tryphon, which the Patriarch Arsenios rebuilt to "the size and beauty it now has" in the words of Skoutariotes who was writing in the late thirteenth century. Previously, the church had been made of earth bricks and lay below ground level, so that water formed in a pool on the floor and kept people from entering.[23]

Although such a school represented a significant advance, the instruction it offered was not to everyone's taste. When Gregory of Cyprus, later Patriarch of Constantinople, was a young man in about 1260, he wanted to leave his native island and go to Nicaea which he had heard described as another Athens because of the multitude of its learned men. His parents objected that he was too young to travel so far; he thereupon ran away from home and sailed to Ephesos, where he tried in vain to study with Blemmydes. He then made his way with great difficulty to Nicaea, and began to study only to meet a different kind of disappointment. The local teachers, he complained, taught grammar and poetics (the two subjects endowed by Theodore) superficially, no better than anyone else, and were ignorant of philosophy, rhetoric, and other studies. As far as he was concerned, it was a waste of time to study conjugations and declensions, Homer or Sophocles, but since nothing better was available, he stayed in Nicaea until the recapture of Constantinople brought new opportunities.[24]

The complaint of Gregory reveals that the local curriculum stressed pagan literature, no doubt *progymnasmata* of the kind which had always formed the basis of Byzantine education, and that such classical learning had no appeal for such a pious student. This reaction need not have been typical, however, for the speeches of Theodore Laskaris and Metochites clearly reveal that Nicaea became and remained a major centre of education in the empire of the thirteenth century, until replaced by Constantinople where Greek letters began to flourish after the reconquest. Several manuscripts of classical writers are known to have been copied in the Empire at this time, but none has been specifically assigned to Nicaea.[25]

An incidental anecdote reveals that education of a less formal kind was also available at Nicaea. A certain Hyacinth, who had been a monk in the West, came to the capital and settled in the Church of the Archangel Michael near the patriarchate. There, he supplemented his living by giving elementary instruction to children until he was denounced to the Patriarch Arsenios because, by so doing, he was violating his vows as a monk. The Patriarch, however, recognising that he was a man of some skill, made him his friend and confidant. Hyacinth eventually accompanied Arsenios to Constantinople after its recapture and there gained some notoriety as the avid supporter of his friend in his dispute with the Emperor.[26] The story reflects the normal situation that churchmen played a prominent role in primary education, but also suggests that such instruction was in demand, since an unknown monk could easily set himself up as a teacher.

So far, this narrative has dealt with the Church and the learning associated with it – that is, entirely with the Christians, but they were not alone in the city, nor was their learning the only kind available. The ancient Jewish community, last encountered in the ninth century, evidently survived into the Laskarid period, and had members who knew Hebrew. It has left only one monument, the tombstone of a certain Abraham ben Meier, a craftsman, who may have lived at this time.[27] He might also have been one of the last local Jews, for Vatatzes ordered all the Jews of his dominions to embrace Christianity.[28] This rare persecution was continued by Theodore II. The occasion and reasons for it are unknown, nor is it certain whether it marked the end of the Nicene Jews, who are not mentioned again.

The age of Vatatzes and his son, which came to an end when the latter died of epilepsy at an early age in 1258, was marked not only by the kind of learning displayed in Theodore's speech on Nicaea, but by important works of architecture. These involved reconstruction of the walls with the addition of an entire outer circuit, along with the building of several churches; all will be discussed below.

The archaeological record of the age, in so far as it consists of standing or known buildings, is substantial, the richest of any period in the city's history. Excavation, on the other hand, has been extremely limited, with only the ancient theatre presenting any evidence, and much of that enigmatic. The theatre had long since been abandoned and used as a quarry and a graveyard, and a dump. The Laskarids built a small church here and a larger building, preserved only in fragments.[29] Otherwise, the theatre was filled with burials, some of them dated by coins of Vatatzes and sgraffiato pottery of the thirteenth century. Most remarkable among them are the skeletons of thirty-seven men, all hastily buried together in the lower part of the cavea. The bodies seem to have been unceremoniously tossed one on another; some were naked, some wrapped in simple cloth. Others had been dismembered, and were buried in wooden boxes. Most bore clear traces of blows and cuts from weapons. All were of a Nordic type foreign to Anatolia.[30]

This gruesome collection of bones raises many questions, and illustrates not only some conditions of the time, but also the deficiencies of the sources. The young men who found their last resting place in the theatre were evidently foreigners, most probably Latin mercenaries of the kind whose existence is attested in the city. They appear to have died fighting, since some were practically hacked to pieces. The obvious association is with a war, but no fighting is recorded around Nicaea at this time, nor does it appear likely that soldiers who died in the imperial service would receive such a crude burial. The men, therefore, may have been victims of a faction fight or mob violence. The possible occasions are intriguing to contemplate, but can only be left to the imagination, for the historical record has no explanation to offer. If nothing else, though, these skeletons suggest that the times were perhaps less tranquil than they otherwise appear.

A second mass burial in the theatre suggests another local disaster. It consists of numerous skeletons, mostly of infants and children, buried in evident haste in shallow earth. They seem to have been the victims of a plague or epidemic, otherwise unrecorded in the sources.[31]

NOTES

[1] Heisenberg (1920) 97-112.
[2] Laurent, *Regestes* 1308, with details from an unpublished text.
[3] Akropolites 101.
[4] Laurent, *Regestes* 1261; see below, 110-114, for its setting.
[5] Golubovich, *Bibliotheca* 1. 161f.
[6] For what follows, see the full account in Golubovich (1919) 428-445.
[7] Latins formed an important part of the Laskarid army at all times: see Angold (1975) 188-201.
[8] Akropolites 71f.
[9] Zepos, *Ius* I. 659-666; Dolger, *Regesten* 1956.
[10] Blemmydes 7.
[11] For a summary appreciation of higher learning during the Nicene period, see Hunger (1959) 125-128; see also n. 25 below.
[12] For what follows, see Angold (1975) 179.
[13] Blemmydes 55, 60; but note that Blemmydes went to Smyrna to study with Karykes, who apparently taught there as well as (or rather than) in the capital.
[14] Blemmydes 60, 63.
[15] *Ibid.* 7-16.
[16] *Ibid.* 16f.
[17] *Ibid.* 22, 63-70; Golubovich (1919) 434.
[18] Akropolites 49f. The scene of Hexapterygos' activities is not clear from this passage, for Vatatzes is quoted as having brought students from Nicaea to study. The interview apparently took place in Nicaea or Nymphaion, where Vatatzes usually resided. If the latter, the teaching will have been done in one of the southern cities of the kingdom.
[19] Theodore frequently mentioned Nicaea in his letters, in reference to his presence there, or that of others including the Patriarch, but never with specific information; see the index to the edition of Festa.
[20] Akropolites 106f.; cf. 177.
[21] Theodore Laskaris, *ep.* 217, pp.271-76; cf. Skoutariotes 512 (*ap.* Acropolites 291).
[22] For the career of Sennacherim, see Angold (1975) 180, with Dolger, *Regesten* 1913a and Wilson (1983) 219; for the comment, Pachymeres 1.205 (=B I.149)

[23] Skoutariotes 512 (*ap.* Acropolites 291).

[24] Gregory of Cyprus 178f.

[25] On these, and for a pessimistic appraisal of Nicene education, see Wilson (1983) 218-225.

[26] Pachymeres I. 383 (=B I. 294).

[27] The inscription is published in Schneider (1943) 36 no. 69, with a translation. It is carved on a stone reused in the base of the minaret of the mosque of Kutbeddin. The only published photograph appears to be that in *Iznik* (1943) 28. My colleague Professor Lester Segal devoted much effort to transcription and photograph, and made valuable suggestions about the readings; my sincere thanks to him. According to Professor Segal, the inscription probably contains a date of which only the first letter may be read; that indicates the thirteenth century or later. In any case, the inscription must antedate the mosque, built in 1418; by that time, if not long before, the Jewish cemetery would appear to have been disaffected.

[28] Dolger, *Regesten* 1871, on which see Sharf (1980).

[29] See below, 109,119.

[30] See Yalman (1984, 1985, 1986, 1988, 1989), with the useful summaries in *AS* 35 (1985) 197f. and 36 (1986) 198f.f.

[31] Reported in Yalman (1990) 383f. and (1991) 382f. There was also a third, more regualr graveyard around the church; see below, 109.

9. The Return to Constantinople and the Last Byzantine Phase: 1258-1331

When Theodore II died in 1258, he left behind a small son to continue the dynasty under the protection of his old friend and adviser, George Mouzalon. Nine days after the Emperor's death, however, a party of the aristocracy, which had never been favorable to him, carried out a coup, murdered Mouzalon and installed Michael Palaiologos as regent. He soon turned this position to his own advantage, took the title of Despot, and installed his friends and relatives in high positions. Finally, at the end of 1258 or the beginning of 1259, Palaiologos was crowned Emperor by Patriarch Arsenios at Nicaea.

Prior to the coronation, the regent had gone to Philadelphia to inspect and fortify the frontier. He sent the Patriarch, with the bishops and clergy, ahead to Nicaea, then, when his tour of inspection was finished, he and a great retinue came to the city for the coronation. According to an agreement with the Patriarch, the young Emperor was to be crowned first, and then the regent, but Palaiologos by trickery and intimidation managed to secure his own coronation and to postpone that of the child. After the ceremony, the whole assembly made a solemn procession to the royal palace, with the new imperial couple riding ahead, wearing their royal diadems, while young Laskaris followed, content with a veil of pearls and precious stones. Palaiologos, recognising that the population of Nicaea was not favorable to his usurpation, made every effort to conciliate them by throwing silver coins among the crowd, and by giving speeches and military displays of jousts and polo. Satisfied with his great promises for the future, the citizens relaxed and even began to imitate his style of wearing the beard. Those who predicted dire consequences were ignored. After a few days at Nicaea, Palaiologos and his retinue left the Patriarch and returned to Nymphaion.[1]

The Patriarch was far from pleased at the course of events, especially when it became evident that the new Emperor had no intention of crowning John Laskaris. Consequently, late in 1259, he resigned his office and left Nicaea, walking from the patriarchate to the city gate, and then to the monastery of Agalmates near the wall, accompanied the while by great crowds. During the night, he quit the church to take up residence in the monastery of Paschasios near the Drakon river. When the clergy learned of his abdication, all the bishops who resided in Nicaea wrote letters begging him to return.[2] In his stead,

Michael chose Nikephoros, Bishop of Ephesos, who arrived at Nicaea with a great deal of gold from his former see, which he distributed in an effort to conciliate the clergy and people. His efforts were in vain, for the population would have nothing to do with him, but demanded the return of Arsenios, and the clergy remained so adamant that the Emperor had to move against many of them. Most of Arsenios' supporters were driven from Nicaea and forced to become monks, prominent among them Manuel, bishop of Thessalonike who was confined in a monastery on the shore of the Ascanian Lake.[3]

By 1260, Michael's power was consolidated and he could contemplate his main goal, the reconquest of Constantinople. As a first move in that direction, he besieged the fortress of Galata, the Venetian outpost on the opposite shore of the Golden Horn, and for this employed a force of highly skilled archers from the region of Nicaea. His attack roused the hopes of the new Patriarch Nikephoros, who left Nicaea after a short stay, descended to Helenopolis, and from there sailed to meet the Emperor; he anticipated that the recapture of the former capital would enable him to settle far from Nicaea and its hostile population.[4] Unfortunately for both, the siege failed. Palaiologos returned to Nymphaion, and Nikephoros died of disease at Nicaea early in 1261. Michael, yielding to the feelings of the people, then restored Arsenios.

During these years, the patriarchate grew in wealth. As the state expanded, it had greater resources to devote to the Church and consequently made important additions to its land holdings. Theodore II, during his short reign, added to the territory which Vatatzes had donated in the theme of Optimaton by contributing several villages. Michael Palaiologos, similarly, during the first years of his reign before 1261, gave more land, with villages on the Gulf of Nicomedia and the rest of the imperial olive groves near Fort Saint George, of which a part had already been donated.[5] The Church thus gained resources just as it was about to leave Nicaea forever.

On 25 July 1261, the long awaited great event, the recapture of Constantinople, happened unexpectedly when the general Strategopoulos and a small body of troops managed to enter the city. The news soon reached Nicomedia, where Michael Sennacherim, the former teacher of Nicaea, gloomily remarked on hearing it: "What do I hear? This has been saved up for our days! How have we sinned to survive to see such terrible things? No one can hope for any good now, since the Romans are once again walking in the City."[6] The warning, of course, proved accurate, for the brief glory of recapturing the capital was followed by increasing threats from the West, internal turmoil, and the loss of the Byzantine heartland in Asia Minor.

The first sign of trouble, the prelude to disaster in Anatolia, occurred in the region of Nicaea within a year of the reconquest. A revolt broke out in Trikokkia, a place in the mountain pass near Nicaea (presumably east of the city, overlooking the road to the Sangarios valley). Its inhabitants, who made their living from farming, defended the frontier by their skill in archery and their intimate knowledge of the rough mountainous country. These men, already hostile to Michael because of his usurpation, were led to revolt by his transfer of troops from the eastern frontier to the Balkans (the archers employed at the siege of Galata, for example, probably came from this region), and by his systematic policy of confiscating the land and removing the privileges of the *akritai,* or frontier guards.

Consequently, when a blind child, who was announced as the deposed John Laskaris, appeared among them, they enthusiastically embraced his cause and proclaimed him Emperor. Michael sent the regular troops against the rebels, who for a time held them off successfully because of their knowledge of the country. When the imperial force attempted to burn the forests and thus deprive the rebels of cover, they found themselves shot at from the heights and at a constant disadvantage because of the terrain. Finally, the diplomacy and bribes of the Emperor proved more effective: some of the rebels submitted, but, ominously, others fled to the Turks. The rest were subjected to harsh penalties and would have all been exiled, had they not been the only defenders of the frontier.[7]

The transfer of the capital naturally involved the emigration of civil and ecclesiastical dignitaries from Nicaea to Constantinople, but some at least maintained their wealth in the former capital. In 1264, the Emperor came into dispute with two high Church officials, John Bekkos and Theodore Xiphilinos. As a result, Michael, who was using this as a pretext to strengthen his control over the church, ordered the houses of the offending prelates demolished, their vines uprooted, and the men brought to him in person. Although both managed to take refuge in churches in Constantinople, imperial agents were sent to Nicaea to take action against their property, which evidently lay there rather than in Constantinople. It appears from this that the economic base of some, if not most, of the aristocracy remained at Nicaea.[8]

The following year saw a curious event in the city, a symptom of the troubles which were soon at hand. On 23 February 1265, in the middle of the morning, a rumor suddenly spread that the Mongols, who had crushed the Seljuk Turks in 1243 and were spreading their power through Anatolia, had arrived at Nicaea in great numbers. According to the story, they had slaughtered the guards at the gate, entered the city and were killing everyone in sight. The city fell into complete panic. A great crowd gathered and started rushing around, while others sought safety by hiding in houses and tombs. Nicholas Manouelites, the *prokathemenos,* or governor of the city, accompanied by his garrison troops, came out to see what was happening and put himself at the head of the crowd. They were joined by the prisoners from the local jail, who escaped when they heard that the city had been taken, even though the prison was called "Lethe" ("Oblivion") because of its great security. The augmented throng, led by the governor, rushed to the east gate, where attack was most likely, only to find that nothing had happened. From there, they hastened to the other gates, and last to the sea gate, where attack was least probable, only to find no trace of the Mongols. It finally turned out that the rumor had been started when people heard a group of women, in procession behind an image of the Virgin, imploring God in tones of lamentation to spare the people from the Turks and Mongols. The hearers mistakenly thought that the women were weeping because the city had actually been taken, and spread the rumor which caused total panic. When the news of these events reached Constantinople, the Emperor sent a letter castigating the population, pointing out how irrational their fears were since the Mongols had only just arrived in Asia Minor from Persia, and warning them to stay on their guard in the future. The incident reveals not only a state of mind – a population swift to panic at the thought of attack from the east – but a present reality: the long-established enemy, the Seljuks, with whom a *modus vivendi* had been reached, were now weakened and largely replaced by the far more formidable Mongols at a time when the Byzantine defences were being undermined by the actions of the government. Although Nicaea was still some distance from the frontier, confidence could no longer be placed in the system of defence, especially since the arrival of the Mongols and weakening of the Seljuk state had released bands of nomadic tribesmen who were constantly raiding Byzantine lands. Incidentally, the account also shows that Nicaea had a prison of some repute (the city had long since been a place of exile) and was governed, as the cities of the Lascarid state normally had been, by a *prokathemenos,* an official appointed by the Emperor.[9]

The role of Nicaea as a prison became especially important during the last decade of Michael's reign, when internal troubles grew as a result of his proposals for union of the Greek and Roman Churches, which roused widespread hostility. One of the first victims of the emperor's displeasure was the well-known rhetorician Holobolos, who was exiled to the monastery of Hyacinth because he objected to the proposals. After the union became a reality in 1273, many other churchmen joined him in Nicaea.[10] The powerful walls of the city also provided a convenient means of detaining foreign potentates or their relatives. When the Bulgar Prince Terter married the sister of the Tsar Asen, he sent his now inconvenient first wife and their son to the Emperor who had them imprisoned in Nicaea. Later, when Terter became king, they were released, and the son, Svetoslav, in his turn eventually succeeded to the Bulgar throne.[11]

Among the victims of the persecutions of 1274 was a native of Nicaea, Theoleptos. At the time of the Union, he was a young man of twenty-five. He left his wife and children, joined a band of ascetic monks, and denounced the Emperor. He was thereupon arrested, but was eventually released and became a hermit in the vicinity of Nicaea. There, people flocked to him from the city as a holy man, even though he was not a priest. Later, before 1285, he became Bishop of Philadelphia and enjoyed a highly distinguished career.[12] The same period saw the Bishop of Nicaea, Theophanes, rise to great prominence. In opposition to many of his colleagues, he supported the Union and participated in the negotiations for it, being sent on embassies to the Pope in 1274 and 1280. His activity, however, is almost certainly to be seen in the context of Constantinople rather than Nicaea, for, as previously, it was the custom of leading churchmen to reside at the capital where they could rise to prominence.[13]

Toward the end of his reign, Michael became obsessed with conspiracy, and reacted violently against his enemies, real or imagined. The year 1280 claimed two notable victims. Basil, Bishop of Adrianople and nephew of the former Patriarch Germanos, fell under suspicion and was exiled to Nicaea; he was blinded before he entered the city, described as a fort *(kastron)*. The case of John Angelos, son of Michael, despot of Epiros, was more serious as revealing the deficiencies of Byzantine resistance to the Turks. John had been gaining considerable success against them, apparently using Nicaea as his base. The glory he seemed to be winning made him an object of suspicion and jealousy to the Emperor who had him brought in chains from Nicaea, blinded and exiled.[14]

The main efforts of the restored Byzantine government were necessarily directed toward the West, which presented the more immediate threat as its powers attempted to restore the Latin Empire. It was thus only toward the end of his reign that Michael made an expedition to Anatolia to visit the frontier and strengthen it against the marauding Turks. He travelled via Nicomedia to the Sangarios valley where he inspected the fortifications and was appalled by the poverty and weakness of the region and its defense. Unable to accomplish anything significant against the Turks, he returned to Prusa and Mysia. The patriarch, John Bekkos, planned to join Michael, and sailed to Kibotos, then followed the highway toward Nicaea as far as Ennaton, evidently a post at the ninth mile from the city. He stopped there, hesitating to continue because he had no money to give to the population of Nicaea who expected some largess. Consequently, he returned to Pythia and the capital.[15]

The Patriarch had more success the following year when Empress Anna died. Her body was brought to Nicaea, where the Emperor, Patriarch, and the clergy soon arrived for the funeral. This time, Bekkos was better provided, and was able to give presents to the population.[16] These incidental mentions, as well as the accounts considered above, indicate that the population of Nicaea had become notably turbulent and independent-minded, perhaps as a result of the loss of prestige resulting from the transfer of the capital, combined with the growing Turkish threat, which transformed the city into a major bulwark of the frontier at a time when that frontier was being increasingly neglected.

Michael Palaiologos died in 1282, leaving provision in his will for the Monastery of Kellibara which he founded in the capital. He endowed priests and monks in various churches of the kingdom associated with his foundation, among them two monks in the Church of the Holy Trinity in Nicaea, a city which he had much reason to remember.[17]

Michael was succeeded by his son Andronikos II, whose long reign (1282-1328) saw the collapse of the Byzantine power in Asia Minor. When Andronikos came to the throne, the Empire still controlled the richest parts of the west, with the fertile valleys of the Aegean region from Bithynia to Caria. At his death, only a few forts in the northwest, Nicaea precariously among them, were holding out like islands in the Turkish flood. His reign nevertheless saw some striking events in the city, one of them destined to add to its eternal renown.

In 1290, the Emperor, who had campaigned in Asia Minor as a prince, embarked on a long tour which was to last three years. He stayed in Nicaea, visited the frontier regions of the Sangarios, then moved via Lopadion to Nymphaion which he made his headquarters. His visit to Nicaea, the occasion for strengthening the walls, was momentous for a less material reason: it saw the beginning of the career of Theodore Metochites who, at the age of only twenty, composed his Nicene speech and delivered it before the Emperor. Andronikos was so impressed that he took the young man into imperial service, even though his father was in disgrace, and gave an impetus to the great success Metochites was to achieve. The speech, which forms the subject of the present work, is the last great tribute to the city whose form, as defined by its walls, was then over a thousand years old. Within a generation, Nicaea was forever lost to the Turks; Metochites lived to see its fall, an event he survived by only a year.[18]

Nicaea appears on only two other occasions during this reign, the first casual, the other ominous. In 1294, Theodore Mouzalon, one of the highest officials of the Empire, died. His body was taken to Nicaea to the monastery of Tornikios where he had acquired the right of burial with his wife's dowry.[19] Less than a decade later, in 1302, a Turkish commander destined to play a great role in history first appears in the records of Byzantium, and, for that matter, in any historical source. The contemporary historian Pachymeres, in describing the battle of Bapheus near Nicomedia, mentions that Osman had been attacking the area around Nicaea when he learned of the Byzantine expedition into Anatolia and joined forces with the leader of the Turks of Paphlagonia to inflict a decisive blow to imperial hopes of reestablishing control in Asia Minor.[20] This Osman, who appears as a minor tribal chief, casually mentioned, was to prove the greatest adversary of the Empire by building a state on its eastern frontiers which would soon overwhelm Byzantine Asia Minor and eventually destroy the Empire itself.

The threat posed by Osman became an oppressive reality in 1306, when Turkish forces advanced far into the western parts of Bithynia. They ravaged the lands around the gulf of Nicomedia, and cut Nicaea off from the coast. Instead of taking the direct routes from the Gulf, communication was confined to an overgrown and disused road from the port of Kios to the lake, proceeding from there by water to the sea gate of the city. The other gates could not be opened safely, for fear of the Turks who were blockading the city by land. Even this route was dangerous, and passage was made by night. The Emperor, in one of his many futile efforts to rescue his Anatolian possessions, sent a force to the region of Prusa, but it was easily defeated, and further losses followed. If Nicaea escaped capture now, it was because of diplomacy, not military force. Andronikos made an alliance with the Mongols who brought Osman and his Turks into submission; the city had twenty years of respite.[21]

It was probably during these years that Nicaea acquired something of great value and badly needed, a new saint, who revealed himself in the city under curious circumstances. Knowledge of him comes entirely from a speech written in the early fourteenth century by Constantine Akropolites, son of the historian George Akropolites. He rose to high positions, wrote numerous works on theology and hagiography, and died in about 1324.

The account opens with a formal, brief praise of Nicaea which gives special attention to the learning for which the city had long been famed:

> Πόλις ἀρχαία, πόλις περίφημος, Σάγγαριν ποταμὸν τῶν ὁρίων προβεβλημένη, παρὰ δ' αὐτὰς τὰς τῆς Ἀσκανίας λίμνης ὄχθας ᾠκημένη, ἣν μὲν ἐκ μακροῦ περιφανὴς καὶ περίβλεπτος. Βιθυνίας τε προκαθημένη καὶ τῶν περιρρεόντων ἕνεκεν ἀγαθῶν ἐπιεικῶς περιαδομένη. Χρόνου δὲ προϊόντος καὶ τῶν καθ' ἡμᾶς πραγμάτων ἀλλοίωσιν εἰληφότων, καὶ ἐπὶ μέγα δόξης τὰ κατὰ ταύτην προύχώρησε καὶ κατ' ἐπωνυμίαν τὴν νικῶσαν ὡς ἐν ἁμίλλῃ πρὸς τὰς ἐν ἕῳ πόλεις πάσας ἠνέγκατο· λογίων γὰρ ἀνδρῶν εὐμοιρήσασα, σπουδὰς διαφόρων, ὡς εἰπεῖν, παιδευμάτων ἀνέδωκεν. Ἔνθεν καὶ λογίμους ἄνδρας ἀνέβλαστε καὶ τῶν ἐκεῖθεν καρπῶν ἡ τῶν Ῥωμαίων ἀφθόνως ἀπήλαυσεν, ὡς ἐντεῦθεν βασιλεῖς τε καὶ πατριάρχας τὰ μεγάλα πρὸς τοὺς κύκλῳ καὶ πόρρωθι φιλοτιμεῖσθαι καὶ ἐναβρύνεσθαι. Τοίνυν καὶ τὰ πρωτεῖα μετὰ τὴν πρώτην ταύτῃ πάντες ἀπένεμον.

> An ancient city, a revered city, founded on the banks of the Ascanian lake with its boundaries extending to the Sangarios river, it was long conspicuous and admired, presiding over Bithynia and suitably celebrated for the good things which abound. As time went on and our situation changed, her accomplishments advanced her to great glory and made her the victor

in accordance with her name, as if in a contest with all the cities of the East; for, happy in the possession of learned men, she spread about, as it were, the enthusiasm of her distinguished pupils. Then she produced famous men and the Roman empire abundantly enjoyed the benefits which came from them. As a result of this, the Emperors and Patriarchs were special objects of emulation and pride for those near and far away. Everyone therefore assigned her the first rank after the first (city; i.e. Constantinople).[22]

The saint, whose name at first was unknown, was buried in a cemetery for strangers in the suburb of Agalmates (apparently named for an ancient monument, *agalma*) two miles from the city. After resting in obscurity for many years, he appeared in a dream to a local peasant who had a blind daughter, promising a cure if the man found his body and brought it into the city. The peasant followed the directions, but found many bodies in the same spot, and was in a quandary until that of the saint was miraculously revealed.

The body was loaded onto a wagon and brought to Nicaea, arriving at the gates before dawn, when they were still shut. As soon as they were opened, the peasant entered with his sacred burden, not knowing which way to proceed. Monks who met him contested for the honor of possessing the new relic, but his oxen kept moving until they came to the Church of Saint Tryphon, beyond which they would not budge. The body was duly installed in the church and immediately began working miracles. First, the peasant's daughter, as promised, was cured of her blindness; then all who had eye trouble, including Akropolites' (unnamed) teacher who was almost blind, obtained relief. Not only did the saint's body work cures, but the medallions of other saints, which he wore on his chest, had the same effect even at a distance (though all cures stopped when they were stolen) as did the iron staff with a cross which rested in his hand.

No one yet knew who the saint was; the people, and especially the local priest, naturally became curious. One morning at dawn, the priest beat the sounding board which summoned the faithful to prayer and opened the doors of the church in order to light the lamps and set candles on spits before the holy icons. To his astonishment, he found the lamps and candles already burning, the church full of light, and an old man of distinguished appearance standing by the font. The stranger identified himself as the saint, a native of Lampsakos who had joined the army, married, and had seven children, all of whom had died. He thereupon took his iron staff with a cross and became an ascetic on Mount Olympos, descending to Agalmates only shortly before his death. His name was John. The priest told this story to Akropolites' teacher, who in turn urged his pupil to write the account. It ends with a prayer for help against the Agarenes whose daily attacks were devastating the land.

The Last Byzantine Phase: 1258-1331

This narrative has many features of interest, the most notable being the discovery of the saint whose career as a holy man might have escaped notice altogether had not his body been revealed. The credulity of the people, too, is striking, for all were willing to accept the holiness of the unknown stranger without having a clue to his identity. Whatever the truth of the life and miracles of Saint John the Merciful the Younger (so called to distinguish him from the emperor John Vatatzes, who was himself honored as a saint long after his death), the circumstantial details bear every mark of authenticity. The gates of the city were locked at night and a voyager had to wait till dawn for admittance. At that moment, a wooden clapper was struck to announce the first service of the day, churches were opened and their candles were lit. The Church of Saint Tryphon, as will be seen, was a real place, the scene of a famous recurrent miracle, and the suburb of Agalmates was a real place outside the walls. It contained the monastery in which Patriarch Arsenios took refuge after his abdication. Finally, the Agarenes – for so the antiquarian language of Byzantium called the Turks – were a real menace whose daily attacks were indeed to be feared late in the thirteenth century.

Nicaea only appears in history again on the eve of a fundamental change, its transformation from the Christian city it had been for a millennium into a centre of the Moslem Turks. One of the final mentions constitutes the last formal praises of the city, found in the funeral oration which Nikephoros Choumnos devoted to Theoleptos of Philadelphia, a native of Nicaea, in about 1325. It deals, however, not with present realities, but with the glory of the Nicene Church:

> οὗτος ἐγένετο, καὶ πατρίδος τῆς Νικαέων, τῆς δευτέρας ἔμοιγε Σιών. Ὡς γὰρ ἐκ τῆς πρώτης καὶ πρῶτος ὁ κατὰ Χριστὸν νόμος ἐξῆλθε καὶ λόγος, τὸ τῆς σωτηρίας ἡμῶν κήρυγμα· οὕτω δὴ καὶ αὖθις, τοῦ νόμου τούτου κινδυνεύοντος, αὐτοί γε οὗτοι οὓς ἔφημεν πατέρας, ὑπὲρ Χριστοῦ, τῷ ζήλῳ καὶ τῷ πυρὶ τούτου ζέοντες καὶ θερμοί τινες ὄντες ὁπλῖται, τὰς τοῦ Πνεύματος μαχαίρας, γλώσσας τὰς ἑαυτῶν, θήξαντες τῇ εὐσεβείᾳ, οὐ πρὸ τῆς πόλεως, ἐν αὐτῇ δὲ τῇ πόλει βάλοντες τὰς αἱρέσεις ἀπέκτειναν, οὐκ εἰς τὰς πρωΐας μόνον, ἀλλὰ καὶ μέχρι παντός, ἐξ αὐτῆς τῆς πόλεως καὶ πάσης ἄλλης ἧς ὁ Χριστὸς κύριος ἐξωλοθρευκότες. Τοιαύτην ἐκεῖνος ἔσχε τὴν πατρίδα, εὐσεβείας μητρόπολιν·

> His native country was Nicaea, the second Zion in my opinion. Just as the first law and word of Christ, the announcement of our salvation, came from the first Zion, so later, when that law was in danger, these very fathers whom we have mentioned, seething with enthusiasm and fire for Christ, and being His avid champions, sharpened the swords of the Spirit – their tongues –

with piety; they struck down and killed heresies not in front of
the city, but in the city itself; they annihilated them from that
city and from every other of which Christ is Lord, not just for
those early days, but for all time. Such a country did he have,
the metropolis of piety.[23]

These sentiments show that the ancient role of the city in the history of the
Church was not forgotten, even though Christianity was soon to become a
memory in the place which had given it definition. In 1329, news reached the
capital that the new Turkish chief, Orhan, son of Osman, who had already
made tremendous gains in the expense of the Empire, was besieging Nicaea.
His forces were blockading the city, which was threatened both by war and by
starvation. The inhabitants were reported as ready to go over to the Turks if no
help were forthcoming. The new Emperor, Andronikos III, made an attempt
to save the situation by leading an army into Anatolia, a land where Byzantine
power barely survived beyond the coasts. Together with his chief general John
Kantakouzenos (whose eyewitness account provides the details of the campaign), the force advanced and on the third day reached the vicinity of
Philokrene, halfway to Nicomedia on the north shore of the gulf. Here the
Byzantines met Orhan and were overwhelmed. The defeat removed the last
hope of saving any part of Asia Minor or of stopping the Ottoman advance;
within a few years, virtually nothing remained except a few precarious toeholds on the coast.[24]

The Byzantine defeat doomed Nicaea. Finally, on 2 March 1331, the city,
which had long resisted blockade, surrendered on terms. Its walls had enabled
it to hold out for two years against the Turks whose strength resided in cavalry
and archers, but they were not protection against the hunger which a blockade
could bring. The conquerors, who were more interested in money than ecclesiastical treasures, sold many sacred books and icons, as well as the relics of
two female saints.[25]

After the conquest, the city sank into temporary eclipse. Its condition at
that time, which has implications for the last Byzantine period, was described
by an indefatigable traveler, Ibn Battuta, who visited Yaznik (as he called it,
using an Arabic form of the Turkish name Iznik) in about 1335. Like others,
he admired the walls which were complex and surrounded by a moat, but
found the area within them practically deserted. The only inhabitants were a
few of the Sultan's men. Its buildings were dilapidated, and the place had a
rural rather than urban aspect, since it contained houses scattered among the
fields and orchards which filled the area within the walls. The water supply
was from shallow wells, and the land fertile, producing excellent walnuts,
chestnuts, and grapes.[26]

In its first years under the Ottomans, Nicaea thus barely preserved the appearance of a city. To some extent, this must have been due to the emigration which would have been continuous for the previous half century or more as the frontier moved ever closer and the Turkish raiders became more successful and ubiquitous. People naturally would leave to seek the apparent security of the capital or the European provinces, while those who stayed behind had to face not only attack but the constant disruption of agriculture which could only have brought a reduced supply of food with greater danger of famine and disease.[27] It is quite probable that the Turks found a place in which only a small population survived. But even at its height as a capital, as the speech of Metochites will show, Nicaea contained much open space, and the area of the Roman theatre, the one part known from excavation, was always desolate and abandoned. Byzantine Nicaea, in other words, had not filled the area within the walls, though it had probably never been so reduced as it was at the time of the conquest.

The Christian community dwindled rapidly, from natural causes as well as conversion to Islam, whether forced or chosen. Two letters of the Patriarch, written in 1338 and 1340 reveal a situation for which the solutions were drastic. Those faced with conversion had two choices: martyrdom, for which there were many noble precedents, or, perhaps more realistically, maintaining the appearance of apostasy, but inwardly remaining Christian. According to these texts, the open profession of Christianity seems not to have been an available alternative.[28]

In spite of this gloomy picture, there were still some professing Christians in 1354 when Bishop Gregory Palamas arrived as a captive of the Turks. Since he was allowed considerable freedom of movement within the town, he enquired where the Christians lived and was directed to the neighborhood of the Monastery of "the Blessed" Hyacinth. He was delighted by what he found: a beautifully decorated church set in a cool courtyard shaded by abundant trees and containing a well. He took up his lodging there and the next day ventured out to see the east gate. He admired the high and powerful fortifications – now useless – and stepped outside where he engaged a Turkish religious teacher in a long theological discussion.[29] With this brief description, the long history of Christian Nicaea comes to an end.

The subsequent fate of Turkish Iznik, which saw a brief flourishing followed by a long decline, falls outside the scope of the present discussion.[30] The city soon recovered from its desolation to become the site of elegant mosques and numerous religious foundations, but construction had largely ceased by the late fifteenth century. Later, Iznik became a famed centre of pottery manufacture, which, however, seems not to have brought a general recovery. When the first European travelers arrived in the sixteenth century, they found the city in the state it preserved until recently, a place more remarkable for its past than its present, with few inhabitants scattered through the ruins. Recent decades, however have brought a notable change; the town has become a prosperous regional center and a convenient and exceptionally attractive resort for weekends from Istanbul. The area within the walls, which still stand in a remarkable state of preservation, is rapidly filling with houses. They obliterate much of the past, leaving the delapidated remains of a few churches with the massive substructures of the Roman theatre as reminders of the splendid past of a city whose history reaches back, unbroken, for more than two millennia. Its brief moment of glory, as the capital of an Empire, has still left many traces, well worth the effort of finding and admiring.

NOTES

[1] Pachymeres 1.139-149 (=B 1.98-105); for the usurpation of Palaiologos, see Geanakoplos (1959) 33-46.
[2] Pachymeres 1.159 (=B 1.111f).
[3] Pachymeres 1.165ff (=B 1.117ff.); Akropolites 179ff.
[4] Pachymeres 1.167f. (=B 1.118f), 1.173 (=B 1.122).
[5] Zepos, Ius 662.
[6] Pachymeres 1.205 (=B 1.149).
[7] Pachymeres 1.259-267b (=B 1.193-201). For a clear account of this revolt in a broader context, see Lindner (1983) 14f.
[8] Pachymeres 1.299 (=B 1.227).
[9] Pachymeres 1.317-325 (=B 1.244-250); for the *prokathemenos,* see Angold (1975) 264 ff.
[10] Pachymeres 1.501, 503 (=B 1.391, 394).
[11] Pachymeres 1.567 (=B 1.447f), 2.57, 267; Gregoras 1.133.
[12] Choumnos, *Epitaphios* 203-212.
[13] Pachymeres 1.493 (=B 1.384), 1.637 (=B 1.505f.); for his career, see *PLP* 7606.
[14] Basil: Pachymeres 1.393 (=B 1.303); John: *ibid.* 1.613 (=B 1.485).
[15] Pachymeres 1.623 (=B 1.493f); for the campaign of Michael, see Lindner (1983) 16.
[16] Pachymeres 1.631f. (=B 1.499).
[17] Palaiologos, *de Vita sua* 473f.
[18] Andronikos' tour is discussed by Laiou (1972) 76-84 on the basis of the unpublished *Basilikoi Logoi* of Metochites; for the career of the latter and his speech at Nicaea, see Ševčenko (1975) 24-37. The walls and the speech will be treated in detail below.
[19] Pachymeres B 2.193.
[20] Pachymeres B 2.332; for these events, see Arnakis (1947) 127-132 and Lindner (1983) 25f.
[21] Pachymeres B 2.412-414; for the circumstances, see Arnakis (1947) 142-55.
[22] The translation cannot reproduce the elegant play of the verbal prefixes *pro-* and *peri-* in the original. The text is published by Polemis (1973) with full discussion. It nowhere indicates the date of the events, but the mention of Akropolites' teacher, who heard of the Saint just after he had been revealed, being an old man, going blind, gives an indication. Akropolites was born in about 1260 and was thus a student in the following decade. It seems likely, therefore, that the Saint appeared in the late thirteenth century.
[23] Choumnos, *Epitaphios* 188.
[24] Kantakouzenos 1. 341-360, cf. Gregoras 1.433 and Chalkokondyles 22f. Arnakis (1947) 176-88 provides the best modern account of the battle and its consequences.

[25] Kantakouzenos 360-363; cf. Gregoras 1.458. The date is provided by an anonymous short chronicle, *Chron. Brev.* 1.79.24.
[26] Ibn Battuta 2.452f.
[27] On conditions in Asia Minor at this time, see Vryonis (1971) 250-58.
[28] Miklosich and Muller 1.183f., 197f.
[29] Palamas 18.30.
[30] For Turkish Iznik, see the excellent study of Raby (1976).

10. The Walls of the City

When Nicaea was capital of the Empire, it was surrounded by a massive and impressive double rampart consisting of a high inner wall, a lower outer wall or *proteichisma,* and a ditch. These fortifications, not by accident, resembled those of Constantinople, and were the subject of specific praise in the speeches of Laskaris and Metochites. Such an elaborate system of defence was the product of a long evolution, which saw constant rebuilding and modification over the thousand years during which the walls had been in use. These changes to the largest and best preserved monument of the Byzantine city enable practically every period of its history to be traced in stone.[1]

Hellenistic and Roman Nicaea was surrounded by walls which Strabo described in the first century. These have entirely disappeared, leaving as their only trace the triumphal arches of Vespasian and Hadrian which were incorporated in the later city gates. The history of the present rampart begins in the chaotic days of the late third century when western Asia Minor was threatened and overrun by the Goths. Gallienus (253-268) began and Claudius Gothicus (267-270) completed a powerful and carefully built circuit wall which was such an object of local pride that it appears on coins of Nicaea issued by the usurpers Macrianus and Quietus (260-261). These walls were the base on which all later fortifications were built.

The new rampart formed an irregular pentagon almost exactly five kilometres long, which defined the circuit followed through the Middle Ages. It was built on a far more substantial scale than most other walls of the time, and so solidly that much of it has survived all the troubles of past ages to remain standing even now. Walls and towers alike consisted of a core of rubble densely packed in mortar and covered with a facing [Fig. 2]. The curtain walls were faced with fieldstones so laid that flat sides faced outward, and the joints between them were filled with mortar. This facing was anchored to the core by bands of brick, laid four thick, which stretched though the body of the wall, each thus providing a bonding and a smooth foundation for the next layer of masonry. The towers had a facing of brick, some of which stretched deeper into the core to provide a bond.

This original wall was single, perhaps with a ditch before it (the ditch is first mentioned in the eleventh century). The towers, which were semicircular with a diameter of eight to nine metres, stood about sixty to seventy metres apart. Their projection enabled the approaches to the curtain wall to be covered by fire from two sides. Twin towers flanking the gates offered additional protection at the most vulnerable points. By standing above the wall, they also provided a greater range of fire from their upper platforms, suitable for the installation of artillery such as catapults which could strike the enemy and his machinery at a distance. Vaulted chambers in the towers at the level of the wall-walk had no opening to the outside and were apparently intended for storage of supplies. Posterns in many if not most of the towers enabled the defenders to launch surprise sallies. The curtain wall, about four metres thick, supported a wall-walk reached by stone stairs built against its inner face. This walk, defended by battlements, provided the main defensive zone of the wall.

Although seemingly simple, these high and solid walls were far more elaborate that those which defended most of the cities of Asia Minor against the Gothic menace. These generally were much thinner (usually about 1m50), lacked towers and were hastily built of whatever reusable material was at hand.[2] Nicaea thus had an exceptional system of defence from the beginning, by far the most imposing in the whole region.

The walls evidently performed their function without major change during the relatively tranquil years of Late Antiquity, when only the revolt of Prokopios in 365 involved the city in a siege. The Persian invasions at the beginning of the seventh century are likely to have affected Nicaea, but no text mentions the place, nor do the walls show any work which may be associated with these events. Thereafter, however, Nicaea became one of the great military bases of the empire and was frequently the scene of bitter fighting. Such activity brought many changes to the walls.

In 715, the ephemeral Emperor Artemios took refuge behind the walls of Nicaea, and in the following year the region was attacked by the Arabs. The city probably did not suffer on either of these occasions, but the great attack of 727, when two Arab armies besieged the city, inflicted severe damage. Parts of the walls were knocked down, but the Arabs were unable to enter the city. After their withdrawal, considerable repairs were necessary. These provided the occasion for a general rebuilding of the walls, now almost five hundred years old.

The Arabs appear to have concentrated their attacks of the neighborhood of the north and south gates, where repairs were most extensive. The walls and towers west of the Istanbul gate were completely rebuilt: the walls received a new stone facing, and the old round towers were converted into larger rectangular structures. In all cases, the new facing was far more elegant than the old, with marble blocks and column drums from ruined buildings laid in regular courses of ashlar and cemented with mortar [Fig.3]. The work was commemorated in one of the few inscriptions which still survives in its original place on the walls [Fig.4]. It celebrates the divine help which subdued the boldness of the enemy, names Leo III (716-741) and his son Constantine as the builders, and shows that the project was executed by the *curopalates* Artavasdos, who was then general of the Opsikian theme, son-in-law of the Emperor, and one of the most powerful figures of the day. The text, though in prose, is written in a poetic style and contains traces of iambic verses to suggest that it might have been based on a poem, perhaps one devoted to the victories of Leo.[3]

Analogy of masonry and mortar has enabled other sections of the wall to be attributed to this time. The towers and walls east of the South Lake Gate are evidently part of this project, as are the spur walls which connect the fortress with the lake shore. In addition, the whole circuit was raised by a new wall-walk and parapet of reused material, most of it consisting of seats from the ancient theatre [Fig. 2]. As a result, the defensive system was greatly strengthened, and Nicaea was better enabled to fulfill its role as military base and capital of a large strategic province at a time when it was constantly exposed to attack.

A century later, when the constant attacks of the Arabs had diminished and the Byzantine state was preparing to move on the offensive, the government of Michael III (842-868) carried out a major program of strengthening the defences of Asia Minor. This activity is especially evident at Ankyra, the main bastion and road junction of the central plateau, and is attested at Smyrna. Nicaea appears to have received the greatest attention of any fortress, with changes and improvements which produced the first redesign of the defensive system since its inception.

The most striking aspect of the new plan went beyond the normal reconstruction and consolidation by adding new towers between the old on the southeast and east walls, where the configuration of the fortress presented long straight flanks to an attacker. In this way, the number of towers, and thus the firepower and defensive strength of the wall, was doubled. The new towers at first sight resemble the old, and were apparently built in conscious imitation of them, in order to preserve a harmonious appearance in this part of the wall [Fig.5]. Like the original towers, they were faced with brick, but differed by resting on a base of reused material which in turn stood a metre and a half above the base of the old wall, evidently because of a rise in ground level in the intervening six hundred years. Most of these towers were defended from inner chambers with loopholes suitable for archers, and from their upper crenellated platforms where catapults could be mounted. Some had an additional chamber with loopholes or larger embrasures through which missiles could be shot.

The same project included a major rebuilding of the southwest wall adjacent to the section repaired by Leo III. In this, the new towers bore a facing of spoils and bands of brick, a style of masonry more typical of the ninth century [Fig.6]. It appears that the need for accommodation to an older style was not felt in this section, which had already seen considerable modification. The new walls connecting the towers were quite thin, but reinforced by stone arches which also supported the wall-walk.

The constructions of Michael III are identified and dated to 858 by a series of inscriptions, none on them now *in situ* and some lost but recorded by earlier travellers. Had they not survived, it would have been difficult if not impossible to date the new work with any accuracy, or to associate the parts of it that are built in widely varying types of masonry. In fact, without the inscriptions, nothing would be known of any activity at Nicaea under Michael III, and an important monument would have escaped notice, for the historical record is silent.

Here, as in many other cases, the value of the archaeological evidence for establishing the history of Byzantine cities is evident. Chroniclers and historians of the age necessarily devoted their attention to events in the capital which involved the dominating personalities of the time, as well as to wars and the Church. In most cases, the history of provincial cities, even important ones, is ignored. Nicaea is to some extent an exception, as the previous narrative has indicated; but even here, much went unrecorded, leaving large gaps which the monuments can fill in part. The walls are especially valuable in this respect, for they were constantly rebuilt as long as the city retained its strategic military role. The constructions of 858 are therefore a prime example of the importance of the walls as an historical as well as an archaeological source. They show that Nicaea at the time was considered worthy of significant imperial attention and expense and that it played a major role in the organisation of the offensive to the east and in the consolidation of the regions already under imperial control. Nevertheless, it is not possible to determine the proximate causes of the work. General considerations of policy will account for the new design of the east wall, but the rebuilding on the southwest implies that those walls were already in bad repair, even severely damaged, perhaps as the result of an otherwise unknown earthquake. In any case, Michael III may assume a place as one of the great benefactors of Nicaea.

Although the next two centuries were a period of relative peace and prosperity, the walls were constantly in use and had to be maintained. The first attack came not from a foreign invader but from civil war when the rebel Bardas Skleros besieged the city in 978. His forces inflicted such damage on a great tower near the south gate that it came to lean over and to be known as the tower of Gonatas, because it seemed to be bending on its knees *(gonata)*. This tower was the scene of the most determined assault of the First Crusade whose forces finally undermined it, a signal for the capitulation of the city. The tower had been large and dominated the circuit at a point where it made a right angle. It was thus an essential element in the defences, and the breach made by its collapse could not long be allowed to remain open. Consequently, Alexios Komnenos plugged the gap by erecting a small bastion of seemingly

The Walls of the City

hasty construction [Fig.7]. It was faced with all kinds of spoils, many of them gravestones taken from a Muslim cemetery [Fig.8]. These incidentally constitute the only surviving material record of the short-lived Seljuk state based at Nicaea.

The Crusade typically inflicted far less damage than nature had a generation earlier. In 1065, a great earthquake flattened much of Nicaea, including major churches and stretches of the walls. This necessitated extensive repairs which are especially evident in the eastern section, whether because this part suffered more, or because other parts were more modified by later rebuilding. The repairs introduced a new and distinctive style of masonry, characteristic of the age, the so-called recessed brick. In this, the facing consisted as before entirely of brick, but alternate courses were set back and covered with mortar so that the wall gave the appearance of courses of brick separated by wide bands of mortar [Fig.9]. The facing was tied to the usual rubble core by a network of wooden beams, a system of construction which now appears for the first time at Nicaea. This style continued in use for some time, and appeared in the superstructure of the bastion built by Alexios.

The side of the fortress which had relatively little to fear from attack, the lake front, was extensively rebuilt by Manuel Komnenos, whose work had been identified by its use of a new type of masonry with alternating courses of brick and rubble, and by more elaborate patterns of brick in the facing [Fig.10]. Once again, the immediate causes of this work are unknown. It is perhaps to be associated with Manuel's general program of strengthening the defences of Asia Minor against the now rampant attacks of the Turks. This resulted in the creation of the new theme, or administrative district, of the Neokastra southwest of Nicaea, as well as reconstruction of many fortresses there and on the frontier.

The greatest changes to this rampart, which gave it the form it still preserves, were the work of the Laskarids, executed when Nicaea was the capital of the Empire and when its walls were singled out for especial praise in the two encomia here presented. Although the rebuildings of Theodore Laskaris are visible in every part of the circuit, those of Vatatzes may be considered more fundamental since they added a new wall, doubling the strength and changing the nature of the fortifications.

No sooner had Laskaris established his capital at Nicaea than he looked to its defence by building two great corner towers which still dominate the southern circuit of the walls. The southeast tower, which is built on a high base of spoils and has a superstructure in brick, contains a large square chamber from which the main fire was directed. The brick is decorated with a frieze and a cross [Fig. 11]. An inscription, now lost, showed that the tower was built in 1208, two years after Laskaris gained control of the city. A similar, but undated inscription still adorns the other corner tower.[4] Written in verse, it calls the structure the Tower of Babel, probably because of its impressive size. This, too, has a huge base of spoils, a superstructure in brick and a square chamber. Here, though, the brick is more elaborately decorated, including a good deal of stone surrounded by brick in the so-called cloisonné technique.

The activity of Laskaris was not confined to these towers, for recent analysis has indicated that numerous towers and walls throughout the circuit were rebuilt in his time. Most of the towers are faced with brick and employ a good deal of decoration; they are distinctive also in their large square embrasures, designed for the installation of artillery. The facing was usually bonded to the core by massive squarecut beams. For protection against the elements, especially the rain which could seep into the cracks between the stones and ultimately undermine the facing, the mortar of the whole circuit was extensively relaid. Much of the wall received a shelter coat of mortar, designed both to resist rain and to present a smooth surface in which the hooks of an enemy could gain no grip. As a result, the walls assumed a bright appearance and seemed, as Mesarites happily recounted, to be gleaming white as snow when viewed from the distance. By means of all this work, the fortifications were thoroughly modernised and able to withstand any assault that an enemy of the time might mount. They were also rendered sufficiently attractive to adorn an imperial capital.

The greatest builder in the history of Byzantine Nicaea was John Vatatzes, the author of fundamental change. He doubled the strength of the circuit by adding an outer wall, lower and thinner than the original, but exceptionally well defended. It had the same number of towers as the inner wall, all semicircular with crenellated platforms, while its walls were defended both from loopholes at ground level and from the wall-walk [Fig. 12,13]. By these means, the firepower of the whole was enormously increased. The new wall was built on the scarp of the old ditch, and a new moat, which has left traces in the small streams which run around the circuit, was excavated in front of it. As part of the same project, the inner wall was raised by about two and a half metres [Fig. 6]. This produced better coordination between the two walls, gave added range to the catapults on the inner towers, and compensated for a rise in ground level since the time of Michael III. Most towers saw the installation of new upper chambers with loopholes or embrasures for the use of crossbow or ballista (a device which hurled a bolt like a long and heavy arrow). Many of them could therefore be defended from two levels of chambers and from the top platform. Most of the work employed a distinctive masonry in which bands of stone alternated with single courses of brick. This was more regular and decorative in the inner walls and by the gates, and less careful in the stretches of the outer wall. The style, as well as the mortar used, is sufficiently distinctive to show that this vast project was the product of a single plan.

As a result of all this, the walls of Nicaea took on a new appearance. Instead of the powerful single rampart that had served the city for a thousand years, it now had a triple system of defence, with the moat, the low outer walls and the high inner circuit. The ensemble closely resembled the fortifications of Constantinople, which similarly were double with a ditch in front. Those of the former capital, however, were on a much larger scale and built in far more careful or elaborate masonry. The resemblance is almost certainly no accident, for the new double walls gave Nicaea an image appropriate to the capital of the Empire. There was also a practical aspect: Vatatzes might need to defend his capital not only against nomad tribesmen, but against more sophisticated enemies. Attack could now be expected both from the knights of the West, whose military technology had by now surpassed that of the Byzantines and from the Seljuk Turks whose massive fortifications dwarf those of the small Byzantine state.

The buildings of Vatatzes, unlike those of Laskaris, are not dated by any surviving inscription. Instead, and most remarkable in view of the nature of the text, their attribution is assured by statements about them in the speech of Theodore Laskaris, son of Vatatzes, delivered at Nicaea before the Emperor, and thus spoken in praise of both. He alone reveals that Vatatzes was responsible for doubling the circuit.

After the Laskarids, when Nicaea resumed its role of important provincial city, the walls saw few changes. Some, however, are relevant in the context of the speeches. Two towers by the lake shore are built in a complex masonry of stone and brick bands which is typical of the early Palaiologan period. [Fig. 14] They quite probably represent repairs carried out in 1290 when Andronikos II was visiting the city and attempting to strengthen the defences of the lands which remained in his control. This visit was the occasion for the speech of Metochites, then a debutant. In it, he devoted much time to praising the walls. Other, later, rebuildings included another general raising of the circuit, with the bolstering of many towers, the addition of new chambers to some, and the blocking of numerous openings. They would be appropriate to a time when new artillery was coming into use and when fewer men were available for defence. They probably represent the last stand of Byzantine Nicaea against the Turks, a time when the new heavy artillery, the trébuchet, was being installed against an enemy whose means of attack were becoming increasingly sophisticated. Nevertheless, it was not weapons which brought down the great walls of Nicaea, but famine and despair. The city finally capitulated when it became clear that further resistance was hopeless and that the capital no longer had the resources to come to its aid. Under its new Turkish masters, Nicaea no longer needed elaborate defences, for the frontier was far and the government strong. Consequently, there is virtually no work on the walls which can be attributed to the Ottomans, under whom the fortress began to sink into the romantic decay which is now its most immediately striking characteristic.

This rapid survey of the long history of the fortifications shows clearly how the city's history is written is stone. Virtually every period of its existence is reflected in changes made to its most essential building, the one structure without which it could not have survived. From the third century to the fourteenth, the walls provided a system of defence which was constantly maintained and elaborated, and generally successful. The only time the city was taken by storm was in the First Crusade; otherwise famine or treachery had to do the work which men and machines could not accomplish. The walls reveal that the third, eighth, and ninth centuries were periods of great activity – ages when new enemies had to be faced, or when a base had to be provided for further conquests – but that the most impressive and substantial changes were the work of the Laskarids, who devoted to the city the care and glorification due to a capital. Their achievement still stands for all to behold and admire.

NOTES

[1] The following is based on the discussion of Foss and Winfield (1985) 75-120, where full details may be found.

[2] For walls of the third century, see *ibid.* 126-129.

[3] The text is published in Schneider (1938) 49 no. 29.

[4] *Ibid.* 52 no. 37.

11. The Churches and Other Buildings

In his speech on Nicaea (section 10), Theodore Metochites gives a fairly detailed description of a church. Although he begins with a statement about the churches in general, the passage appears to deal with a specific building by describing, in typically allusive language, its plan, decoration and surroundings. The survey which follows was undertaken in the hope of identifying the church. It will discuss all the churches known to have been built or standing in the thirteenth century [Fig. 15, 16], as well as those attested only in earlier times. An identification will then be attempted and after it, a description of the city in the days when it was capital of the Byzantine state. Naturally, such a reconstruction cannot be complete because of the deficiencies of the sources and especially of the archaeological record, but an attempt will at least provide some material background for the speeches and an impression of a place which had such a significant role in the history of Byzantium. It will begin with the most famous church.

The Monastery of Hyacinth

A church which has appeared frequently in these pages, and is best known to students of art and architecture because of its unusual plan and remarkable mosaics, is the Church of the Virgin in the Monastery of Hyacinth, generally called by its modern name, the Church of the Dormition. Alone among the churches of Nicaea, this has been studied in considerable detail, a fortunate circumstance since it is now destroyed and knowledge of its decoration depends entirely on photographs made before the First World War.

The church was founded by a certain Hyacinth, priest, monk, and abbot. His name appears in the mosaics, on the column capitals, and in the form of monograms on a marble plaque which gives his full titles [Fig. 17]. None of these provide any unambiguous evidence to tell when he lived. That was certainly before the late eighth century, however, for another abbot of the monastery attended the council of Nicaea in 787. Plan, mosaics, and a recently discovered, though undated, inscription suggest that the church may have been built in the late seventh century, a remarkable achievement for an age when little civil or ecclesiastical construction is attested.[1]

The monastery next appears in connection with Saint Constantine the Jew, in the late ninth century. After his voyage to Cyprus, where he acquired the sacred hand of Saint Palamon, Constantine returned to Nicaea and deposited the relic in the Church of the Virgin at the Monastery of Hyacinth, an establishment famed for the devotion of its monks. The next role of the church is more impressive, and surprising. In 1209, the patriarch Michael Autorianos presided over a synod which met in the external *pronaos* of the church, an area given to the Patriarch as his *kathisma*. The significance of this passage will be discussed below.

Whether or not the church normally served as the patriarchate, it continued to function as a monastery under the Laskarids. When the Calabrian monks who accompanied the bride of Vatatzes to Nicaea in 1241 decided not to return home, they were allowed by the patriarch to enter the Monastery of Hyacinth. The church was also used as a place of confinement and royal burial. The former Emperor Alexios III, captured when fighting alongside the Turks in 1211, was sent to the monastery and eventually died and was buried there. In 1222, he was followed by Theodore Laskaris whose wife had already been buried in the church. A long inscription in verse dated to 1211 indicates that a certain Manuel *prinkips* also had a tomb in the church. It shows that he was of the Komnenos family, and connected with the rulers of Sicily. He was apparently Manuel, nephew of Alexios III, but the identification poses many problems which have not been entirely resolved.[2] In 1240, the abbot of the monastery, Methodios, was elected Patriarch. He only served three months before dying and being buried in the church over which he had presided. Consideration of the mosaics and remains will put these burials into a context. Finally, the distinguished orator Manuel Holobolos, when he fell into disfavor with Michael VIII, was exiled to the monastery.

Alone among the churches of Nicaea, the Monastery of Hyacinth survived into modern times, continuing to function without interruption under the Turks, and even being restored in the nineteenth century. Its last mention in a Byzantine source occurs early in the Ottoman period, in 1354, when the learned Bishop Gregory Palamas was brought to Nicaea after he had been captured by the Turks. He found the church, which was then the centre of the surviving Greek community, and rested in the shade of its garden. The whole place was delightful for him: the precinct contained not only a well-decorated church, but a well and a grove of trees. This is the last description of any consequence until modern scientific investigation began.

The church [Figs. 18, 19, 20], universally known in the modern literature as the Church of the Dormition, has attracted much attention because of its unusual plan and its striking mosaic decoration.[3] The building was not large – about 22$^{1}/_{2}$ metres long and 21 metres wide, with the narthex extending beyond the main body of the church about 3 metres on each side. Its plan featured a central cruciform nave crowned by a dome resting on four massive piers. Structurally, the nave and the sanctuary formed one space, but a *templon* decorated with marble plaques bearing crosses, corresponding to the later iconostasis, functionally divided it into two units. The nave was separated from the side aisles by an arcade rising from rectangular pillars with marble plaques installed between them. The central space was thus defined as something distinct from the rest of the church. A narrow passage connected each aisle to a side apse, and nave and aisles alike opened onto the narthex.

This plan has affinities with those of a whole group of churches whose chronology is in much dispute. The principle upon which the church was constructed involves a central dome resting on heavy pillars and the predominance of the central chamber over the residual idea of a basilical plan. Since this is typical of the architecture of Justinian and appears to reflect the plan of Hagia Sophia in Constantinople, a date in the late sixth century has been advanced. The most recent analysis, however, suggests that the church may have been built a century later.[4]

In the course of its long existence, the church was naturally repaired many times. The most substantial rebuilding followed the earthquake of 1065, which, as already noted, was one of the greatest disasters ever to strike the city. Although the Church of Hyacinth is not specifically mentioned, analysis of the structure shows that it suffered massive damage. As a result, the narthex was completely rebuilt, as were the dome and its supporting arches. Within the church, a new templon was erected, and much new decoration installed. This work gave the church the appearance it still had in modern times. A further rebuilding affected the chambers beside the apse, where the *diakonikon* received a prismatic dome. The style of architecture and masonry has suggested a date in the thirteenth century. The work is probably to be attributed to the Laskarids, who seem also to have been responsible for various repairs in brick and rubble carried out in the main body of the church.

Until 1921, the church preserved a rich and remarkable decor. Mosaics covered the upper parts, while walls and floors were adorned with marble. The surviving mosaics covered the conch of the apse, the arch of the *bema*, and parts of the narthex, and appeared on the pillars which supported the dome. In earlier times, they had probably covered all the upper surfaces of the church, for rubble from the rebuilding of the dome in 1807 included many mosaic cubes.[5]

The mosaic of the apse portrayed a standing figure of the Virgin holding the Christ child, with rays descending on her from on high. This directly adjoined the decoration of the *bema* arch which featured the *hetoimasia*, a backless throne on a footstool supporting a decorated Gospel, with a nimbate dove above it, symbolic of the triumph of the Church. This covered the top of the arch, while figures of four archangels holding standards inscribed with the *trisagion* adorned the lower parts. The outer face of the arch which joined apse and *bema* contained a biblical inscription with the monograms of Hyacinth at the beginning and end. Below these mosaics, the eastern piers which supported the dome bore mosaic icons of Christ Antiphonetes and the Virgin Eleousa. The narthex contained other mosaics: the Virgin *orans* in the lunette above the main entrance to the nave, and, in the vault adjoining it, an eight-branched cross surrounded by saints and Evangelists.

These mosaics represented a combination of the original decor with several changes and repairs. Study of the apse mosaics in particular has revealed developments important for understanding the history of the church.[6] The inscription, the rays descending on the Virgin's head, and the *hetoimasia* are part of the original decoration, as shown by the monograms of Hyacinth. The figure of the Virgin, however, was the result of major changes. In a first stage, the original figure was replaced by a large cross. This in turn yielded to the image of the Virgin photographed in modern times. Similarly, the original figures of the archangels were removed, eventually to be replaced by others of the same type. An inscription proclaiming that a certain Naukratios restored the sacred icons accompanies the later archangels. All this visibly manifests the effects of iconoclasm. Destruction of the images of Virgin and archangels was a typical product of the ideology of the eighth century, especially of the reign of Constantine V (740-775); the cross could be attributed to that time. The restoration of Naukratios has been plausibly attributed to the period just after the final restoration of the icons in 843. The surviving ensemble, therefore, was a major example of the art of the ninth century.

The other mosaics were later: those of the narthex were dedicated by the grand hetairiarch, or commander of the imperial bodyguard, Nikephoros, in the reign of Constantine X (1059-1067) as part of the redecoration after the great earthquake of 1065. Similarly, the mosaic icons of the pillars have been assigned to this time. The church thus contained mosaics of three periods: the original (late sixth century), the mid-ninth, and the late eleventh. It is all the more to be regretted that none has survived.

The rest of the church was decorated with a degree of luxury compatible with the mosaics. The walls of the nave were sheathed in marble, and the floor was decorated with a multicolored *opus sectile* which spread out like a carpet before the altar. This flooring, which appeared in the nave and the room beside the apse, was a product of the eleventh century rebuilding. A marble plaque with fine incrustation which was later built into the floor, however, seems to have been the altar table of the same period. The *templon* also suffered in 1065. It was rebuilt with square pillars instead of columns and new marble plaques were installed. It is not clear whether two plaques from the church with floral and geometric design which may be attributed to this period are part of the templon screen.

The church, as noted, was the site of several burials. Two tombs survived within the building, one in the south aisle, the other in the narthex.[7] The first consisted of marble plaques which formed the facade of a sarcophagus and were set in a lunate niche. This tomb was originally decorated with a mosaic that showed the Virgin and Child flanked by Constantine X and the hetairiarch Nikephoros. It thus belonged to the official who rebuilt the church after 1065. The inscription on in indicated that the monastery had been granted by the emperor to Nikephoros as a *pronoia,* that is, he was to enjoy its revenues, but at the same time had the obligation of restoring it. The other tomb, decorated with marble plaques, could not be dated or identified.

The written sources and the material evidence reveal that the Church of Hyacinth had a rich history. Its founder cannot be identified, but he apparently lived, built the church, and presided over the monastery in the late seventh century. His name was featured in the building, and his memory preserved in the tenth century, when he was revered as a holy man of the remote past. His church appears to have survived the great earthquake of 740, and thus to have been the one church which the sources record as left standing. Not long after, though, its mosaics succumbed to iconoclastic zeal, and their figured representations were replaced. In 787, its abbot Gregory attended the Council of Nicaea which temporarily reestablished adoration of images, but it remained for Naukratios (who has not been identified) to restore the images of the church in the mid-ninth century.[8]

The earthquake of 1065 provoked the greatest changes. The damaged church was entrusted to the great hetairiarch Nikephoros who rebuilt it extensively, with special attention to the narthex and dome. He replaced or added several mosaics, including that of his own tomb, which stood in the south aisle. Early in the Laskarid period, the church gained the additional distinction of being the seat of the Patriarch, if only for a time (the question will be considered below), and the tomb of Emperors, princes, and other dignitaries. It also received the rebuilding evident in the chambers by the apse and in the walls. The church stood, still in good repair, in the fourteenth century, when it continued to function as a monastery. As such, it must have had numerous other buildings during the Byzantine period, but no trace of them has survived. Practically nothing is left of the church now, after its destruction by the Turks in 1924, but the preserved record enables it to be reconstructed and to serve as the best known example of the churches which formed such an important part of the life of the city.

The Church of Hagia Sophia

As the site of the Seventh (and last) Ecumenical Council in 787, Hagia Sophia is the only church in Nicaea associated with an important historical event. At that time, over 300 bishops and a great crowd of monks assembled in front of the *ambo,* and proceeded to hold seven sessions in the building. Hagia Sophia was presumably chosen for the meetings because it was the cathedral, a role it certainly played in 1065 when it was shaken and collapsed as the result of the earthquake. These are the only occasions when the church appears in history, though by implication it suffered in the quake of 740 which left only one (unnamed) church standing.[9]

The substantial remains of a basilical church still stand in the very centre of Nicaea, at the intersection of the two main streets. Now called the Aya Sofya Camii (Mosque of Hagia Sophia), it has generally been identified as the site of the Council. The name, however, appears to be modern, applied, perhaps, from knowledge of local history or because, as in other places, the name of Hagia Sophia may be given to a major mosque converted from a church, by analogy with Constantinople.[10] In the nineteenth century, the building was called the Mosque of Orhan because that Sultan had converted the greatest church of Nicaea into a mosque, and his *tughra*, or monogram, was reportedly visible over the entrance.[11] In earlier times, it apparently bore the name of Ulu Cami (Great Mosque).[12]

Despite the confusion of names, it seems likely that the present building was indeed the church transformed by Orhan soon after the Ottoman conquest. It is the only local mosque which was once a church, and it is larger than any of the other known churches, a situation which presumably prevailed in the fourteenth century. Its location in the exact centre of the city indicates considerable importance and seems to strengthen the identification with Hagia Sophia, the metropolitan church. Yet problems remain: the structure seems small for such a populous assembly as the Council; the church is never mentioned after 1065; and the patriarch, as noted, had his seat elsewhere in the Laskarid period at least. An alternative theory, by which Nicaea once had a much larger basilica – as might be expected in an important late antique city – and that this was destroyed in the earthquake of 1065 and never rebuilt, could also be entertained. Without more substantial evidence, however, the question cannot be resolved, and the mosque commonly known as Hagia Sophia may be accepted as such, allowing a margin of doubt.

The church in question is a basilica built of brick and measuring about 30 by 22 metres [Fig. 15]. It has a central nave with a single apse and side aisles which end in small domed chambers without apses; and once had a narthex some 6½ metres deep. The present appearance of the church is the result of rebuildings which have been variously interpreted.[13] All agree that the original structure was built with lower courses of a fine marble ashlar (now visible at the east end) and a superstructure in brick. This initial period has been assigned to the fifth or sixth century. At that time, a colonnade, or perhaps pillars, separated nave and aisles and the apse contained a *synthronon*. A small rectangular apsidal chapel attached to the southeast corner of the church may belong to this period. Thereafter, the church was extensively rebuilt. The side aisles were divided off by long heavy pillars of brick, a new floor was laid more than a metre above the old, the apse was redesigned to become polygonal on the exterior, and the *synthronon* was partially buried; the domed chambers were added and considerable repairs were made to the walls. The chapel received a new floor of reused marble with a fine decoration in *opus sectile*.

Brounoff, who studied the building in 1927, distinguished three periods of rebuilding according to the masonry employed: a first which favored brick was responsible for the new internal pillars; a second rebuilt the apse in brick with wide mortar joints and made other repairs; a third erected the domed chambers using mortared rubble with bands of brick. Using analogy and known earthquakes, he dated these respectively to the eighth, eleventh, and thirteenth centuries. A decade later, A.M. Schneider surveyed the building and was able to make some small trial excavations. He concluded that the piers and the domed chambers were contemporary, representing only one period of rebuilding in the eleventh century, and that other minor repairs were later.

Although there has been no further discussion, the chronology of the church may in fact be illuminated by a source not previously used, though long available – by comparison of the masonry with that of the city walls, for which a detailed chronology has been proposed.[14] Such analogy would first suggest that the earlier theory which distinguished several periods is to be preferred, for the masonry of the church has close parallels in the walls, even to the extent of using similar kinds of mortar in corresponding types of masonry.

The brickwork of the piers and dividing walls of the church, which all agree to represent a secondary period, finds its closest analogy in the facing of the towers built by Michael III in 858. Both use bricks set close together in fairly irregular rows, in an arrangement quite distinct from that employed in earlier or later repairs. The mortars are even more striking. The inner walls and piers of the church use a light grey mortar with large amounts of broken brick and black pebbles in equal proportion. This mortar appears in the fortifications only in sections dated to the ninth century, and is quite distinct from that used in other periods. Such close parallels would indicate an unexpected date – the mid-ninth century – for the main reconstruction of the church, and associate that with the work of Michael III, who would thus have devoted considerable attention to both the spiritual and physical welfare of the city. The reasons for rebuilding the church at this time are unknown; it is possible that an unattested earthquake was responsible, as it may have been for the extensive work on the walls.

The other periods of repair likewise employ masonry which has parallels elsewhere. The brick with wide mortar joints used in and around the apse is closest to that of the narthex of the Dormition, added after the quake of 1065. The domed chambers and the final rebuilding of the apse are executed in courses of mixed spoils and rubble separated by single, double, or triple bands of brick. In the domes, the arches around the windows have alternating voussoirs of brick and stone, and the whole addition is reinforced with a network of wooden beams. This masonry, as Schneider noted, is close to that of the outer wall, built by Vatatzes. Here, too, the mortar offers confirmation, for these parts of the church employ a whitish mortar with small black pebbles which appears consistently in the outer walls and in other sections attributed to Vatatzes. Stylistically, the mixed brick and stone of the arches would suit a Laskarid date.

There is every reason to suppose that the internal decor of Hagia Sophia approached the richness of that of the Dormition, but little has survived. Bits of mosaic and marble revetment found in the excavations give a hint of the former appearance of the central nave and perhaps other parts, while fragmentary frescoes survive in the *diakonikon* to show that it once bore numerous figures of saints and apostles.[15] Far more impressive is the pavement in *opus sectile* which forms a square 3m60 on a side before the entrance. This contains an elaborate arabesque of colored marble around a central circle, and is one of the finest of its kind surviving. Traces of similar work were found in the south aisle, but the marble floor of the apse and *bema* was simpler, with a rectangular geometric design. Those pavements have been dated to the eleventh century.[16]

Hagia Sophia therefore appears to be a basilica of the fifth or sixth century (no closer dating has been proposed, nor does evidence for one seem apparent), extensively rebuilt in the ninth under unknown circumstances, but probably in connection with the work on the city walls. The great earthquake of 1065 provoked the rebuilding of the apse and other sections and was responsible for a redecoration which included the marble pavements and probably mosaics and marble revetments on the walls. A final transformation was effected in the mid-thirteenth century when the apse received a new outer facing and the domed *prothesis* and *diakonikon* were added. The frescoes in these chambers probably date to this time. The whole project no doubt reflects the role of Nicaea as the capital of the Empire, and the attention lavished on it by the Laskarids.

The Church of Saint Tryphon

In Laskarid times, the Church of Saint Tryphon had special fame as the scene of a miracle reenacted annually when the lilies which grew by the saint's lamp were cut in mid-winter and bloomed again out of season. The event captured the imagination of the age and was celebrated by Theodore Laskaris in his encomium on the Saint, and by Metochites in his speech on the city, in which this church is the only one mentioned by name.

Saint Tryphon was of special importance to Theodore, to whom he had appeared in a dream in 1254 when the imperial army was about to engage in a difficult campaign in Europe. After the Saint urged him to cross the Dardanelles, Theodore won a decisive victory and gained control of the city of Berrhoia.[17]

The Churches and Other Buildings 105

As a sign of his regard for the saint as patron and protector not only of himself but of the whole state, Theodore put his image on the coinage. Silver coins show Emperor and Saint standing together holding a *labarum* whose base rests on Tryphon's miraculous lily. Silver and billon issues show the full length figure of the beardless Saint wearing a tunic and holding a cross; he is flanked by lilies. The smallest denomination, in copper, simply had as its type the lily of Tryphon.[18]

Theodore's encomium of Saint Tryphon, couched in the language of his speech on Nicaea, deserves considerable attention for the vivid image it gives of the crowded festival which took place on 1 February, the Saint's day, and the occasion for the annual repetition of the miracle of the lilies. It shows the popularity of the cult and the devotion of the Emperor to the Saint from whom he had received valued inspiration when he crossed from Asia into Thrace on campaign.[19]

Οὕτως ἠγωνίσατο ὁ γενναῖος καὶ τοιαύτας τὰς ἀμοιβὰς ἔλαβε, τὰς ἐπουρανίους καὶ ἐπιγείους, ἐκείνας περὶ αὐτόν, ταύτας διὰ τοὺς προσκαλουμένους αὐτόν· ἀνθεῖ γὰρ καθ' ἑκάστην τὰ θαύματα, ῥαίνει τὰς δωρεάς, πλημμυρεῖ τὰς εὐεργεσίας. Δράμετε ἄνθρωποι οἱ νοσοῦντες πρὸς τὸν ἰατρόν, οἱ αἰτοῦντες πρὸς τὸν χορηγὸν τῶν καλῶν αἰτημάτων, οἱ πάντες πρὸς τὸν πάντα μεσιτεύειν δυνάμενον εἰς Θεόν· καὶ μηδεὶς στραφήτω κενός, τὴν προαίρεσιν φέροντες καὶ τὰς εὐεργεσίας ἀντιλαμβάνοντες· οὐ γάρ ἐστι τοῦτο δεόμενον ἐξετάσεως· ὁ κόσμος βοᾷ, καὶ τὰ ἔργα κηρύσσει διαπρυσίως καὶ γνησίως ὡς καλοῦ προμάχου καὶ ἀσφαλοῦς ἡ πόλις τῶν Νικαέων· ἐν ταύτῃ γὰρ τὸν ἀγῶνα τοῦ μαρτυρίου διήνυσε καὶ τανῦν ἐν ταύτῃ τέλει τὰς μεγαλουργίας, κρίνων ἀνθήσεις παραδόξους καὶ ἐκβλαστήσεις ἐνιαυσιαίους καρποφορεῖ εὐλογίας, ὢ τοῦ θαύματος, ἐν παγετῷ καὶ χιόνι τε καὶ χειμῶνι ἀνθεῖ τὸ κρίνον τῇ τοῦ μάρτυρος λυχνίᾳ ἐγκείμενον. Μετὰ γὰρ τὴν ἐκκοπὴν τούτου συντελουμένου ἐνιαυτοῦ, καθ' ἣν ὥραν τὸ ἑωθινὸν τελεῖται ὑμνῴδημα καὶ τοῦ ἀθλοφόρου καλλιεπῶς ἐξᾴδονται τὰ ἐγκώμια, τὸ ξηρὸν ἐκ τοῦ πάραυτα ἀχρόνως βλαστάνει τὴν αἴσθησιν διαφεῦγον κατὰ βραχύ. Καὶ ὁρᾷ τότε τὸ πλῆθος τὰ τοῦ Τρύφωνος θαύματα· τοῦτο βασιλεῖς ἐθεάσαντο πατριάρχαι τε ἑωράκασι· τοῦτο σέβεται ὁ λαὸς πᾶς, πιστὸς μᾶλλον ἐκ τούτου στηρίζεται· δαίμονες δραπετεύουσι τῇ θαυματουργίᾳ, νοσήματα φυγαδεύονται, αἰτήσεις πιστῶν πληροῦνται, μία πανήγυρις τότε πάνδημος, ὅτε δὴ τελεῖται αὐτό, βρεφῶν, νηπίων, μειρακίων, ἀνδρῶν, γερόντων, πρεσβυτῶν, γηραλέων, γυναικῶν, κοσμίων, στρατευομένων, ὑποτελετῶν, ἱερέων, μοναχῶν ὁρῶσα καὶ σκιρτῶσα αὐτῷ πᾶν γένος καὶ ἡλικία πᾶσα· οὐ γάρ ἐστι τὸ γιγνόμενον ὡς ἐν γωνίᾳ καὶ ὑποσκίῳ τόπῳ τινὶ γινόμενον, ἀλλ' ἐν ἐκκλησίᾳ Θεοῦ. Διὰ τοῦτο δεῖ πάντας τὸν μέγαθλον Τρύφωνα διὰ θαύματος ἐγκωμιάζειν ὅτι πολλοῦ. Ἐμὲ δὲ καὶ μάλιστα καὶ ὅσον κατ' οἶκτον ὃν ἔλαβον παρ' αὐτοῦ ἀξιοπρεπῶς ἀμελεῖ καὶ ἐπιτέρπεσθαι ταῖς τούτου μεγαλουργίαις καὶ ἐπιγάννυσθαι καὶ ἐνθουσιᾶν, ὡς ὁ θεοπάτωρ Δαυῒδ ἐπὶ τῇ καταπαύσει τῆς κιβωτοῦ, ἵνα θαυμαζομένου τοῦ δούλου, ἡ τιμὴ διαβαίνῃ πρὸς τὸν δεσπότην.

In this way, the noble saint achieved martyrdom and received its rewards – heavenly for him and earthly for those who call upon him. He makes miracles bloom every day; he showers gifts; he lavishes favors. You men who are sick, run to the doctor; you who seek, to the fulfiller of good requests; and everyone to him who has the power to mediate everything before God. Let no one return empty-handed, as they bring their choices and in turn receive his kindness. This does not need investigation: the world shouts it out, and the city of Nicaea loudly and truly proclaims his works as those of a noble and dependable champion. In this city, he completed the struggle of martyrdom, and now here he accomplishes his great works. He brings his blessings to fruition in the incredible yearly blooming and sprouting of the lilies – what a miracle! The lily which lies in the lamp of the martyr blooms in the frost and snows of winter. When a year has passed since it was cut, the dry bulb suddenly blooms, almost escaping perception, at the hour when the morning service is celebrated with hymns and the praises of the victorious martyr are sung in beautiful language.

The crowd sees the miracles of Tryphon: emperors have seen it, patriarchs have observed it, and the faithful are greatly strengthened by it; because of the miracle, demons run away, diseases are banished, and the prayers of the faithful are granted. When the miracle takes place, there is a universal festival – of infants, children, adolescents, men, old men, elders, the aged, women, laymen, soldiers, officials, priests, and monks – every kind and age of people sees it and jumps with joy. For what happens does not happen in a corner or some shadowy place, but in the church of God. Everyone, therefore, should praise the great victor Tryphon as much as possible for his miracle; as indeed should I especially because of the mercy I received from him, and I should rejoice in his great works and exult with enthusiasm, just like the divine father David when the ark came to rest, so that when the servant receives a miracle, the honor redounds to the master.

The miraculous was not the church's only distinction, for Theodore II established his new school in it, with its teachers of grammar and rhetoric, and the Patriarch Arsenios accordingly undertook a major rebuilding. By this time, the surrounding ground level had risen so that the vestibule of the church often filled with water and the congregation had trouble entering. The reconstruction, which is not described, evidently remedied the situation, perhaps added new walling (the church is described as previously built of "earthen bricks"), and no doubt included provision of space for the school. Another miraculous event brought the church into history for the last time, toward the end of the thirteenth century when the body of Saint John the Younger arrived, and the saint's identity was eventually revealed. The church housed the saint's body and thus entertained new throngs of pilgrims just as it vanishes from history.

The fate of the church, and even its identity, sank into oblivion for almost seven hundred years until construction in the street which leads to the north or Istanbul gate in 1947 unearthed remains of a Byzantine church [Fig. 16]. This was of the cross-in-square plan, with four central columns to support the long-vanished dome, three apses, and a narthex. It measured about 12 by 22 metres and was constructed of mortared rubble with bands of brick. The west facade was ornamented with pilasters and blind arcades, while the interior had evidently once been adorned with mosaic and a pavement of *opus sectile*. A marble plaque with a floral cross and a marble altar found nearby apparently came from the church. Ruins in adjacent fields in a similar masonry suggested that the church had a series of side rooms. In some parts of the main building, a different kind of masonry with thin bricks, and openings of the south wall blocked with mortared rubble indicated rebuilding, perhaps extensive.[20]

These remains were soon identified with the Church of Saint Tryphon because the possibly thirteenth century date corresponded with the rebuilding of Arsenios and the side buildings were appropriate to the school which had been installed at the church.[21]

In fact, the whole structure could represent the Laskarid rebuilding, for its masonry of rubble and brick bands as well as its decoration would correspond with the Laskarid style which is now well defined.[22] In that case, the work of Theodore and Arsenios would have been fundamental, as the text of Skoutariotes suggests when it mentions that the Emperor "built the church and gave it the beauty it now has," while the statement that it had formerly been of brick suggests that the new material was different – such as the stone and brick masonry discovered. Such suppositions, though indicated by the remains, are not necessary for establishing the identification, though they might strengthen it. Confirmation comes from the last miracle associated with the church. The oxen which drew the cart bearing the body of Saint John the Younger from the suburb of Agalmates entered Nicaea through a gate and stopped on a street when they arrived before the church of Saint Tryphon. Since Agalmates apparently lay to the north, the cart would have entered through the Istanbul gate, and followed the main road which leads to the nearby church.[23] The identification therefore seems well assured.

Three Laskarid Churches

Three churches which have recently been investigated appear to date from the Laskarid period. Remains of the first (Church B) survive immediately to the southeast of the Roman theatre; they consist only of vaulted substructures but are sufficient to provide considerable information.[24] They indicate a church of 18 by 12 metres with a single apse and a narthex, probably of the cross-in-square plan [Fig. 16]. The lower level – the only one preserved – contains three long rectangular vaulted chambers, five others of varying shapes and sizes, and seven walled grave chambers. The lower courses are of spoils and rubble alternating with single, double, or triple bands of brick while the vaults are entirely of brick. The walls employ a lime mortar with large black grains of sand and some light-colored gravel. Some (if not all) the rooms of the crypt were decorated with frescoes of geometric and floral design.[25]

Nothing remains of the upper level except some cut sandstone blocks which may have been part of the flooring. Finds from the graves and excavated parts included pottery of the eleventh to thirteenth centuries, among it a decorated and inscribed communion cup dedicated by a certain Manuel. The style of construction, with an alternation of rubble and brick bands, corresponds closely with that of the recent parts of Hagia Sophia and the outer city wall. It suggests a date in the mid-thirteenth century which may be confirmed by the use of the distinctive light mortar with small black inclusions, characteristic of that time.

The second church (Church C) stands by the main street just north of the Yenishehir or southern gate.[26] It is larger than the previous – $22^1/_2$ by $18^1/_2$ metres – and has a rather different plan [Fig.16]. The west door led to the narthex which in the turn opened onto the central nave and two side aisles. They all ended in apses. A large dome crowned the nave, which was separated from the aisles by walls. The centralised plan so created is reminiscent of the Church of Hyacinth. Walls are of mixed spoils and rubble, single bands of brick, and occasional cloisonné; they employ a lime mortar with large grains of sand. The church was elaborately decorated inside and out. The west facade had pillars, blind arcades, and decorative brick, while the narthex walls bore mosaics and the floor was paved with *opus sectile*. Stylistic considerations suggested a date in the thirteenth century; it is confirmed by the distinctive masonry and mortar.

Neither of these thirteenth-century churches bears an inscription or any indication of name or dedication. It is nevertheless possible to propose identifications. John Vatatzes is recorded to have built the nunnery of Saint Anthony within the walls and to have endowed it with olive groves in the vicinity of Fort Saint George.[27] This is the only church specifically mentioned as a new construction of the time, but the Monastery of Tornikios, in which Theodore Mouzalon was buried in 1294, was most probably a foundation of Demetrios Tornikios, who died in 1247. He had been a man of tremendous influence and chief minister of Theodore I and Vatatzes.[28] Although other churches may have been built without being mentioned in the sources, it is possible that these two correspond with those just described: Saint Anthony with the church near the south gate, and the Monastery of Tornikios with that near the theatre. This church with its grave chambers in the lower level suits the indication that Mouzalon had the right of burial in the church from his wife's dowry. The crypt would thus have been intended for tombs of the founder and his relations.

The third church is a small, three-aisled basilica with narthex [Fig.16], built over the orchestra of the ancient theatre. Apart from semi-circular niches adjacent to the apses of the side aisles, it is of a simpler plan than the rest. It appears to have been a mortuary chapel, for it is surrounded by an extensive graveyard. Its masonry finds such a close parallel in that of towers of Theodore Laskaris that assignment to his reign seems certain.[29]

This survey shows that Nicaea contains the remains of six churches built or modified during the Laskarid period. Hagia Sophia and the Monastery of Hyacinth were much earlier structures, one a basilica, the other a domed church with a centralised plan. Of the Laskarid foundations, Saint Tryphon was an inscribed cross church, as was apparently Church B by the theatre (perhaps the Monastery of Tornikios), while the plan of Church C (possibly Saint Anthony) was apparently influenced by that of the Hyacinth church; the chapel in the theatre was a basilica. All, however, have important elements in common.

The masonry of the Laskarid churches consistently employs spoils and rubble alternating with brick bands, and uses decoration on the facade. Blind arcades and pilasters appear at Saint Tryphon and Church C; the latter also has some decorative brickwork. The churches were richly decorated within. Hagia Sophia had a remarkable pavement of *opus sectile* somewhat more elaborate than that of Hyacinth. These were both the product of the eleventh century, but the fashion persisted and traces of such floors have been found in Saint Tryphon and Church C. Mosaics adorned those two churches (and of course the Monastery of Hyacinth, works of an earlier age), while frescoes of the period have survived in Hagia Sophia and left traces in Church B. The two new churches, therefore, fit naturally into the context of the architecture of Nicaea when it was the imperial capital.

The Patriarchate and the Church of the Fathers

The sources reveal the names of several other churches in use under the Laskarids, but also raise some difficult questions about two of the most important, the patriarchate and the Church of the Fathers. The lesser churches may be considered first.

When Mesarites settled in Nicaea in 1208, he took up residence in the Church of Christ *tou Bolenou* within the city walls, a dependency of the Monastery of Ano Lakkous.[30] The Monastery of Christ the Savior *tou Kophou* appears in the same year when a manuscript brought from Constantinople was deposited in it; the same church was the recipient of manuscripts donated by Constantine Laskaris during his brief reign. In 1240, Patriarch Germanos was buried in the Church of the Virgin Kyriotissa in the city, and in 1254 the Monk Hyacinth began teaching children in the Church of the Archangel Michael near the patriarchate. It is probable that the small Church or Chapel of the Trinity, which had only two monks and was left by Michael VIII to the Monastery of Saint Demetrios in Constantinople, already existed at this time. Another chapel or church stood near the residence which the patriarch assigned to the Latin ambassadors of 1234; it cannot be located.

These churches all stood within the city walls. It is probable that there were several others just outside, in the graveyards where early saints had been martyred and laid to rest. Only one, the Monastery of Agalma, is attested in this period. It appears in history when Patriarch Arsenios spent the night there after he abdicated the throne in 1260. Described as lying next to the city walls, it probably stood outside them to the north: the Patriarch continued from there to the coast, and would thus have left the city by the road which passes through the Istanbul gate. The statement that it stood next to the walls seems to contain an element of exaggeration, for the name indicates that the monastery lay in the suburb of Agalma or Agalmates, where Saint John the Younger was buried. The account of his life shows that this was two miles north of the city, and thus probably in or near the Roman necropolis.

Laskarid Nicaea plainly had a good number of churches, among which monasteries were especially prominent. Of the ten or eleven churches so far considered (the chapel assigned to the Latins could have been one of the churches already mentioned), five were monastic and two more were dependencies of monasteries; the status of one, Saint Michael the Archangel, cannot be determined.

As an imperial capital, Nicaea was the seat of the patriarch. He would naturally have had a cathedral, though not necessarily one newly constructed for him; he most probably took over the existing metropolitan church. References to the patriarchate, however, raise the difficult question of its identification.

According to a synodical act of 1209, the patriarch Michael presided in the outer *pronaos* of the Monastery of Hyacinth, which had been given to him for a *kathisma*.[31] This seems to indicate an exonarthex, a structure which the Church of Hyacinth lacks. The church did, however, have a narthex which in the seventeenth century contained a bishop's throne known as the Chair of Constantine because of its reputed antiquity.[32] Part of the church (perhaps an outer porch) therefore served as the seat of the patriarch in 1209, as it did for the local bishop in Ottoman times. The monastery, however, continued as such into the fourteenth century, and the space in question seems far too small for the permanent installation of the patriarch and the body of officials and clerks who necessarily formed part of the retinue.

In 1232, when a synod met to discuss restoring the unity of the churches of Nicaea and Epiros, the patriarch presided in the domed rotunda (θολωτῷ ᾠάτῳ, or perhaps better, θόλῳ τῷ ᾠάτῳ) at the patriarchate.[33] This rotunda, apparently otherwise unattested, may be added to the list of ecclesiastical buildings standing in the thirteenth century. Its location is unknown, nor does mention of it reveal the site of the patriarchate.[34] Finally, in 1234, when the Latin delegates arrived in Nicaea, they wanted to be taken "*ad maiorem ecclesiam*," that is, to the cathedral, and some of their disputations were held in the "*domus patriarcae*," the patriarchate.[35] Neither is further identified or described, but the text shows that the patriarch of the day had a cathedral and a palace.

At first sight, the size, central location, and history of Hagia Sophia seem to identify it as the cathedral. The liturgical requirements of the time, however, indicate a different solution. A Byzantine emperor needed a cathedral in which a coronation ceremony could be performed. For this, the church had to have a dressing room, a large *ambo*, and a gallery where the emperor could appear to be acclaimed after the coronation. The Church of Hyacinth alone meets these requirements: one of the chambers beside its apse could have served as a dressing room, a surviving sixth century *ambo* [Fig. 21] may have come from the church; and galleries ran above the aisles and narthex.[36] Hagia Sophia, on the other hand, has a suitable space for a dressing room but never had galleries. The evidence therefore suggests that the Monastery of Hyacinth was the patriarchal cathedral not only in 1209, but for the whole period when Nicaea was capital of the Empire.

Instead of being taken to the cathedral, the weary Latin delegates were shown a church where the First Council is supposed to have met, its walls decorated with a painting representing the holy fathers of that assembly. This church, which cannot now be identified – except to say that it was distinct from the cathedral – raises the question of the Church of the Holy Fathers, famed in the early Middle Ages. According to a tradition which reaches back at least to the eighth century, the First Council met in one of the churches still standing in the city. Such an assumption, of course, was incorrect, for Eusebios clearly shows that the Council met in the imperial palace, but its acceptance and growth in the Dark Ages is hardly surprising in a city whose greatest claim to glory was the Council.

The holy fathers of the Council gave their name to a church which first appears and is most frequently mentioned in the Dark Ages. In 727, when the Arabs attacked Nicaea, their forces battered down part of the walls in the vicinity of the Church of the Holy Fathers, but were unable to take the city because of the prayers of the faithful and the efficacy of the holy images of the fathers. These were still revered in the early ninth century, when Theophanes, the chronicler of these events, was writing.[37] In the same period, the church was the goal of the Anglo-Saxon pilgrim Willibald who made an excursion from Constantinople, where he stayed from 727 to 729, in order to see the site of the Council and the form of the church where it met.[38] He described the church as similar to that of the Mount of Olives whence Christ ascended into heaven, particularly in its lack of a roof, and remarked on the images of the fathers depicted on its walls. The comparison with the church in Jerusalem gives a clue to its appearance which will be considered below.

The images had great fame in an age which saw much controversy about the use of such representations. They also stirred the imagination of a superstitious public who willingly saw in them the work of Constantine, a visible survival of the first triumph and organisation of the Church. According to an iconodule text of the mid-eighth century, Constantine himself had set up an image of Christ in Nicaea, as well as that of the Council which also showed the Emperor receiving a crown from an angel.[39] Patriarch Nikephoros, writing around 820, described the image in similar terms, mentioning the fathers and Constantine and adding the detail that it was in shining mosaic and still preserved in his day.[40] The mosaics, then, were one of the major attractions of the church and widely famed. They appear to have originated before the time of Leo III and to have survived the first period of iconoclasm, presumably because their subject was considered historical rather than purely religious. They seem also to have survived the great earthquake of 740, which is supposed to have left only one church standing. Plainly, as already seen, this statement must be an exaggeration, for both the Dormition and Hagia Sophia, like the Church of the Holy Fathers, were products of earlier ages and were standing long after 740. It is perhaps best to interpret the text as meaning that only one church escaped damage. In any case, the mosaics remained to be admired in the ninth century, but their subsequent fate is uncertain.

The historical record is silent until 1065, when the Church of the Holy Fathers, "where the synod against Arius was held and orthodoxy was proclaimed and shone brighter than the sun," collapsed as a result of the earthquake.[41] Nevertheless, a church purporting to be the site of the Council and bearing a depiction of the fathers on its walls was shown in 1234 to the reluctant Latin ambassadors.[42] Although this is the last account of the church, an inscription indicates that it still existed in the late thirteenth century. This fragmentary document, apparently to be dated to 1291, records that the monastery was a substantial establishment, with a clergy of forty-two monks, twelve priests and twenty-four deacons. It stood on a lot of about 25 by 45 meters (the dimensions are described in detail) and possessed three *proasteia,* or suburban properties. This indicates that the church survived the earthquake, but of course does not prove that it was the actual site of the Council.

So far, it has not been possible to identify the church with any surviving building, in spite of valiant efforts. The sources nevertheless give an idea of its plan and location, sufficient to suggest that the church cannot be any of the standing buildings. The clue to its appearance comes from Willibald's comparison with the church of the Ascension in Jerusalem which he also visited on his pilgrimage. He described this church as being open at the top and with columns so close to the walls that anyone who could pass behind them would be freed from his sins. In the centre of the building, on the spot where Christ had ascended, was a square column of brass with a lamp on it.[43] This selective description may be supplemented by the narrative of the French Bishop Arculf who made his pilgrimage around 670. Like Willibald, he was struck by the lack of any roof or vault, a circumstance he attributed to the miraculous nature of the footprints of the Lord, which did not allow any covering above them. He noted that the altar stood on the west under a narrow covering. Arculf also described a brass cylinder in the middle of the building, so constructed that the holy footprints could be seen within it, and remarked that eight glazed windows on the western side of the round church were filled with lamps which illuminated the path from the Vale of Josaphat. The text includes a drawing which indicates that the church was an open rotunda, probably with a double colonnade.[44]

The Church of the Ascension has been studied; its history and plan are well known. It was built by a rich patron Poemenia before 378 on a peculiar plan, a rotunda with a narthex and covered altar, but open to the sky so that the path which the Lord had followed to heaven would never be blocked. The unpaved central part preserved the holy footprints; they were later covered by a sort of brass tower where the sacred dust which they generated was stored and distributed. There were two colonnades, one very close to the wall. The church stood until 614, when it was destroyed by the Persians, but was rebuilt by Patriarch Modestos in 638. It is figured in the mosaics of Sta. Pudenziana in Rome and may have served as the model of the Dome of the Rock in Jerusalem.[45]

The resemblance between the two churches which struck Willibald suggests that the Church of the Fathers was also a rotunda with an open roof. Such a plan is highly exceptional, and the reasons for its use at Nicaea can only be imagined. No known church there is of this shape, but the building where the synod of 1232 met naturally enters into the question. That was a domed rotunda at or near the patriarchate. If it were physically part of the patriarchal church, it would be possible to imagine a complex structure like, for example, the Holy Sepulchre in Jerusalem, where a rotunda is attached to a basilical church. In that case, the church of the Holy Fathers would also have been the cathedral, and the remarks above would have to be modified accordingly. On the other hand, the vague wording of the text does not justify such an assumption, and the rotunda in question is perhaps best seen as a martyr's tomb or an old baptistery adjacent to the patriarchate. A parallel for such an arrangement is near at hand, in Prusa, where a round building which adjoined the main church was later converted into the tomb of Osman, founder of the Ottoman state and conqueror of the city.[46]

Some of the problems surrounding the Church of the Holy Fathers seem incapable of resolution, but its general plan is clear, and its location can be established, at least approximately. Theophanes records that the church stood near the part of the walls which the Arabs demolished. Their attack was most destructive in the vicinity of the Istanbul gate, where a large section of wall had to be rebuilt soon after. Consequently, it is probable that the church stood in the northernmost part of the city, west of the Istanbul gate, and not far from Saint Tryphon's. No trace of a church has been found there, nor has any rotunda ever been reported. This famous church, whose origins probably far antedate the Dark Ages, though they certainly do not go back to the Council, may therefore be considered as lost.

Earlier Churches

The churches directly attested for the Laskarid period may have been only a small proportion of those actually in use in the capital. Among these were no doubt many which are never mentioned in the sources, as well as some surviving from earlier ages, and attested only then. Several earlier churches are known by name and occasionally location; they may be considered in order of their appearance in history.

A text attributed to Amphilochios of Ikonion deals with a miracle which Saint Basil supposedly performed at Nicaea during the reign of Valens (364-375). The narrative concerns a dispute between orthodox and Arians over possession of the local cathedral; if authentic, it would reveal the presence of a cathedral church (of unspecified plan or location) long before the construction of Hagia Sophia. Unfortunately, the text appears to be apocryphal, and of a much later period; therefore no conclusions may be drawn about the early cathedral. The same narrative also mentions the Church of Saint Diomedes, situated outside the walls, close to the city.[47] This is no doubt a real church, dedicated to a local martyr and surviving in the Middle Ages, whenever the text was actually written. It seems not to appear again in history.

The only other ecclesiastical buildings mentioned in late antique texts are the churches, monasteries, and nunneries built or restored by Justinian; nothing further is known of them. A surviving structure is perhaps to be associated with the churches. This is a domed chamber almost 4 metres high, built underground and reached by steps, just to the east of the Church of Hyacinth. A marble pillar bearing a large cross suggested that it was a baptistery, but its subterranean location may make identification as a sacred spring more likely.[48]

The other attested churches appear in the ninth century and later. Theodore of Studios addressed a letter to an (unnamed) abbess of Nicaea, thus indicating the existence of a nunnery. He also wrote to Joseph, abbot "of the Potters," a monastery which may have been so named because it stood in the quarter where pottery was made. Joseph is also supposed to have built churches, apparently at Nicaea.[49] Bishop Alexander in the tenth century refers to his decoration of the Church of Rufinaous, which may have been in Nicaea. The life of Saint Neophytos, of which a section has been discussed above, reveals that he was martyred and buried between the city walls and the lake shore, a spot later dignified by a fine church, still standing when the life was written (eleventh century or earlier). Because of the location of his church, the Saint was considered as being in the forefront of the city's defences, since he protected the approach from the lake.[50] Finally, Saint Theodote, a martyr of the great persecution, is supposed to have been buried at Nicaea, and probably had a church there; whether her relics were among those of the female saints sold by the Turks in 1330 cannot be determined.[51]

Any or all of these churches might have been standing in the Laskarid city, but none is attested at that time. Their brief mentions, though, at least give the impression of a vital ecclesiastical life in all periods of the city's Christian existence, and show that the cult of the local martyrs (of whom Saint Tryphon was the most famous) was constantly of importance.

Some churches are represented not by texts but by traces of their internal furnishings, of which a quantity have been preserved in the museum of Iznik. Among them are an *ambo* of the fifth or sixth century [Fig. 21], a range of capitals, including some which imitate late antique styles [Fig. 22], and decorated marble plaques [Fig. 23, 24] of all periods from the sixth through the eleventh centuries.[52] Some of the plaques come from the Monastery of Hyacinth and have been discussed in that context. As for the rest, their provenance appears to be unknown, but they may still serve as illustrations of local sculpture in the Middle Ages, mute witnesses of churches which have disappeared.

The Church of Metochites

With the evidence for the churches of Nicaea in mind, it is now possible to address the question with which this chapter began. The tenth section of the speech of Metochites contains a description of a church which at first sight appears conventional, since it is introduced by phrases about the churches in general. It soon proceeds to such detail, however, that the author appears to be describing a real and specific building. The details should enable the church to be identified, if indeed it corresponds with any of those which are known. Although Metochites never names the church, there is a strong likelihood that, in his allusive way, he is referring to some well-known establishment rather than to a place whose obscurity would have left his auditors unmoved. It is therefore probable that his church was noted at the time, and thus one which finds a place in the historical record. Of those, one may be eliminated from consideration: the church of Saint Tryphon appears in a following section, and is clearly not the subject of the present description.

Metochites begins with the interior decoration of the church, starting at the top.[53] The ceiling was adorned with paintings (or perhaps mosaics) of gold and variegated colors; they continued down the sides to cover the upper walls. A revetment of colored stone (probably marble) distinguished the lower walls, while the floor was richly paved with cut stone. Obscure language makes the architecture harder to apprehend. The church had colonnades, but there were also columns of varying dimensions in its centre. Their capitals and bases were richly decorated, and inlaid with gold. Images, some of them decorated with gold and precious stones, embellished the interior, as did sacred offerings, vessels and books. On leaving the church, the visitor beheld a grassy meadow and grove of trees, many of them cypresses.

The details of this rhetorical description are not always easy to follow. It is difficult, therefore, to establish a certain identification, but the case for the Church of Hyacinth (the Dormition) seems the strongest, even though some parts of the description, if taken literally, are hard to reconcile with the remains. Upper parts with mosaics which stretched down the side walls are a notable feature of that church, which had marble revetment on the walls of its nave, and floors paved with *opus sectile*. Colonnades of a sort separated the nave from the aisles, but they were short, consisting of a triple arcade resting on rectangular pillars. The curious phrase about "deceiving the eye" could have reference to the large piers which supported the dome; these were so designed that the parts which adjoined the "colonnade" resembled the other pillars or columns.[54] The columns which rose within the church could have belonged to a ciborium which has disappeared, or to the *templon* screen. The elaborate carving of capitals and bases probably refers to these rather than to the columns of the church, which were quite simple, their capitals decorated only with sculptured monograms. Colonnades and columns therefore do not correspond exactly with the text, nor does the most notable feature of the church, its dome, find a place in the description. On the other hand, when allowance is made for the obfuscation of rhetoric, the degree of correspondence might appear adequate.

The decor and architecture of Hyacinth's church may thus suit the description. The most convincing parallel, however, comes in the following section where Metochites describes the grove which meets the eye as one leaves the church. A century and a half later, Gregory Palamas was also struck by the rich growth of trees which overshadowed the courtyard of the monastery. It seems likely, therefore, that Metochites had this church in mind. Consideration of the others, which do not suit the description, will offer some negative confirmation.

The Church of Hagia Sophia would appear to be another plausible candidate. It, too, had mosaics in the upper parts, revetments on the walls and a floor of cut marble. The church has no dome and is of a basilical plan ideally suited to colonnades. Its aisles, however, are separated from the nave by solid masonry piers which resemble walls. Furthermore, it is unlikely that a church built at the intersection of the two main streets would ever have been surrounded by a grove. Even if trees stood on two sides, anyone leaving would have seen not them, but a busy street. Hagia Sophia, therefore, may be excluded from consideration.

Likewise, it would be difficult to accommodate the description to any of the other churches attested for the thirteenth century. Church B (Monastery of Tornikios?) was of the cross in square plan and thus devoid of colonnades, while the aisles of Church C (Saint Anthony?) were defined by walls rather than columns. It is of course conceivable that the Rotunda of the Fathers, if it were still standing, could have met the description since it had a central colonnade. Yet Metochites gives no hint of the famous image of the fathers, even though he dwells at length on the Council. In any case, no conclusions are possible since the church does not survive. In sum, it seems probable that the Church of Hyacinth was the object of Metochites' praise. Since it was one of the two most renowned churches of the time, it is reasonable to suppose that he would have included it in his speech, however cloaked in obscurity. If, as it appears, this church was the seat of the Patriarch, its prominence in the speech would be even more justified.

Secular Buildings

Although the churches are relatively well known, the record of other buildings, public or private, is remarkably thin, especially for the Middle Ages. The most famous and important building of Late Antiquity was the imperial palace where Constantine had summoned the First Council. It long survived: Valentinian I went there after his proclamation as Emperor, the usurper Prokopios interned one of his opponents in it, and Justinian repaired it. In the mid-fourth century, the city still preserved its Hellenistic regularity and contained closely set high buildings along its straight streets. It is likely that they filled much or all of the area within the walls.

By the time of Justinian, however, the urban fabric had deteriorated. Part of the palace had collapsed, the aqueduct was broken, and the lodging and baths of the postal officials had long been ruined. These structures, too, may be added to the meagre list of civic buildings. All have disappeared except the aqueduct, whose remains have not been dated: the lower parts could be Justinianic. All these were repaired by the Emperor who in addition built churches, monasteries, and nunneries. In the sixth century, therefore, it is probable that Nicaea had the full complement of public buildings which characterised cities of the age, though, like many others, it was in a decidedly delapidated state.

Sources for the early Middle Ages have little to add. A seal of the tenth or eleventh century reveals the existence of the *xenodocheion,* or hospice, which would also have served as a centre for charitable works. Its importance is shown by the high rank which its director bore. The archaeological record suggests that the aqueduct was rebuilt in the ninth century, perhaps at the same time as the walls.[55] Most significantly, the excavations of the theatre reveal a major change, completed by the Dark Ages: one of the most characteristic buildings of the ancient city had gone out of use and been transformed into a quarry and a dump. It would seem that this district at least was in decay throughout the period, but no reasonably clear picture of urban life can be reconstructed before the thirteenth century.

Laskarid Nicaea

More abundant sources, especially the speeches of Laskaris and Metochites, allow an impression of the city in the years when it was the imperial capital to be reconstructed.[56] Although there are many gaps, the city appears more clearly at this time than any other.

A visitor to this capital would first have been impressed by the walls. Theodore Laskaris repaired and strengthened them, adding the coat of light mortar which made them gleam like snow when seen from afar. They were rendered even more imposing as a result of the work of Vatatzes, who raised them, and added the outer wall and ditch, reproducing on a smaller scale the appearance of Constantinople. No other fortification in the kingdom could compare.

When such a visitor passed through one of the gates into the city, he would have been struck by its verdure and fertility. Both Laskaris and Metochites praise this aspect of local beauty: by likening the whole place to a grove, and by remarking on the grassy meadows and luxuriant trees which confronted the eye outside the Monastery of Hyacinth. Anyone who has seen Nicaea will appreciate and sympathise with such a description, for the city and region are indeed marked by fertility and charm. Yet from the point of view of urban life the trees and meadows have a sinister aspect, for their abundance indicates that large parts of the city within the walls were empty of habitation. The excavations of the theatre, combined with the historical circumstances and parallels from other sites, would naturally suggest that much of the urban area was ruined and desolate during the Dark Ages. Yet some changes should have been apparent by this time, for all sources agree that Laskarid Nicaea was a great city.

Continuing evidence from the theatre clearly shows that one part of the city was still desolate, for the massive ancient structure was now being used as a graveyard. Similarly, the presence of monasteries and praise of the peace which allowed their inmates to meditate is not indicative of a bustling metropolis. It is probably no accident that one of the monasteries (if it is correctly identified) was built next to the theatre. The one monastery certainly identified, that of Hyacinth, had long stood in the southeastern part of the city. In the thirteenth century, it was surrounded by verdure and thus probably lay outside the built-up area of the central city.

Nicaea, of course, did have some sort of urban centre. Metochites mentions its tall and closely set buildings (or houses) and a contemporary source, a poem of the great scholar Nikephoros Blemmydes, praises its wide streets full of people.[57] These are reminiscent of the description of the fourth-century city, with its regular streets and buildings. The palaces of Emperor and Patriarch were doubtless of some magnificence; so far, neither has been certainly located. Recent excavation to the theatre, however, has uncovered remains of what appears to be a substantial building of this period. It has long walls, some decorated with frescoes, and at least one apsidal chamber. The excavator has raised the possibility that this may be the Lascarid palace – perhaps appropriate to the highest point in the city – but confirmation must await further excavation. If the suggestion is correct, the area of the theatre would be seen as far more important than now appears, and the small church might turn out to the private chapel of the Emperor.[58]

Other civic buildings included baths, a hospital with provision for epileptics (there may have been two separate establishments), a poorhouse, workshops for weaving, and a jail called Lethe. The baths were no doubt fed by water from the aqueduct which Theodore Laskaris appears to have repaired. It entered the city through the walls, north of the east gate, and provided an abundant supply of water for houses and for the numerous fountains which graced the city.[59] All were material expressions of the wealth of emperor and patriarch, whose generosity would have left its visible mark. Although no buildings are specifically mentioned, it is likely that the lake front, too, was a busy place, constantly in use by fishermen and trades and no doubt the site of the fish market. If the Church of Saint Diomedes were still standing (as seems likely) it would have been the centre of a thriving district.

Other known buildings are religious, and it is these which appear to have made the greatest impression, for Metochites dwells at length on the monasteries and churches. The former apparently occupied a good deal of land within the walls; the churches may have been scattered through the city, though the few whose locations are known were on the main streets: Saint Tryphon near the north gate, Hagia Sophia in the center, and Saint Anthony (?) near the south gate. The church of the Fathers was apparently located in the vicinity of Saint Tryphon. The latter, in addition, contained the school established by Theodore II. Others also had some facilities for primary education, attested specifically at Saint Michael's near the Patriarchate.

Laskarid Nicaea was certainly a large and important place by the standards of the time, however it may have declined from its classical magnificence. Its streets were wide and probably lined with houses, churches, and others buildings to give the impression of a thriving and well-populated place. Yet substantial parts were empty, occupied by fields, groves, and monasteries. All were surrounded by walls whose strength and beauty were greatly admired. They sheltered a green and pleasant city, busy in the centre and along the main streets, quiet and perhaps a bit ramshackle in the outlying districts, yet no doubt deserving of all the praise it received.

NOTES

[1] For the history of the church see Janin (1975) 121-128 as well as the passages cited in the previous narrative. The most recent attempt at dating is that of Mango (1994) 353.

[2] They are discussed at considerable length in van Dieten (1985).

[3] For architecture and decoration, see Wulff (1903), Schmit (1927) and Peschlow (1972).

[4] The early dating was proposed by Schmit (1927) 20; cf. Mango (1976) 172.

[5] See Schmit (1927) 21. The church was a casualty of the war between Greece and Turkey. By 1921, when it was first possible for outsiders to visit the region of Nicaea which had been a war zone, the church had suffered considerable vandalism, being looted and despoiled of its sacred furnishings, apparently by the victorious Turkish troops as they reoccupied the area. In 1924, it was blown up. The reports of the destruction are quoted in the article of H. Leclercq in *DACL, s.v.* Nicée.

[6] The essential studies for the chronology of the mosaics are Underwood (1959) and Mango (1959).

[7] See Wulff (1903) 181-186; cf. Feld (1970) 175; tomb of Nikephoros: Mango (1959).

[8] Lipsic (1964) proposed identification with a known abbot of the Studios in Con-stantinople; as Janin (1975) 123 remarks, this is a natural suggestion for which there is no proof.

[9] Council: above 22-25; earthquakes: Attaliates 91 (1065), Theophanes 412 (470).

[10] As at Edirne and Vize in Thrace.

[11] Von Hammer (1818) 113.

The Churches and Other Buildings 121

¹²So J. Covel reported in 1677; see Raby (1976) 159, 181. Identification of the Ulu Cami as Hagia Sophia is perhaps strengthened by the early Ottoman chronicler Asikpasazade who wrote (p.32) that Orhan tranformed the great church, 'ulu kilise,' into a mosque.

¹³For the building history, see Brounoff (1925) and Schneider (1943) 10-17.

¹⁴See Foss and Winfield (1985) 79-120.

¹⁵For these, see Alpatoff (1926).

¹⁶Fully discussed in Eyice (1963). This floor offers a useful parallel to a similar floor at Montecassino: Bloch (1985) 51f.

¹⁷Skoutariotes 514 (=Acropolites 291f.).

¹⁸Hendy (1969) 330-6; cf. Laurent (1958) for the significance of the lily on these coins.

¹⁹The text is from *AASS* Nov. 4 356, for David and the ark, see 2 Samuel 6.

²⁰See the detailed report of Eyice (1948) who saw the remains soon after they were unearthed. When Anthony Bryer visited in 1967, footings of the apses were still visible by the side of the road. They had disappeared by 1971, and no trace is now to be seen. My thanks to Dr. Bryer for his comments.

²¹Papadopoulos (1952).

²²Laskarid architecture is presented and analysed in the fundamental study of Buchwald (1979).

²³Janin (1975) III determined that Agalmates lay north of the city.

²⁴Excavated and published by Yalman (1979).

²⁵Yalman (1979) 466. They apparently resembled the frescoes of the fourth century hypogaeum outside the city (above, p.14), but certainly cannot be used to determine such an early date for the present church.

²⁶Described in Eyice (1983).

²⁷Gregoras 1.44. The chrysobull of Michael VIII of 1272 (*Ius greco-romanum* 661) mentions the landholding and indicate that the church was a nunnery.

²⁸Pachymeres 2.193; cf. Janin (1975) 120 for the proposed founder.

²⁹For this and for the other minor churches, see Janin (1975) III-25 *passim* and their various mentions in the present discussion.

³⁰Mesarites, *Bericht* 35.

³¹Hadzipsaltes (1964) 141f.; the relevant passage is quoted in Laurent, *Régestes* 1210.

³²See the references in van Dieten (1985) 72 n.42 and Raby (1976) 162f., 183 n.36. In modern times, the bishop's throne stood in the nave, then the apse; it was apparently a work of the eighteenth or nineteenth century: Wulff (1903) 12 n.3; Schmit (1927) 9.

³³Laurent, *Régestes* 1261.

³⁴But for a possible identification, see below.

³⁵Golubovich (1919) 430, 436.

³⁶For these requirements, see Bryer and Winfield (1985) 240. The existence of galleries in the monastery of Hyacinth is generally assumed, though it has been brought into doubt for the period after 1065: Peschlow (1972).

³⁷Theophanes 406; for what follows see the detailed, though necessarily inconclusive discussion of van Dieten (1985) 63-76.

³⁸Willibald, 41, 70.

³⁹*Nouthesia Gerontos* 25.

⁴⁰Cited in van Dieten (1985) 67.

[41] Attaliates 91.
[42] Golubovich (1919) 428.
[43] Willibald 32f, 67.
[44] Arculf 246f.
[45] The evidence is presented in some detail in Vincent and Abel (1914) 2. 360-419, to be corrected by the results of subsequent excavations: Corbo (1960).
[46] On this, see Eyice (1963a) 375-78. and in more detail Eyice (1963b).
[47] For these, see above 11f. The Church of Diomedes is apparently not identical with the monastery of the same dedication which was one of the refuges of Patriarch Arsenios in 1260; that seems to have been situated farther west, in the vicinity of the Drakon river: Janin (1975) 89.
[48] Schneider (1943) 17.
[49] See Janin (1975) 118, 114 and above p.25.
[50] *Vita Neophyti* 250.
[51] *Synax CP* 156, Delehaye (1937) 219, and for the relics, Gregoras I.488.
[52] For the plaques see Ulbert (1969) nos. 59-74 (without illustration) and (1970) nos. 20, 32-35, 42.
[53] The text is printed below, 178-180.
[54] See Fig. 20 and the photo in Mango (1976) 168, usefully placed in the context of other churches of similar plan.
[55] See Foss and Winfield (1985) 88f., where no dating is proposed; but the type of mortar corresponds with that used in the walls of Michael III.
[56] Use of Metochites in this context is not entirely anachronistic since it is unlikely that the city saw major change in the thirty years between the return of the capital to Constantinople and the speech of Metochites.
[57] Blemmydes 113, a poem on the Monastery of Sosandra founded by Vatatzes near Magnesia.
[58] See Yalman (1989) 307: cf, *AS* 38 (1988) 179.
[59] The two palaces are attested in the report of the Latin embassy of 1234 and the imperial palace again at the coronation of Michael VIII (see above, 74 and 83). Hospital and poorhouse: Blemmydes 113 and Metochites sec. 8; baths, weaving: Metochites secs. 8, 18; the jail appears in connection with the panic of 1265: above, 86. Aqueduct: Laskaris sec. 12, Metochites sec. 11. On hospitals and poorhouses and their importance in Byzantine times, see Constantelos (1968) 152-84, 157-69.

12. Introduction to the Speeches

The speeches of Laskaris and Metochites, both works of the thirteenth century, are the longest texts which deal with Nicaea and thus a fundamental part of its historical record. Both were delivered on the site in the presence of Emperors – John Vatatzes and Andronikos II – and both therefore represent detailed views of the city according to the taste and interests of speaker and audience, expressed in a suitably elevated language.

These speeches are the culmination of a long tradition of praise of Nicaea, which stretched from Classical times into the fourteenth century; many examples have already been presented. Most of them are brief, fragmentary, and usually devoted to specific events and places; these speeches alone give a comprehensive view of Nicaea, at least those aspects of it considered worthy of emphasis. Their value lies in the image which they present, and in themselves as examples of encomia, a genre with a long history as part of the rhetoric which was fundamental to Byzantine education and literature.

The language of the speeches is difficult, often obscure. In order to convey its meaning we have therefore provided translations as literal as possible, but necessarily at the expense of the eloquence of the Greek. We have not edited the texts ourselves, but reproduce the published version of Sathas for Metochites, and, thanks to her kind permission, the new text of Laskaris by Dr. Sophia Georgiopoulou. She will publish it with full critical annotation in the context of a general study of Theodore Laskaris. Where we differ from those texts, we have so noted in the commentary which follows the speeches. This is intended to be summary, and primarily to treat matters of historical or topographical interest; our attention to philosophy will be sporadic, since there are many far better qualified to discuss this aspect of the works. To aid the reader, the commentary contains a summary of each section of the speeches.

Rhetorical productions like these are something of an acquired taste for the modern reader, and it may seem difficult at first glance not to share the judgment of Edward Gibbon on such products of the Byzantine mind:

> In prose, the least offensive of the Byzantine writers are absolved from censure by their naked and unassuming simplicity: but the orators, most eloquent in their own conceit, are the farthest removed from the models whom they affect to emulate. In every page our taste and reason are wounded by the choice of

gigantic and obsolete words, a stiff and intricate phraseology, the discord of images, the childish display of false or unseasonable ornament, and the painful attempt to elevate themselves, to astonish the reader, and to involve a trivial meaning in the smoke of obscurity and exaggeration. Their prose is soaring to the vicious affectation of poetry: their poetry is sinking below the flatness and insipidity of prose.[1]

Nevertheless, the works are worth considering in their context, for they represent a tradition which found much appeal in a complex and ornate rhetoric and never ceased to emulate its masters. The speeches may best be appreciated if some attention is devoted to this tradition.

The bases of Byzantine education were grammar, taught in the primary school, and rhetoric, which encompassed or led to most other subjects and was essential for anyone who hoped to advance in a public career. The study of rhetoric had an ancient history and had produced a vast literature long before the Byzantines. They, however, appreciated it not so much through its ancient exponents as through the works of two late antique schoolmasters which, though generally consigned to oblivion now, were essential reading for the Byzantine student. These are the books attributed to Hermogenes of Tarsos (second-third century) and Aphthonios of Antioch (fourth-fifth century), a series of manuals read through the whole period and consequently the subject of a long series of learned commentaries. Their importance can hardly be exaggerated.[2] These manuals organized the whole subject of rhetoric, gave rules for its use, and provided model speeches for instruction and emulation. Such textbooks of writing and speaking, called *progymnasmata,* were used in the last stages of the study of grammar and the first of rhetoric.

Among the various classes of *progymnasmata,* the encomium, or speech of praise, and the *ekphrasis*, or description, were constantly of use and interest. The former, originally intended to have an individual as subject, would treat his family, upbringing, and accomplishments, all the while adding favorable comparisons with others. The *ekphrasis* was designed to create a vivid image of the subject in clear language, ornamented with the usual figures.[3] The encomium could easily be adapted to treat other subjects, and early became the convenient vehicle for the glorification of countries and cities. The *ekphrasis* could naturally deal with a vast range of subjects. In many cases, the two genres overlapped, so that a speech of praise might contain a good deal of description, or an *ekphrasis* could deviate into lauding what it described. For these, the Byzantines devised a useful term, "encomiastic ekphrasis."

Cities were a natural subject of praise in Roman times, when they formed a vital part of the administrative and economic fabric of the empire, and in Late Antiquity, when chairs of rhetoric were set up in many of them and cities vied to attract the best teachers and speakers. The occasions for such speeches were legion: visits by Emperors or high officials, installation of governors, local festivals, or expressions of gratitude by successful sophists. A city might be the subject of an entire speech, or feature in speeches devoted to individuals or events. The genre was of sufficient importance to justify detailed treatment in manuals of rhetoric composed in Late Antiquity and copied and discussed throughout the Byzantine period.

Actually, the earliest directions for composing the eulogy of a city survive in the Latin of Quintilian (first century AD), whose works are closely tied to the Greek tradition.[4] He prescribed that cities should be praised like men. A speech should discuss their founder, age, virtues, position, fortifications, and citizens. Buildings should be mentioned, along with their utility, beauty, and history. These twin themes of beauty and utility, as will be seen, were fundamental to the whole genre. The brief statement of Quintilian finds a parallel in the "Art of Panegyric" attributed to Dionysius of Halicarnassus, though apparently of later date.[5] It tells how to praise the city where a festival *(panegyris)* was being held. The speaker should treat the site of the city, its founder, its accomplishments in war and peace, its size if great, its beauty if small, its temples and dedications, public and private buildings, its river if it has one, and its traditions. Similarly, the famed Hermogenes ordained that the origins, development, culture, character, plan, and accomplishments of a city were suitable topics for praise.[6]

These concise statements laid the general plan which an encomiast might follow. A far more detailed treatment, however, was available, and is of great interest here as giving a full view of how such a speech should be constructed and what elements it should contain. This is the chapter "How to Praise a City" in the work of Menander the Rhetor, a native of Laodicea in Phrygia who wrote in the time of Diocletian. As the main source for the subject, his work merits some consideration.[7]

Menander first gives general directions for praising a country. There are two main headings: position (in relation to the land, the sea and the sky, this last including the climate) and nature (its landscape and fertility). Both the pleasing and useful aspects of each category should be stressed. He gives specific examples; they show, naturally enough, that objectivity was not the aim of such speeches, any more than the mere presentation of factual material. The content was to be arranged to show the subject to its best advantage, and its characteristics, whatever they were, should be complimented. The medium, of course, was adaptable to praise quite opposite qualities, should the need arise, as seen in Quintilian's remarks of large and small places.

The main essay, "How to Praise a City," is the most important because of its specific instructions. These are arranged according to the main topics: the site, its nature, harbors, the citadel, origin and development, and accomplishments. Most of these could have a direct application to Nicaea.

When praising a site, the orator should consider every item in both its pleasing and useful aspects. He should treat the climate, and agricultural products; relation to the mainland, the sea, the surrounding country, (here he should include springs, rivers, and lakes), and neighbors. Nature, in this context, is topography: whether the city is in mountainous or flat country, to be presented with its various advantages (or disadvantages, for it was always important to stress merit by pointing out the defects of the opposite case).

In his discussion of history, the encomiast should treat the city's founder, its antiquity (praising youth or age, as appropriate), its original inhabitants, and its development. More important were its accomplishments, to be treated in four headings: political system, science, crafts, and peculiar abilities (such as athletics or rhetoric). All were to be judged according to the cardinal virtues of justice (which included public and private piety as well as good treatment of foreigners), temperance (the good behavior of the inhabitants), prudence (laws, customs, and importance of practitioners of wisdom, such as rhetors and sophists), and courage (in war or adversity).

In general, Menander wrote, some praises were appropriate to cities at all times, others suitable for special occasions. Among these were festivals and arrivals – of the speaker in his native city or of governors or other high officials. In his directions for speeches of arrival, the Rhetor gives further points about cities.[8] The *prooimion* should express the speaker's joy at beholding the city (this could be omitted in speeches of a general patriotic nature) and praise of the founder. Then site and nature and the topics already presented should be treated. An epilogue should deal with the fame and wealth of the place, its notable buildings, and those of the surrounding territory.

Generations of Byzantine speakers studied the work of Menander and put it to practical use. By expanding on Aphthonios and Hermogenes, it exercised an influence which can most readily be seen in the long series of encomia on Constantinople. The praises of the capital are naturally far longer and more elaborate than those of Nicaea (with the exception of the present speeches) but the two types have much in common, and a valuable study devoted to the former illuminates the long development in which these speeches have a definite place.[9]

As the new capital grew rapidly in the fourth century, it attracted a host of influential and learned men, among them many skilled in flattery. Highly developed encomia were already written at that time, most notably by the famous orators Themistios and Himerios. Both treat the beauty of the place – its buildings and decoration; the advantages and attraction of its site; its importance as a centre of education and virtue; and both stress its role as a second Rome and a ruling city. In all this, the influence of manuals like that of Menander is obvious. Other late antique speakers followed a similar pattern, though taking account of a present reality: from being an emulator of Rome, Constantinople became a new Rome, better than the old, as the Western Empire sank into decline. They also introduced a new element indicative of a fundamental cultural change by praising the Christian piety evident in the capital. This aspect became especially important in the Dark Ages, and played a major role in subsequent encomia. When the Empire was at its height, numerous speeches treated Constantinople as the centre of the world and of civilization, using all the elements considered. Laskaris and Metochites, therefore, could draw on a long tradition if they needed inspiration beyond that provided by the handbooks or Nicaea itself. They also had a local tradition whose surviving fragments have been mentioned in the course of this study. These may now be seen in the broader context of encomia.

The only surviving late antique praises of Nicaea are of the mid-fourth century, in the *Expositio totius orbis*.[10] Its brief paragraph treats only the appearance of the city, a subject which might find its place near the end of a formal encomium. In another age, the Council of 787 also brought accolades, quite different from any so far considered.[11] Because of the circumstances, these deal only with a relevant specific point: the Christian piety of a place which had been the seat of two councils and had thus played a major role in establishing and defining orthodoxy. Although these cannot be considered as encomia, they introduce an element which will form an essential part of such speeches.

The Christian glory of Nicaea is first combined with the stock elements of praise in the anonymous introduction to the life of Saint Neophytos, written before the eleventh century.[12] This follows the rules by briefly mentioning the site and its nature, along with that of the surrounding country, and touching upon the buildings, the inhabitants, and the lake. Then, it devotes equal space to the piety of the city expressed in the First Council. By introducing the element of Christian piety, the subject of the speech of 787, it corresponds with contemporary praises of Constantinople and foreshadows the content of the longer praises. Even more concisely, the verses of John the Geometer manage to introduce the main elements of site and nature: vines, fields, trees, gardens, animals, and the lake.[13]

Finally, the Latin of William of Tyre offers such parallels to conventional praises that it seems derived from a Greek original. His brief description treats the location of the city in the plain, yet not far from the mountains; wealth and advantages of the country; the lake; the fortifications; and the large population.[14] It could almost have been taken from one of the handbooks, even though written by a Latin far from the site. Although none of these praises is of much length, they contain elements common to the tradition and perhaps give an indication of the local precedents available to Laskaris and Metochites, to whom this discussion may now turn. Their speeches will be treated in reverse order of chronology, since that of Metochites adheres more closely to the tradition. Both will be more easily apprehended from a brief outline, which may also serve as an introduction to their content.

The speech of Metochites is an *oeuvre de jeunesse,* the work which marked the beginning of his career. It was written when he was twenty years old and delivered before the emperor Andronikos II who was staying in Nicaea in 1290 during his inspection of the eastern frontier.[15] Metochites was born in Constantinople, where his father George was a high government official. When the father fell from favor into exile in 1283, the family moved to Nicaea, and here Theodore received his secondary education. Because of his precocious skill with letters, Metochites was able to compose the present speech; its effect was immediate. The successful orator was taken into the imperial service and launched on a career which soon made him the most powerful minister in the Empire.

The skill and learning displayed in the speech are impressive. So is the complex obscurity of the style which has no doubt kept it from becoming better known. The initial impression is of a carefully executed work, which also has the rare merit of providing some concrete information. It seems all the more astounding as the product of youth. Yet a closer inspection reveals that much of it is conventional, following the precepts and models of the schools, though introducing a certain bombast and convoluted language of its own.[16]

Metochites devotes his *prooimion* (sections 1-2) to his own inadequacy before such a great subject; a brief mention of the city's history (3) follows. More substantial is the discussion of the site (4-6) which treats its relation to the sea and mountains, its lake and rivers, and the rich products of its land. In all cases, both pleasing and practical aspects are stressed. The city itself occupies a long section (7-12). It treats the walls; the buildings, in particular the monasteries; a church (discussed above); the gardens; and the church of Saint Tryphon. The churches lead to the piety of the city in the form of the ecumenical councils (13-15), and its accomplishments in preserving the Empire when Constantinople had fallen (16-18). The peroration praises the Emperor to whom the speech was addressed. In all this, the author's close dependence on the tradition, as he follows the prescribed subject and arrangement, is clear. This speech is easy to outline and to compare with the precepts of Menander, or with other similar encomia. There is no doubt that it is a good example of the genre. Its language, of course, is individual and original. Some of these points will be considered at more length in the commentary.

The speech of Laskaris, on the other hand, is far more difficult to categorize. It was also the work of a young man, though not necessarily a debutant in public life. The author and later Emperor Theodore Laskaris was born in Nicaea in 1222, on the day when his father, John Vatatzes, came to the throne. He received his education there, much of it from Blemmydes, who greatly influ-

Introduction to the Speeches 129

enced him. As a prince of considerable intelligence who studied with the greatest scholar of the age, Theodore acquired profound knowledge of many fields, and a skill with words which he expressed in a style considered elegant by the standards of the day.[17] One aspect of this elegance was a careful avoidance of concrete or vulgar fact, a feature long established in Byzantine literature, especially in letter writing.[18] This, combined with the love of obscurity and difficult words which permeates Theodore's writings, has meant that relatively little is known of his life, and that few of his works can be fit into a scheme of development.[19] Thus the speech on Nicaea remains undated, and its relation to Theodore's other works has not been established.[20] Nevertheless, it provides one useful clue; it was delivered in the presence of Vatatzes, and thus before 1254; the author was no older than thirty-two. The circumstances, however, can only be conjectured.

The introduction of the speech (section 1) summarizes the qualities of Nicaea before shading into a long declamation on the learning there displayed (2-6). This includes an extravagant simile likening the city to a mind in which the citizens move around like thoughts, as well as a comparison with Athens, to the detriment of the ancient city: Athens lacked the Christian piety which Nicaea demonstrated at the first Council (7). After another introduction (8-9), Laskaris turns to the city itself, praising its groves, monasteries, walls, crops, and water supply (10-12) before turning to the most emotional part of the speech. This deals with recent events, or, in terms of the handbooks, the accomplishments of the city (13-15): Nicaea preserved the empire when Constantinople had fallen to the Latins; it concludes with an elaborate medical metaphor. Finally, the peroration (16-17) praises the Emperor and the city, nurse of a generation.[21]

The differences between these two speeches are easy to see. Metochites follows the rules more closely and gives far more information than Laskaris whose speech almost entirely eschews the concrete in favor of a high-flown and often emotional rhetoric. By the standards of the modern day, when clarity and information are valued, the speech of Metochites is far superior and so it has been judged.[22] Considering the probable aim of the writers and interest of their audience, however, it is surely Laskaris who should be awarded the palm. The superiority of his speech is manifest in its departure from convention, in its unexpected changes of topic, and in most of the qualities which moderns detest. Laskaris succeeds in conveying almost no information at all, but instead creates an emotional atmosphere which culminates in the peroration likening the city to a nurse and mother. In the process, he employs a smooth and elegant language, maintains contact with real and imaginary auditors, and indulges in some intricate and highly obscure metaphors. It is difficult to believe that the audience did not go away satisfied, with warm feelings about the city and the speech, however little of it they may actually have understood.[23]

For the Byzantines, especially of this period, vapidity and obscurity were not the vices which Gibbon, looking down from the heights of Reason, so eloquently condemned, but virtues to be attained after long years of study and practice. Even a swift perusal of speeches and letters of the time will reveal that style was far more highly esteemed than content, and that a style which lifted the subject as far as possible above the level of vulgarity (and intelligibility) was avidly to be sought.[24] Since Laskaris excelled in the qualities which his age admired, his speech rises above that of the young Metochites, whose style is by comparison stilted and whose text, however much its descriptions and information might appeal to a modern taste, is tied more closely to its conventional models and displays little of the flights of rhetoric and emotion of the learned prince.

NOTES

[1] Gibbon, *Decline and Fall*, chap. 53, in the section entitled 'Decay of Taste and Genius'; ed. Bury 6. 10f.

[2] For a clear treatment of these authors and their importance, see Clark (1957) 177-212; cf; Kustas (1970), Hunger (1978) 75-88, and Kennedy (1983) 273-325 *passim*.

[3] The terms are defined and discussed in the works cited in the previous note; the treatment of Hunger (1978) 92-120, especially 104f and 116f. is particularly helpful.

[4] Quoted in the introduction to Menander, xxiv.

[5] [Dio. Halic.], *Rhet.* 257.

[6] See Menander, xxvii f.

[7] The following is based on Menander 28-42.

[8] Menander 94-114.

[9] See the comprehensive study of Fenster (1978) for what follows.

[10] See Above, 9.

[11] See Above, 20ff.

[12] See Above, 33ff.

[13] See Above, 34.

[14] See Above, 53f.

[15] The date was first proposed in Ševčenko (1962) 137ff.; cf. (1975) 25f.

[16] Note the judgement of Fenster (1968) 183f.: 'Der Verfasser bei allen stylistischen und sprachlichen Virtuosität nicht verleugnen kann, dass er nach den Vorschriften und Musterbildern der rhetorischen Handbücher vorgeht.' For Hunger (1978) 173f., however, the speech is superior to that of Laskaris.

[17] But not by modern standards: cf. Pappadopoulos (1908) 160: 'L'idée est pour ainsi dire noyée sous les flots d'une rhétorique pompeuse.'

[18] On that, see Karlsson (1962) 14f.

[19] The biography of Pappadopoulos (1908) reflects this problem by providing remarkably little information in its 192 pages, which are closely based on the writings of the Emperor. For Laskaris and his intellectual significance, a shorter work, Dräseke (1894) may also be consulted pending publication of the major study of S. Georgiopoulou.

[20] Fenster (1968) 180 is perhaps hasty when he writes: 'Dieses Jugendwerk.... ist ....ein mit antiken Reminiszenzen und Gemeinplätzen volgestofftes rhetorisches Progymnasma.' Nevertheless, he considers it of higher quality than the speech of Metochites.

[21] Compare the outline and discussion of Fenster (1968) 178-183 and, for an appreciation of the speech in the context of Byzantine humanism, see Hunger (1959) 136f.

[22] See above, n.16.

[23] Eugenia Petrides, who was kind enough to read through speech and translation, made the illuminating remark that it reminded her of speeches she had heard in high school in Greece. In other words, it conveys feelings in a way which may still be appreciated.

[24] See, for example, the comments of Karlsson (1962) 14f., and the valuable discussion of obscurity in Kustas (1973) 63-100; for the importance of these elements in the time of Metochites, see Ševčenko (1962) 51-67.

Θεοδώρου Δούκα τοῦ Λάσκαρι ἐγκώμιον εἰς τὴν μεγαλόπολιν Νίκαιαν

1. Ἄνδρες ὦ Νικαεῖς, ἡ περιφανεστάτη πόλις ὑμῶν ἐξ αὐτῆς καὶ μόνης τῆς ὄψεως ἐμποιεῖ πολὺ τῇ λογικῇ ψυχῇ τὸ τερψίθυμον, ἔκ τε τῆς περὶ κύκλωσε τοῦ ἔνδον χώρου καλοτειχίας, ἔκ τε τοῦ ἀξιολόγου μεγέθους ταύτης καὶ ἰσορρόπου, ἔκ
5 τε τῆς θέσεως, ἔκ τε τῶν θριγγωμάτων, τῶν πυργωμάτων, τοῦ τῶν ἀμφοτέρων ὑψώματος, τῆς περιφανεστάτης ὕλης καὶ ἐξαιρέτου τῆς οἰκοδομῆς, τῆς κατασκευῆς καὶ ἐντέχνου μεθόδου τῆς αὐτῆς σπαρτιάσεως· ἔκ τε τῶν ἔνδοθεν καὶ τῶν ἔξωθεν, τῶν ἰδίων, τῶν οὐσιωδῶν, τῶν ἐπουσιωδῶν, τῶν ἐκ τῆς
10 τοῦ τόπου καλοκἀγαθίας συρρεόντων καθεκάστην πάντων τῶν ἀγαθῶν, καὶ ἐξ ὑμῶν, ὦ σεμνοὶ ἄνδρες, τὴν κοσμιότητα καὶ κατ' ἦθος λογικὴν παιδείαν ἀσυγκρίτων. Τότε καὶ γάρ ἐστι πόλις πόλεων, καὶ βασιλὶς βασιλίδων, καὶ ἄρχων ἀρχόντων,
15 καὶ ὑπερέχων ὑπερεχομένων, καὶ καταλλήλως θάτερον θατέρου ἐξαίρετον τῇ τιμῇ ὁπόταν ὑπερβαίνῃ τῇ λογικότητι.

Theodore Doukas Laskaris
In Praise of the Great City of Nicaea

1. Men of Nicaea, your most illustrious city, from the very sight of it alone, gives great pleasure to the rational mind—by the firm wall which encircles the grounds within, with its remarkable size and symmetry, by its situation, its battlements and towers and the height of both of them, the most magnificent and choice material of its structure, and the arrangement and skillful method of its construction—by all that is within, and all outside; by all that is its own, and by its essential and adventitious qualities; by all the good things that flow in every day from the excellence of its site; and by you, honorable men, incomparable for your refinement and the education in reason that is a part of your character. For it is then that a city is above other cities, and a queen above queens, and a ruler above rulers, a superior above superiors—appropriately distinguished in rank one over the other—when it excels them in the use of reason.

2. Ὅτι μὲν γὰρ πολλαὶ πόλεις βρίθουσαι χαρισμάτων ὀλβιότητι παμπληθῶς, καὶ κοσμούμεναι μύρων πολυτελείᾳ, καὶ ταῖς ἐκ γύρωθεν καλλωπιζόμεναι τῶν ὧν ἔτυχον τυχικῶς ἐπιδόσεσιν τόπου, καὶ ταῖς ἐκ πλοίων ποικίλαις συνεισφοραῖς τὰς ἀρχοντικὰς συνεισφορὰς βρύουσαι, ἀληθὲς ὁμοῦ τε καὶ πρόδηλον· οἷον δὲ τούτων τὸ κλέος, τὸ περιλάλητον πανταχόσε κηρύκευμα; εἴπερ λογικότης ἐν ταύταις οὐκ ἐγχορεύει, καὶ Μοῦσαι λόγου οὐκ ὠθοῦσι χορδὴν εὐρυθμίας καὶ εὐταξίας, καὶ μαθημάτων τε καὶ παιδείας οὐκ ἐγχορεύει ἐν ταύταις μεγαλοπρέπεια. Καλὴ μὲν οὖν ἐστὶ καὶ Βαβυλὼν καὶ αἱ ἐν τῇ Ἰνδικῇ χθονὶ πόλεις περικείμεναι· μύρα γὰρ ἐν ταύταις εὐπόριστά τε καὶ ἀγλαά, ὀλβιότης ἐκ χρυσοῦ καὶ μαργάρου πολλὴ καὶ περιφανής, τροφῶν ποικιλίαι, σπατάλης ἐφευρετὸς ἀφορμή, ἀκρασία ἐκ τροφῆς, καὶ εἴ τι ἄλλο πόρρω λόγου ἔχον τὴν οἴκησιν. Ἐπειδὴ γὰρ τὸν περιεκτικὸν τοῦτον δὴ κόσμον ὁ μικρόκοσμος κοσμεῖ, καὶ τῇ ἐκ τούτου ἐξερχομένῃ γνώσει καὶ λογικότητι πάντα ῥυθμίζεται καὶ στηρίζεται, ἐν ταύτῃ δὲ τὰ μὲν μύρα καὶ ἃ προείπομεν βρίθουσι παμπληθῶς, λόγος δὲ οὐκ ἀνθεῖ, καὶ παιδεία οὐκ ἐγχορεύει, καὶ φιλοσοφία οὐ περιέχει, συμβαίνει νεκρὰν εἶναι αὐτήν· ἃ δὲ μύρα καὶ πλοῦτον, ὡς εἴπομεν, κέκτηται, μυριπνοοῦσι πόλιν νεκράν, καὶ κοσμοῦσι θριγγώματα ἄκοσμα· κόσμος καὶ γὰρ πόλεως οὐδέν ἐστιν ἕτερον ἢ ἄνδρες σεμνοπρεπεῖς, λόγῳ καλλωπιζόμενοι καὶ ἐπιστήμῃ φιλοσοφίας, καὶ ἑαυτοὺς καὶ τὴν πόλιν καλλωπίζοντες καὶ δοξάζοντες.

3. Τοίνυν οὖν ἡ νῦν σήμερον Νικαέων πόλις ὑμῶν, κοσμουμένη τῷ λόγῳ τούτῳ τοῦ φιλοπόλιδος τῆς ὑμῶν πόλεως, ἄνδρες σεμνοπρεπεῖς, τῷ ἐρυθρῷ τῆς μεγαλοπρεπείας καὶ ἀληθείας καταστέφει τὰς ὑμῶν κεφαλάς. Ὑψουμένη γὰρ αὕτη μεγαλύνει ὑμᾶς ἀληθῶς· ἐξιστορουμένη σεμνοπρεπεστέρους ὑμᾶς ἀπεργάζεται· τὸ μέντοι γε ὅτι τῶν ἔξωθεν τὰ ἔνδον ἀεὶ ἐνδοξότερα, τὸ δ' ὅτι γε ὥσπερ ἀριπρεπὲς περιβόλαιον αὕτη τῷ λόγῳ τούτῳ ἱστοργουμένη, πολλαχῶς καλλωπίζει ὑμᾶς καὶ σεμνοτέρους ἐργάζεται καὶ περιφανεστέρους ποιεῖ, καὶ

2. That there are many cities abundantly laden with a wealth of pleasures, and ornamented with the variety of charms and beautified all around by the gifts of the situation they have gained by chance, and swelling the revenues of their sovereigns by the great variety of importations brought them by ships, is at once true and obvious. What is their fame, and its proclamation everywhere talked of? If reason plays no role in them, and the Muses do not move the string of harmony and order, of study and education, then magnificence plays no role in them. Lovely indeed is Babylon, and the cities that lie in the Indian land, for their charms are plentiful and excellent, and the wealth of gold and pearls great and splendid, and the variety of foods, that novel starting-point of luxury, and the intemperance arising from luxury, and whatever else is beyond description, have their dwelling there. For since it is the microcosm that gives order to this universal world, and since all things are given harmony and solidity by the knowledge and rational thought that proceed from it; but in that city the charms and the other things we mentioned plentifully abound, yet reason does not flourish, and education plays no role, and philosophy does not excel; it follows that that city is dead. And the perfumes and the wealth, which, as we said, it has, are perfuming the corpse of a city, and decorating ill-formed battlements. For the true adornment of a city is nothing other than distinguished men beautified by thought and by the knowledge of philosophy, and so giving beauty and fame both to themselves and to the city.

3. Thus does the city of you Niceans now, today, as it is honoured in this speech of a patriotic lover of your city, distinguished men, crown your own heads with the purple of grandeur and truth. For when it is itself elevated, it makes you truly great, and when it is described, makes you more distinguished: first, because the internal character is always more esteemed than the externals; and then, because, like splendid clothing woven by this speech, it beautifies you in many ways and makes you more honorable and more illustri-

ἐξ ὑμῶν ὡς ἀληθῶς ἔχουσα τὴν ὀλβιότητα ἀντιστρέφει περιφανεστέραν τὴν φυλακήν, ὡς τέκνα κατέχουσα καὶ ἀγλαΐζουσα ὑμᾶς ἀγαθῶς, τοὺς ἐξ ὧν λαμβάνει τὴν ὕπαρξιν, καὶ ὥσπερ ἔμψυχα φέρουσα τὰ πυργώματα καὶ ἐν ζωῇ τὰ περιτειχίσματα καὶ ὅλη αὕτη λόγου γνῶσιν πλουτοῦσα καὶ μητρικὸν σέμνωμα ἔχουσα πρὸς ὑμᾶς ἐκπέμπει τὸ ἀγαθόν. Τῷ τοί γε καὶ ἀντιστρεφομένης ἐξ ὑμῶν εὐμοιροῦσα τῆς σεμνοπρεπείας, πόλις ὑπάρχει πόλεων, ὡς ἔχουσα τοὺς ἔνδοθεν διατρίβοντας περιφανεῖς ἐκ λόγου ἢ ἐκ χρημάτων καὶ πλείστης δορυφορίας.

4. Ἐγὼ δὲ καὶ νοῦν θεῖον εἴπω τὴν πόλιν, τοὺς ἀγαθοὺς ὑμᾶς πολίτας ἔχοντα ὥσπερ τινὰ διανοήματα εὐγενῆ, ἀντιβαλλόμενα πρακτικῶς καὶ θεωρίᾳ μιγνύοντα πρᾶξιν, καὶ βαθμίδας λόγου ἐν βαδίσματι καθαρῷ ἐπιβαίνοντα, καὶ ὁλοκλήρως ἐκ λογικῆς ἰσχύος αὐτὰ ἑαυτὰ κοσμοῦντα, καὶ τὸν οἰκεῖον οἱονεὶ νοῦν τὴν πόλιν περιτειχίζοντα, περιφανεστέραν ἐργάζονται τοῦ Μηδικοῦ πλούτου καὶ τῆς χρυσῆς καθ' Ὅμηρον σειρᾶς τε καὶ οὐρανίας. Οὕτω δὴ ἡ ἡμῶν πόλις βασιλὶς ὑπάρχουσα πόλεων καί, ὥσπερ τις εἴπῃ, τὶς νοῦς, ὑμᾶς τοὺς τροφίμους ταύτης περιτειχίζουσα, ἀγλαότερον ἔχει τὸν ἦχον, καὶ περιφανέστερον τὸ ἐξάκουσμα, καὶ σεμνύνεται σεμνυνομένη, καὶ στηρίζει στηριζομένη, εἰ καί τις ὑπάρχει ταύτῃ ἀντίπαλος, καὶ ὑμᾶς ἐλλιμενίζει τῇ ἑδραιότητι. Τότε καὶ γὰρ σῶμα λάβῃ τὸ ἀκλινές, ὁπόταν τῶν μερῶν τε καὶ μελῶν εὐμοιρήσῃ τῶν ὑλικῶν ὀργάνων ἀρίστῃ τῇ πρώτῃ συμπήξει τῆς εὐρυθμίας· καὶ πόλις τὰ οἰκεῖα μέλη τοὺς ἐγχωρίους ἀνέρας βλέπουσα λογιότητι κοσμουμένους, εἰδοποιεῖται καὶ ἀγλαῶς καλλωπίζεται τὸ εὔρυθμον. Λόγου γὰρ ἔνδοθεν ἔχουσα μαργαρίτας, καθεκάστην αὐτοκρατορεῖ καὶ ὑπερβαίνει ἐν ὑψώμασι πόλιν ἐκ πόλεως, λόγον ἔχουσα καύχημα.

5. Ἀλλ' εἴπῃ τις καὶ τὰς Ἀθήνας ποτὲ ἀκμαζούσας τῷ λόγῳ, καὶ τῇ παιδείᾳ σεμνυνομένας καὶ γεγαννυμένας ταῖς ῥητορικαῖς ἀντιθέσεσι, καὶ κομψολογίᾳ πολλῇ ἦχον πεμπούσας,

ous. And as it truly has its prosperity from you, it returns the care you gave it, with an increase of splendour, holding you as its children, kindly glorifying you, you from whom it has its existence. And bearing its towers, as if they were living, and the walls as if they had life; and all of it being enriched with the knowledge of reason, and having the dignity of a mother, it sends forth to you all that is good. And in return being well endowed by you with majesty, it is indeed a city among cities, since it contains inhabitants made illustrious by learning rather than by wealth and a great army.

4. And I call the city also a divine mind, having in it you good citizens like some noble thoughts, vigorously debating and mixing practice and the steps of reason with theory, walking in a pure path, doing themselves honour, altogether by the force of reason, and building walls around their own, as it were, mind, this city; they make it more illustrious than the wealth of the Medes or the golden heavenly chain of Homer. Thus this city of yours, which is a queen of cities and, as one might say, a sort of mind, by surrounding you whom it has nourished in its walls, obtains a more splendid echo and a more illustrious sound; and it is honoured by giving honour and is strengthened by giving strength, even if someone should be a rival to it, and gives you a harbour by its stability. For as a body attains stability when it is so fortunate as to have the best original composition of its parts, its limbs, and the harmony of the material organs; so a city which sees its own members, the men who live in it, dignified with eloquence, is given a form and is splendidly beautified by its good harmony. For having within it the pearls of reason, it reigns as emperor every day and exceeds in elevation any city among cities, having learning for its boast.

5. But, someone might say, Athens once abounded in learning, and was famed for education and enjoyed the contests of rhetoric, and gave forth a great sound of magniloquent

καὶ ταῖς οὐρανίαις ἀψῖσι προσεγγίζειν νομιζούσας, ὥστε
καὶ εἰς ἀθεΐαν, τὸ παράδοξον, μᾶλλόν γε πεσεῖν τοὺς αὐτῶν
οἰκήτορας καὶ στερηθῆναι λόγου, οἱ τῷ δακτύλῳ σαλεύειν ἐν
λόγῳ δοκοῦντες ξύμπασαν γῆν· ὃ δὴ λέξαι τις· τοῖς ἀντιποί-
νοις πληχθήσεται ὁ ἀὴρ ἐξ ἄλλης γλώττης, καὶ τοῖς ἐκείνου
ὠσὶν ἀκοντισθήσονται ἕτερα πολλῷ πλέον φέροντα τῇ πόλει
τὸ μεγαλοπρεπές, καὶ τῇ φερωνυμίᾳ τὴν νίκην συναρμόζον-
τα, καὶ ἄμφω ἀφοσιοῦντα τῇ Νικαέων τὰ νικητήρια. Καὶ
γὰρ ταῖς χρυσαῖς Ἀθήναις ἀληθῶς ἦν ποτ' ἦν λόγος εὐθα-
λής, ἀκμάζων, εἴ εἴπῃ τις, καὶ συνακμάζων τῇ πόλει καὶ προ-
εστώς· ἀλλ' οὐκ εἰς ἄκρον ἡ λογιότης τῶν αὐτῶν οἰκητόρων,
οὐδ' εἰς τέλος ἀγαθὸν ὁ σκοπός, οὐδ' ἔνδοξον τὸ ἐργόχει-
ρον· ἐπειδὴ μᾶλλον ἐκ τούτου τοῦ κτίστου ἐπελανθάνοντο,
ὅπερ ἀντιστρόφως ἔδει γίνεσθαι. Λόγου γὰρ εὐμοιροῦντες
ἐλάτρευσαν ἀλόγως εἰς αἰσχύνην τοῦ λόγου τοῦ διδακτοῦ τοῖς
ἀλόγοις, τὸ μέγα τῆς ἀλογίας νοσήσαντες νόσημα.

6. Ἐνθαδὶ δὲ ἡ Νικαέων αὕτη λαμπρόπολις διττῶς πλουτεῖ
τὸ φιλόσοφον, ἔκ τε τῆς ἔξωθεν ὑποβάθρας σοφίας, ἔκ τε τῆς
ὑπερκειμένης ταύτης θεογνωσίας. Αὕτη καὶ γὰρ πολλαχῶς
ἐστὶ τὸ φιλοσοφεῖν· ταῖς δυσὶ δὲ ταύταις τὸ πᾶν συναγόμενον,
φιλοσοφοῦσι μὲν καὶ ταῖς Ἀριστοτελικαῖς καὶ Πλατωνικαῖς
καὶ Σωκράτους ἐπιστήμαις οἱ ταύτης οἰκήτορες, ὡς ῥητο-
ρεύειν οὐκ ἐλαττονούμενοι οἱ τοὺς πάλαι Δημοσθένην καὶ Ἑρ-
μογένην μιμούμενοι, μένος πνείουσι, σεμνὰ κατ' ἦθος ῥέοντες
μελισταγῆ ῥητὰ διὰ γλώσσης ῥοιζούσης ἦχον χρυσοῦν, τῷ
ποιητικῷ τε ῥυθμῷ θαμίζοντες τὰς ψυχάς, καὶ ταῖς τῶν ἰύγ-
γων ᾠδαῖς παῦλαν διδόντες τοῖς θηριώδεσι τῶν ψυχικῶν δει-
νῶν ἀναστήμασιν, ἄλλην ἄλλως τε πᾶσαν παιδείαν ἐξησκη-
μένοι, περὶ ἧς οὐ καθῆκον λέγειν κατ' ὄνομα, μαθηματικήν
τε καὶ τὴν αὐτῆς ὑπερέκεινα ἰατρικήν, καὶ κατὰ μέρος τὰ
μέρη τούτων ἐπιστημόνως γινώσκοντες.

speech, and was thought to approach near to the vault of heaven; so much that its inhabitants—O paradox!—fell the more into godlessness, and lost their sense; they who seemed, in their thinking, to shake the whole world with their finger. That is what someone might say. Yet the air will be struck by opposing arguments from another tongue and his ears will be the target of other words, which will bring much greater magnificence to the city, and will fashion a victory for the city which bears the name of Victory and both of them will dedicate trophies of victory to the city of Nicaea. For golden Athens once truly had, indeed it had, a flourishing and vigorous learning, which, one might say, reached its height at the same time as the city, and presided over it, but the reasoning of its inhabitants did not reach the highest point, nor was its aim toward the right goal, nor was the undertaking admirable; for by it they became the more forgetful of Him, their founder, whereas it ought to have been the reverse: for being blessed with learning, they worshipped it unreasonably, to the contempt of that learning which can be taught to the unlearned, and suffered from the great disease of unreason.

6. In this way this splendid city of the Nicaeans is doubly rich in philosophy: both in the basic, external wisdom, and in the knowledge of God which is superior to it. Learning is pursued here in many ways; but, to collect them all into those two: its inhabitants study the knowledge of Aristotle, and Plato, and Socrates, so that those who emulate the ancients, Demosthenes and Hermogenes, are not outdone by them in speaking but, breathing forth strength, they pour out their stately honey-sweet words, as is their wont, from a tongue that rustles with golden sound; and they have familiarized their souls with poetic rhythm, and placed a check, from the songs of enchanters, on the wild creations of the mind's skills. And they have trained themselves in every other kind of education which is not necessary to name in detail and especially mathematics, and medicine its superior; and they have learned and understood all of them part by part.

7. Ταῦτα δὲ πάντα οὐ καινόν ἐστι καὶ παράδοξον αὐτοῖς γινωσκόμενα, ἀλλὰ καινὸν τρόπον φιλοσοφίας μίξαντες τῇ θεογνωσίᾳ, εὐαγγελικαῖς καὶ ἀποστολικαῖς καὶ πατρικαῖς παιδαγωγηθέντες θεηγορίαις τὸ πρίν, φιλοσοφοῦσι τὰ θεῖα δόγματα, μετακεντρίζοντες τὸ ἀγριέλαιον εἰς καλλιέλαιον καὶ αἰχμαλωτίζοντες πᾶν νόημα εἰς Χριστόν, τοῦτο ἦν τὸ καινόν. Ἐκ τούτου καὶ γὰρ ἡ Νικαέων λαμπρύνεται παμπληθῶς ὥσπερ τις κρήνη· καθαρωτάτη καὶ γὰρ αὕτη καθεστηκυῖα, πλημμυροῖ τὰ χεύματα τῆς εὐσεβείας, πᾶσαν ἄλλην πόλιν ἐπάρδουσα, ἀπορροίας οἱονεὶ τοῖς ἐπὶ τὸ πεδίον οἰκουμένοις χωρίοις ἐκ τῆς πρώτης ἀκρωρείας μεταδιδοῦσα, σχοῦσα τὴν τοῦ ὕδατος ἔκβλυσιν· ὃ δὴ ποιοῦσα, κορεννύει ψυχὰς πενήτων καὶ μὴ πενήτων. Βρύει γὰρ ἡ χάρις τὰ δόγματα· ἐπιδέχεται αὕτη· μεταδίδωσι τοῖς ὥσπερ ἔτυχε· λαμβάνουσα μὲν πλουτεῖ, μεταδιδοῦσα ἐνσεμνύνεται καὶ ἀμφοτέρωθεν ἀκτινοβολεῖ, διττῶς φιλοσοφοῦσα τὰ ἐξαίρετα. Ὁπόταν καὶ γὰρ εἰς ταὐτὸ συνδράμωσι φιλοσοφία καὶ εὐσέβεια, καὶ ἀντιδοτικῶς ἀνακραθῶσι κατὰ θεῖον σκοπόν, ἀστράπτουσι βολίδας πολλὰς καὶ μαρμαίρουσι οἰκουμένην ὅλην σχεδόν, καὶ σὺν τῇ πόλει τοὺς αὐτῆς καλλωπίζουσιν οἰκιστάς.

8. Ἐγὼ δὲ τῇ πολλαχῶς ὑμνουμένῃ τῆς πόλεως καλλονῇ τῷ λόγῳ τούτῳ τῷ χθαμαλῷ ἐκτραπείς, καὶ τοῦ καθήκοντος ἐπιλαθόμενος τῆς ὁρμῆς, καὶ ὁ πόλιν βουλόμενος ἐξιστορεῖν παριδὼν ἐπὶ τῶν πολιτῶν ὥρμησα τὰ ἐγκώμια· ὃ καὶ μηδὲν ὅλως δόξει καινόν, ὥστε καὶ μεμψιμοίρου τυχεῖν ἡμᾶς μοίρας παρ' ἀνδρὶ σκώπτειν ἐπιτηδευομένῳ, ὅτι οὐδὲ πόρρω τοῦ δέοντος ἐπεπράχειμεν ἐκ τῶν ἐμψυχωμένων ἀρξάμενοι καὶ λόγῳ δόντες τὰ πρωτεῖα ὡς λογικοί, καὶ τοὺς πολίτας στηλογραφήσαντες. Ἑπομένως καὶ γὰρ τούτοις αὐτὰ ἅπαντα τῇ καλλονῇ ἐπακολουθήσουσι. Τί δ' ὅταν ἐν πόλει λόγος περιπολῇ, καὶ γνῶσις ἐνδιατρίβῃ καὶ μάθησις ἐκτριβάζηται, ταύτῃ τι φανήσεται ὡς ἐλλεῖπον; οὐδέν, οἶμαι φανήσεται· ἀλλὰ καὶ μάλα γε πάντα ἐν αὐτῇ οἰκοδομήσει ἡ τοῦ λόγου ἰσχὺς

7. All of this is nothing new, and it is nothing unexpected for them to know all this; but that they mix a new kind of study with the knowledge of God, and having first been educated in the divine studies of the gospels, the apostles and the fathers, they now investigate the divine dogmas, grafting the wild olive onto the cultivated, and bringing in every thought, like a prisoner of war, to Christ. This was the novelty. From this the city of the Nicaeans is made altogether splendid like a spring; for, being itself perfectly pure, it causes streams of piety to flow, watering every other city, sharing as it were the outflow from the highest peak with the inhabited places of the plain, having restrained the excess of its water; and, by doing this, it satisfies the soul of the poor and the not poor. For those dogmas are laden with grace; the city welcomes them, it shares them with those whom it meets, in receiving it is wealthy, in sharing it is praised, and in both it shines in glory, pursuing the choicest knowledge in two ways. Since whenever philosophy and piety come together in one place, and are mixed together like lifesaving medicines for a divine end, they dart forth many gleams of lightning; they dazzle nearly the whole world; and they beautify the inhabitants along with the city.

8. I have been diverted in this humble speech by the beauty of the city, celebrated in so many ways and, forgetting the proper aim of my efforts, I, who meant to describe the city, have neglected it, and entered upon the praises of the citizens. This will not appear so wholly novel as to bring on us a share of criticism from a man disposed to mock, for we have done nothing but what is right, in beginning with living things; in giving the first place, as thinking beings, to thought; and in inscribing the citizens on a monument. In succession to these, everything else will follow after that beauty. When reason walks in a city, and knowledge resides there, and learning is pursued there, what will appear to be lacking? Nothing, I think, will so appear. But rather the force of reason will build

βρύειν ἀκαινοτόμητα. Τὰ γὰρ λόγῳ οἰκοδομούμενα ὀλβιώτε-
ρα ὑπάρχουσιν ἢ τὰ μὴ λόγῳ πανταχόσε συναγόμενα, ἀλλ᾽
εἰκῇ φερόμενα καὶ ὡς ἔτυχον τυχικῶς· οὕτως οὖν οἶδεν ὁ
νῦν λόγος διὰ ταῦτα τὴν πόλιν ὑμνεῖν, οὕτως αὐτῆς τὰς χά-
ριτας ἱστορεῖν, οὕτως αὐτῆς διακηρυκεύειν τὸ ὕψωμα· λόγῳ
γὰρ καὶ σοφίᾳ τοὺς πολίτας ταύτης πάντων ἄλλων ὑπερεξαί-
ρων, βασιλίδα πασῶν ἀναγορεύει αὐτήν, καὶ κυρίαν ὄντως
διὰ τοῦ λόγου ὑπάρχουσα τὸ ἀξίωμα.

9. Εἰ δέ τις ἀγροικικῇ μοι βοήσει, πάριδε λόγον τοῦ ἐξυμνεῖν,
καὶ πόρρω πέμψον παιδείαν, καὶ μετάστρεφον τὸν αὐλόν,
καὶ ταῖς τοῦ λόγου χορδαῖς ἔνθες ᾠδὴν ἡδονῆς ὑλικῶς τε
βάδισον εἰς ἐγκώμια τροφῶν καὶ τρυφῶν, ἐπειδή, ὡς ὁρᾷς
συρρέει πλῆθος πολὺ βουλομένων μᾶλλον τρυφᾶν ἐξ ὧν
εὐφραίνονται οἱ πολλοί, ἢ λόγῳ κατ᾽ ἦθος κοσμεῖσθαι καὶ
σεμνύνεσθαι τὰς ψυχάς, πεισθῷ τῷ λόγῳ τοῦ λέξαντος· ὅθεν
καὶ τῶν ἐμψύχων καὶ λογικῶν φυτηκομιῶν φυτῶν ἀποχω-
ρήσας, εὐθὺς πορεύσομαι, ὡς τρυγὼν πτεροκροτήσασα, εἰς
ἄλση Χαρίτων βαδιοῦμαι, τῷ νοΐ, καὶ ποτίμους πηγὰς διειδέστατα βλυζούσας ὕδατα καὶ πανταχόσε διαδραμοῦσα καὶ
κύκλωσε κόσμον ὅλον ἀναπολήσασα, εἰς τὴν Νικαέων πάλιν, οἶδ᾽ ὅτι, πόλιν στραφήσομαι ἐν σπουδῇ, ὡς πασῶν ἄλλων ὑπερκειμένην καὶ βασιλικῶς ἐξηρημένην ἁπανταχῇ. Τί
καὶ γὰρ ἐν ταύτῃ ζητῶν τις οὐχ εὑρήσει, ἢ ποθῶν οὐκ εὐ-
μοιρήσει κατὰ πολύ, ἔκ τε τῶν χαρίτων τοῦ χώρου καὶ τῆς
μεταλλικῆς ἰδιότητος, ἔκ τε τῆς τῶν ἐπικτήτων τερπνότη-
τος, ἅτινα τῷ καλῷ φυσικῶς ὡς ὅλῳ μιμούμενα, συνέρρευ-
σαν εἰς αὐτήν;

10. Ἐν ταύτῃ πλῆθος φυτῶν κύκλῳ φυτουργούμενον καὶ ἔνδοθεν παμπληθῶς· ἣν εἰ ἴδῃ τις ἐκ μακρόθεν, ἄλσος εἴπῃ
ταύτην τῶν δένδρων πανταχόθεν κοσμούμενον τῇ εὐφυλλίᾳ

everything there abounding with permanence, for things built by reason are more fortunate than those put together casually, not by reason, but brought at random and just as they happened to be by chance. In this way, then, the present speech can celebrate the city through these things, and thus record the city's graces, and thus proclaim its sublimity; for by uplifting the citizens of this city above all others in reason and wisdom, it declares it to be the queen of all cities, and to have, on account of its learning, the truly supreme rank.

9. But if someone will rudely shout at me, 'Forget this talk of praise, send education away, turn your flute around and set a song of pleasure to the strings of your speech, and proceed in a material way to praises of food and luxury since, as you see, a great crowd has gathered of people who would rather delight in what gives pleasure to the many than adorn their character with learning and elevate their minds'—let me obey the words of the man who said that. And so, taking my leave of the living and rational fruits of cultivation, I shall travel at once, like a dove beating its wings; I shall journey in mind to the groves of the Graces, to the potable springs that pour out the most transparent water; and after flying about everywhere, and making the circuit of the whole universe, I shall, I know, be glad to return to the city of Nicaea, since it is superior to all others and royally chosen in every sense. For what is there that one seeking will not find here or desiring will not possess in abundance — both from the charms of the land and its mineral character, and from the delightfulness of the additions made to it, which have flowed together into it, as if naturally emulating its entire beauty?

10. In it there is a multitude of crops which are cultivated all around, and abundantly inside. If someone were to see it from afar, he would say it was a grove, decorated as it is everywhere by the fine foliage of the trees, rather than suppose it to be

ἢ πόλιν ὑποτοπάσειε· προσεγγίζων δὲ διανοήσεται εἶναι παράδεισον ἐκ τῆς ἐξερχομένης ὀδμῆς, καλλίστης γε οὔσης καὶ εὐφραντῆς. Ἐκεῖθεν δ' αὖ αὐτῇ πλησιέστερον βαδίσας καὶ ξυντυχών, ἱλαρυνθῇ πάντα τὰ αἰσθητήρια · ἔνδοθεν δὲ χωρήσας καὶ τὰς ποικιλίας τοῦ ἔνδον χώρου, καὶ τὰς θεάτρων ἰδέας, καὶ τὰς τῶν οἴκων εὐπρεπείας περισκοπήσας, οὐκ ἄλλο τι λέξει εἶναι αὐτήν, ἢ πόλιν Χαρίτων καὶ γῆς μακάρων ὑπερκειμένην κατὰ πολύ· ναούς τε περικαλλεῖς σεμνεῖα τε ἀγλαὰ κἀντεῦθεν θεάσεται ἄπειρα, ἐξ ὧν εἰς πλείονα τὸν αὑτοῦ νοῦν θεωρίαν ἀναγαγών, πόλιν εἴπῃ ταύτην θεοῦ, ἀγγέλους ἐκ τῆς πρώτης ὑπεροχῆς βλέπων ἀνερχομένους τε καὶ κατερχομένους ἐν ταύτῃ καὶ ἐκπληροῦντας τὰ προσταττόμενα τοὺς εὐσεβεῖς βασιλέας αὐτῆς.

11. Τῇ γὰρ παντουργικῇ χειρὶ τοῦ Θεοῦ τὰ πρωτεῖα, ὡς οἶδε μόνος αὐτός, αὕτη λαβοῦσα καὶ ταῖς ἀριστουργίαις τοῦ ὑψηλοῦ βασιλέως τήν γε, ὡς εἰκός, ἐπίτασιν τῶν ὧν εἶχε δεξαμένη περιτειχισμάτων καὶ πυργωμάτων, διπλασιάζει τὸ ἀσφαλές, περιτειχιζομένη τοῖς προπυργώμασιν καὶ ἐπενδυομένη τοῖς θριγγίοις θριγγώματα, τῇ τε ὡραιότητι καλλωπιζομένη καὶ στηριζομένη τῇ ἑδραιότητι. Αὖθις τε τὴν τῆς ἰσχύος μονάδα παρὰ τοῦ βασιλέως δυάδι συνενωθεῖσαν τῷ γύρωθεν αὐτῆς περιβοήτῳ ἐνδύματι, ὑπερβαίνει κατὰ πολὺ τὰς πάλαι θρυλλουμένας πόλεις τῆς γῆς· διὸ κυπαρίττων εὐθείας ἀναβάσεως εὐμοιροῦντα αὐτῆς τὰ πυργώματα, καὶ στύλοις ἀδαμαντίνοις ταῦτα παρεικαζόμενα, τὸν τῆς σοφίας εἴπῃ τις οἶκον αὐτὴν παρὰ Σολομῶντι τὸν ἐξυμνούμενον· πολλαχῶς καὶ γὰρ ἐν ταύτῃ τὰ ὀχυρώματα καθεστήκασιν, ἐπεὶ καὶ τὸ τῆς νίκης ὄνομα ἀφωσιώθη ταύτῃ ἀπὸ Θεοῦ.

12. Ἀλλ' εἴπερ ἐρεῖ τις ἕτερος τρυφῆς ἐραστής, μετάδος τῶν χαρίτων ταύτης κἀμοί, ἡδυνθῆναι μάλα καὶ γὰρ ἐκ ταύτης θέλω τὰ αἰσθητήρια, οὐ παρίδω αὐτόν, τῶν τε ὑδάτων αὐτῆς ὕδωρ ἀναλαβόμενος, ἐκπλυνῶ τῆς αἰσχύνης αὐτόν, καὶ κορεσθῆναι προτρέφω καὶ ἀφιλοσόφως κατατρυφῆσαι τοῦτον τῆς ἡδονῆς. Οὐδὲ γὰρ ἔστιν ἐν κόσμῳ τις τροφῆς ἢ τρυφῆς

a city. But as he approaches, he will decide that it is a paradise by the fragrance which issues from it, most lovely and cheering. As he walks nearer from there, and comes up to it, all his senses will be gladdened; and when he has gone inside and has observed the variety of the area within, and the appearance of the theatres, and the splendour of the houses, he will say it is nothing else but the city of the Graces, and far superior to the land of the blessed. And there he will see most beautiful churches, and splendid monasteries in endless number; and leading his thoughts from them into a grand train of reflection, he will call this the city of God, when he sees that messengers from the highest eminence arise and descend in it, and that their commands are fulfilled by its pious emperors.

11. For since it has gained the supreme rank from the almighty hand of God, as He himself only knows; and has received this strengthening, certainly, of the walls and towers which it had before through the great deeds of the sublime Emperor, it doubles its security, walled in with projecting towers and dressing its walls with battlements, adorned with beauty, and firmly fixed with stability. And so again, by having united its single strength to that duality of strength from the emperor, that celebrated vestment around it, it exceeds by far the cities famous of old in the world. Since its towers are blessed with the straight rising of cypresses, and are like pillars of adamant, one might call it the House of Wisdom sung by Solomon. For defences are established in it in many ways, since the very name of Victory has been consecrated to it by God.

12. But if some other lover of luxury shall say 'Give me also a share of its pleasures, for I also want my senses to have pleasure from it,' I shall not neglect him, but drawing water from its waters I shall wash him of his shame, and I shall urge him to be satiated and unphilosophically to rejoice in the pleasure. For there is no lover of food or luxury in the world

ἐραστής, ὃς οὐκ ἐν ᾧ ἐντρυφᾷ λάβῃ κόρον εἴπερ δυνήσεται ὧν ποθεῖ ἐπευφραίνεσθαι ἐν αὐτῇ. Γύρωθεν γὰρ ταύτης καὶ πάλιν ἐρῶ, φυτὰ ὡραιότατα, ἀμπελῶνες ὑπὲρ τὸν ὃν οἶδεν ἡ
10 φύσις ἀριθμεῖν ἀριθμόν, ὕδατα βρύοντα ῥᾳδίως μὲν περαιούμενα, εὐοχετευτά τε τῇ τοῦ ὀχυρώματος ἐν καιρῷ ἀνοικοδομῇ, πότιμά τε αὖθις καὶ διειδέστατα ὑπὲρ κεφαλῆς ἔκβλυσιν σχόντα μέν, κύκλῳ δὲ διόλου τὴν πόλιν περιρραντίζοντα. Οὐ πώποτε αὐτόχθων ἀνὴρ ἄλλου ὕδασιν ἐντρυφήσειεν· ἕκα-
15 στος γὰρ οἴκοθεν ἔχει πηγήν· οὐ ζηλοτυπήσει ξένος τοὺς ἰθαγενεῖς· περιττεύει γὰρ ἡ τοῦ ὕδατος ἔκβλυσις. Ἄνευ σκεπῆς ἢ καὶ ὀρόφου τοὺς ἐπήλυδας ἡ τῶν λειμώνων εὐφυλλία σκηνοποιεῖ· πολλὴ γάρ ἐστι αὕτη καὶ βρίθουσα· οὐκ ἀγρότην ἴδῃς τῶν οἰκείων ἀγρῶν ἐν ταύτῃ κεχωρισμένον τῶν πολιτῶν·
20 ὑπερβαίνει γὰρ ἔξωθεν ἡ ἐξ αὐτῆς παιδεία βλυστάνουσα, καὶ παιδαγωγεῖ καὶ τὰ πόρρωθεν· τούτῳ δὴ τῷ τρόπῳ καὶ οἱ ἀγρόται ταύτης σοφίζονται.

13. Ἀλλ', ὦ πόλις Θεοῦ, δεῖ με γὰρ οὕτω καλεῖν σε οὐχ ἅπαξ, ἀλλὰ συχνάκις διὰ τὰ τῶν σῶν χαρίτων ἐπεντρυφήματα, ἤδη τρέπω τὸν νῦν λόγον πρός σε, καὶ προσλαλῶ σοι γνησιεστέρως, ἐπειδὴ προσεγγίζων σοι τῇ καλῇ, τὰ ζωτικὰ τῆς
5 καρδίας ἐξάπτομαι ὄργανα, ζωπυρηθείς τε ἐνεργείᾳ τῇ ψυχικῇ, ταῦτα σοι νῦν ἐκβοῶ· πολλαὶ μὲν πόλεις ἐποίησαν δύναμιν, πολλαὶ εἰργάσαντο δόξαν, πολλαὶ τὴν τοῦ οἰκείου γένους ἀρχὴν ἐστερέωσαν· σὺ δ' ὑπέρκεισαι καὶ ὑπερῆρας πασῶν, ἐπειδὴ πολλαχῶς ἡ Ῥωμαίων ἀρχὴ μερισθεῖσα παρὰ τῶν
10 ἐθνικῶν στρατευμάτων καὶ ἡττηθεῖσα, πρότερόν τε συμπλακεῖσα καὶ ἁλωθεῖσα τὰς πόλεις καὶ γυμνωθεῖσα τῆς ἐξουσίας, καὶ πᾶσαν γῆν οἰκείαν ἄβατον οὖσαν τὸ πρίν, βατὴν τοῖς ἐναντίοις τῇ δυναστείᾳ παραχωρήσασα, καὶ τῆς πρὶν μεγαλοπρεπείας στερηθεῖσα καὶ τῇ ἀτυχίᾳ εἴπω τι γεγονυῖα σμικροπρε-
15 πής, καὶ βρίθοντα πλοῦτον ἀπολωλεκυῖα, καὶ τὴν βασιλικὴν ὑπεροχὴν τῆς πενίας τῇ λύπῃ χθαμαλωθεῖσα, ἐν σοὶ μόνῃ

who will not be satiated with what he enjoys, if he is able to delight in the things he desires in this city. For all around it, I say it again, are the fairest crops; vineyards beyond the number that nature knows how to count, full-flowing waters, easy to cross, and easily carried by the opportune construction of the city wall, and also potable and most transparent, having their outlet above the level of one's head, and poured in a circle round all the city. Never will one native inhabitant enjoy the water more than another, for everyone has a fountain in his own house: never will a foreigner envy the natives, for the supply of water is overflowing. Without shelter or a roof, the full foliage of the meadows gives cover to those who come there, for it is great and heavy. You would not see in it a countryman, who inhabits his own fields, separated from the citizens: for the education that pours forth from it runs over outside, and teaches even at a distance. And in this way even the country people here are wise.

13. But O city of God!—for I must call you this not once, but many times, because of the luxuriance of your graces—now I turn this present speech toward you, and I shall talk to you more familiarly; since, as I draw nearer to your beauty, I am gripped in the vital organs of my heart, and, kindled into flame by the power of mind, this now I cry out to you: many cities have made themselves powerful, many have gained a reputation, many have established power over their own nation; but you transcend, you have excelled them all. For when the Roman empire had been partitioned in many ways by foreign armies and defeated; and had first struggled, and been deprived of its cities, and stripped of its power; and had yielded up all its own land, formerly inaccessible to them, to be open to the enemies of its government; and had lost its former magnificence, and by its misfortune had been humiliated as much as anything ever was; and had lost abundant wealth, and had humbled its imperial eminence with the pain of poverty; in

ἡδράσθη καὶ ἐστηρίχθη τε καὶ ἐπαγιώθη. Ἀρκεῖ σοι νῦν τὸ ἐγκώμιον· ἔχεις ἐν ὀλίγῳ τὸ πᾶν· τὸ γὰρ τόσον τοῦ πράγματος μεγαλοπρεπὲς ἐν λόγῳ σμικρῷ ἅπασι δεικνύει τὸ ἀληθές·
20 ἐπειδὴ οὐδὲ τὴν τοῦ ἡλίου δύναμιν ἐς τόσον ἐστί τις ἀφρονέστατος ὥστε παρ' ἑτέρων πυθέσθαι μαθεῖν, ἀλλ' αὐτοφυῶς τε καὶ φυσικῶς γνοίη γε ἂν πᾶς ὁ κεκτημένος ταύτην καθαρῶς τὰς φρένας ἐν τῷ νοΐ. Τοῦτο δὴ καὶ τῷ σῷ ὑπάρχει τρόπῳ, ᾧ Νικαέων λαμπρὰ μεγαλόπολις, διότι δίκην πυρσοῦ τὰ σὰ
25 ἐν κόσμῳ κατὰ τῶν ἐχθρῶν ἐξέλαμψαν τρόπαια, ὅτι γε καὶ τὴν βασιλικὴν ὑπεδέξω ἀρχήν, καταδυναστευομένη παρὰ τῶν ἀντιπάλων καὶ ὥσπερ ἀρραγὴς πέτρα ταύτην φυλάττουσα καὶ τὰς τῶν ἐχθρῶν ἀποσοβοῦσα ὁρμάς, ἀμβλύνεις τούτων
30 τὰ δόρατα καὶ καταθραύουσα τὴν τούτων ἰσχὺν καὶ φυλάττουσα τοὺς οἰκείους, ἁμιλλωμένη τοῖς ἐναντίοις ἀσφαλῶς παρὰ σεαυτῇ τὰ ἀνειμένα καὶ ἐκλελυμένα τῆς ἀρχῆς μέρη στηρίζεις.

14. Τῆς γὰρ Κωνσταντίνου τὸ πρὶν ἁλωθείσης καὶ ὑποκλιθείσης τοῖς ἐναντίοις, καὶ νῶτα δούσης τῇ Ἰταλικῇ στρατιᾷ καὶ δουλωθείσης καὶ τὰς ἑτέρας πόλεις οὐκ εὐαγγελικῶς φυλαξάσης, ἀλλ' ὥσπερ τινὸς μύστιδος αὐτὰς παραβλεψαμέ-
5 νης, ἐκθροηθείσης τῆς Ἰταλικῆς ἀλαζόνος φωνῆς ὑπὸ τῆς ἠχοῦς, καὶ τῶν σκύμνων μέσον τῆς ἀρχῆς εἰσδύντων καὶ ἁλωσάντων τὰς πόλεις, καὶ δουλωσάντων τὸ στράτευμα, καὶ ἀμβλυνάντων τὰ ὅπλα καὶ νικησάντων κατὰ πολύ, ὥσπερ μισθωτοῦ τῆς πόλεως φευγούσης, σὺ μόνη μέσον ὥσπερ ὅπλον
10 ἀγχέμαχον εἰσεπήδησας, τῆς Ἰταλικῆς ἰσχύος τὴν σηπεδόνα ἀποκρουομένη, καὶ ἁλυκότητι στρατηγίας δηλονότι καὶ εὐσεβείας τὴν αὐτῶν σεσαθρωμένην ὀφρὺν ταπεινοῦσα καὶ ἀτιμάζουσα, ταῖς δὲ Περσικαῖς ἐπιδρομαῖς ἀντιταττομένη καὶ τὴν ἧτταν αὐταῖς ἀεὶ συναρμόττουσα, στρατηγοῦντος ἐκ σοῦ
15 οἱονεὶ τοῦ πρωτουργοῦ τῆς ἀναλωθείσης Ῥωμαίων ἀρχῆς, μεγαλοθύμου ἀετοδρόμου μεγάλου βασιλέως Θεοδώρου τοῦ Λάσκαρι· νῦν δὲ τῷ θεμελίῳ τούτου ὁ γενναιόφρων βριαρόχειρ μεγαλοφυὴς βασιλεὺς Δούκας ὁ χαριτώνυμος, μυριαχῶς αὔξων τὰ ὅρια τῆς ἀρχῆς εἰς τὴν ἀρχαίαν ἔγγιστά πως

you alone it was established and consolidated and fixed. Now your praise is sufficient: you have, in a little, the whole. For the great magnificence of the object displays the truth to all in one short word; for no one is so totally foolish as to seek to learn the extent of the sun's power from others, but everyone who clearly has sense in his mind will recognise it spontaneously and naturally. And this, splendid great city of the Niceans, is part of your character, too, because your trophies over the enemy have shone out in the universe like a torch; and because you have received the imperial government, oppressed by its opponents, and like an unbreakable rock, guarding it and frightening away the assaults of the enemy, you blunt their spears; shattering their strength, guarding your own people, contending with the enemy, you securely consolidate beside you the lost and broken portions of the empire.

14. For previously, when the city of Constantine was taken, and yielded to the enemy, and ran away from the Italian army and was enslaved, and did not guard the other cities in accordance with the Gospel, but like some initiate pagan, ignored them; when the braggart Italian voice resounded from its echo; and the wild beasts' cubs had got into the midst of the empire, and taken the cities, and subjugated the army, and blunted their arms and greatly overcome them, and that city was running away like a hired hand; you alone leapt, as it were, into the midst of the close fight, beating back the rot of Italian power, and by the salt of your generalship and, obviously, your piety, you humbled and disgraced their unsound pride. And you were set to resist the Persian raids, and you always attached defeat to their side; at the time when there went forth from you to command, like the founder of the ruined Roman empire, that great-hearted, eagle-swift, great emperor Theodore Laskaris. And now, on the foundation he laid, the noble-minded, giant-handed, great-natured emperor, Doukas of the gracious name, increasing the boundaries of the empire in ten

αὐτὴν ἀνάγει μεγαλειότητα. Διὰ τοῦτο σοί, οἶμαι, πᾶς ἔμφρων ἀνὴρ τὰ πρωτεῖα δώσει, ὡς ἀληθῶς ὑπερκειμένῃ τῶν πόλεων ἁπασῶν, ἐπειδὴ καὶ νόμος ἐστὶ τοῦτο· τῷ ἐπιμείναντι χειμαζομένῃ νηΐ κύριον εἶναι ταύτης αὐτόν. Πότερον οὖν τὰς τῶν ἐχθρῶν ἐφόδους σὺ καρτερήσασα καὶ φυλάξασα τὴν ἀρχήν, καὶ τηρήσασα τὸ πολίτευμα καὶ τὸ στράτευμα καθοπλίσασα, καὶ τοὺς ἐναντίους ἀποδιώξασα, ἔδει λαβεῖν σὲ τὰ νικητήρια, καὶ τὴν φερωνυμίαν τῇ πράξει συμμίξασα, πασῶν σὲ κυριεῦσαι τῶν πόλεων;

15. Καὶ γὰρ παλιννοστήσαντος τοῦ θερμοῦ καὶ διὰ τῶν φλεβῶν τε καὶ ἀρτηριῶν παρ' ἑτέρας ἀνωμαλίας μετατραπέντος καὶ διαδοτικῶς προσεγγίσαντος τῇ καρδίᾳ, αὐτοῦ τε πολλαπλασιασθέντος καὶ συστραφέντος καὶ πῇ μὲν σβεννυμένου τῇ ποσότητι, πῇ δὲ σφαδάζοντος ἐκ τῆς ποιότητος, ἐχρῆν ἐξακοντισθῆναι τοῦτο ὅτε καιρός, καὶ διελθεῖν ἐν τοῖς μέλεσι καὶ ἐνθερμάναι τὰ ἐψυγμένα καὶ ἀναζωπυρῆσαι τὰ ἐσβεσμένα, καὶ τῇ ὁλομελείᾳ πάσῃ δοῦναι τὸ ζωτικόν, ὥστε καὶ τῇ θερμότητι τὸ πρὶν νεναρκωμένον σῶμα κοῦφον βαδίζειν ποιῆσαι καὶ εὐφυῶς ταχινοτέρως τε οἴχεσθαι καὶ στρέφεσθαι γρηγορότητι καὶ τῇ ὀξύτητι ὑπερβαίνειν νόμους τοὺς φυσικούς. Τὸ πρὶν γὰρ συναχθέν, ἐξακοντισθὲν τοιαῦτα οἶδε ποιεῖν· τῷ τοί γε καὶ ἡ ἀρχὴ πᾶσα κατ' ἀνάρροιαν ἐν σοὶ εἰσδραμοῦσα τῇ παρὰ τῶν ἐχθρῶν καχεξίᾳ, διωκομένη τε καὶ ἀποκρουομένη, ἀνεζωπυρήθη ἐκ σοῦ καὶ ἔλαβε τὴν ἰσχύν, παρὰ τῆς σῆς ἰσχύος λαβοῦσα τὴν σταθηρότητα, καὶ προέβη τοῖς ἔξωθεν καὶ τὰς νενεκρωμένας πόλεις τῇ τυραννικῇ δυναστείᾳ τὸ πρίν, οἱονεὶ ὥσπερ μέλη καὶ μέρη, ἀνεζώωσε καὶ ἀπεδίωξε τοὺς ἐχθρούς, καὶ τῇ συνθέσει λαμβάνει τὴν ὕπαρξιν, ἣν ἀπόλωλε πρότερον.

16. Τούτων ἐκ σοῦ ηὐμοίρησεν ἡ ἀρχή, τὸ μὲν φυλαχθεῖσα τὸ πρὶν ἐκ τῆς λύμης τῆς ἐθνικῆς, τὸ δ' ὅτι καὶ πᾶσαν διχόνοιαν τῆς οἰκειακῆς ἀρχῆς ἐκκόψασα καὶ ἑνώσασα τὰ διῃρη-

thousand ways, is bringing it back very near to its ancient greatness. Because of this, I think every sensible man will give you the first place, as truly superior to all other cities; for this is also a law, that whoever has remained in a ship overcome by a storm, shall be the owner of it. Then you, who held out through the invasions of the enemy, and protected the empire, and watched over the government, and armed its forces, and drove away its opponents—should you not obtain the prize of victory, and joining the name of victory you bear with reality, should you not rule all cities?

15. For, when the heat has returned and, after some imbalance, has reversed itself through the veins and arteries and, being distributed, has approached the heart, and there has been multiplied and collected, diminished in its quantity yet intensified because of its quality; it had to shoot forth then, when the right time came, and go through the limbs, and warm what had been cooled, and rekindle what was extinguished, and give life to the whole body so that by warmth the body, previously numb, is made to move lightly and naturally, to go more swiftly and turn itself alertly, and to transgress the laws of nature by its speed. For when what has been gathered in is shot out again, it has the power to do such things. So it is that the whole empire, having rushed in and flowed back upon you because of the illness created by the enemy, when it was pursued and driven away, was revived by you; and recovered its strength, drawing its solidity from your strength. It went forth to those outside and to the others which had been deprived of life by the tyrannical government, it revived them like the limbs and members, drove away the enemy and, by putting them together, it is recovering the condition which it had lost before.

16. These are the blessings the empire has received from you: first of all it has been protected from foreign harm, and then has cut off all dissension within its own dominions, and united

μένα τὸ πρίν, σοὶ οὖν δι' ἧς τῆς πρώτης ἐλευθεριότητος ἔτυχε
βασιλικῶς τὰ τῆς νίκης δωρησαμένη πρωτόλεια, νυμφαγωγεῖ
σε ἄρτι τῷ βασιλεῖ, γεννήματα ἐχιδνῶν τῶν δυτικῶν ἀρχῶν
σοὶ προσφέροντι, ἐκφυγόντα δηλονότι ἐκ τῆς ὑποκειμένης
ὀργῆς, τῆς αὐτοῦ τμητικωτάτης ἐν ἀληθινῇ καὶ βεβαίᾳ κρίσει
διακρίσεως· δέδεξο γοῦν τοῦτον ἡ μεγαλώνυμος καὶ ἐνσεμνύ-
θητι ἐν αὐτῷ πολλαχῶς, ὡς νικητῇ μὲν περιπλεκομένη, ὡς
δεσπότῃ δὲ πειθαρχοῦσα, καὶ ὡς ἀετῷ ὑψιβάμονι καλιὰς ἀρί-
στους προσφέρουσα, ἵν' ἐν ταῖς πτέρυξι ταῖς ἑαυτοῦ σκεπάσῃ
τὰ σὰ ἀρχίτοκά τε καὶ νεογνά, καὶ ἐν τῇ πολλῇ τούτου ἰσχύϊ
διαφυλάξῃ τοὺς ἐν σοὶ ἐπικαλουμένους αὐτόν. Διὸ καὶ τὴν νῦν
νίκην ἐν σοὶ ἀποθησαυρίσας ὁ βασιλεὺς ὥσπερ τινὰ θησαυρὸν
ὀλβίως χρήματα βρύοντα, ἀεὶ σὺν τούτῳ καὶ τὴν αὐτοῦ καρ-
δίαν ἐν σοὶ προσαρμόσειεν· ὅπου γάρ ἐστιν ὁ θησαυρός, ἐκεῖ
καὶ ἡ καρδία τοῦ τοῦτον κατέχοντος.

17. Πότερον οὖν καὶ ἡμεῖς τῇ βασιλικῇ ῥοπῇ ἑπομένως ἀκο-
λουθοῦντες καρδιακῶς, καὶ τρέχοντες ἀσμένῳ ποδί, καὶ βα-
δίζοντες ἐλευθέρᾳ ψυχῇ, οὐκ ἀθλιφίας μὲν ὑπαρχούσης αὐτῇ,
πόρρω δέ γε λύπης οὔσῃ καὶ μὴ πασχούσῃ παθήματι, καὶ μὴ
τιτρωσκομένῃ κατὰ πολύ, ἐλευθέρως ὡς ἔφημεν, βαδιούμε-
θα· ἀλλὰ φιλοσοφίᾳ κοσμούμενοι καὶ τῇ ταύτης ἐλευθεριότη-
τι εὐπρεπῶς σεμνυνόμενοι, οὕτω χαίροντες τρέχομεν, οὕτως
εἰσδύομεν εἰς σὲ τὴν καλὴν κουροτρόφον, ἐπειδὴ ἀρχῆθεν ἡμᾶς
εἰς γῆν ἐκ μητρὸς πεσόντας παρέλαβες καὶ ἔθρεψας μητρικῶς,
καὶ περιποιήσω ὡς τιθηνός, καὶ περιφανῶς κατεκάλλυνας· οὗ
χάριν σοὶ τὸν λόγον τοῦτον ἀντιπροσφέρομεν, ὃν δὴ δεδεγ-
μένη σύ, ἡ λαμπρόπολις, οὐκ ἀμοίρους τῆς σῆς μεγαλονοίας
ποιήσεις ἡμᾶς, ἀλλὰ πεποίθαμεν τῶν σῶν μετασχεῖν χαρίτων
παντοδαπῶν, ἵν' ἐξ ἀνάγκης ἐν ταῖς τῶν τροπαίων ἐν σοὶ
ἀρίσταις παλιννοστήσεσι, πολυδόξαστά σοι προσφέρωμεν τὰ
ἐγκώμια, νίκας τε σοὶ προσαρμόζοντες ἐς ἀεί, καὶ ἀντιστρόφως
ἐκ σοῦ τὴν νίκην παγκλεῶς ποριζόμενοι.

what was before torn apart; to you, therefore, from whom it received its first emancipation, it has royally granted the first fruits of victory. It now leads you as the bride to the emperor, who offers you the generation of vipers of the western realms, escaped, obviously, from the vengeance that awaited them, from his own most severe sentence, given in true and solid judgment. Receive him then, you great-named, and be magnified in him in many ways; embracing him as a conqueror, obeying him as a master, and providing him, like a high-flying eagle, with the finest eyries, so that within his own wings he may shelter your old and new births, and in his great strength he may protect those in you who call upon him. So may the emperor, who has now deposited victory in you like a treasure richly loaded with wealth, always attach his heart to you along with it. For where the treasure is, there also is the heart of the possessor.

17. Shall not we accordingly, following the imperial inclination with high heart, and running with happy steps, and proceeding with a free mind, untroubled, and far removed from pain, suffering no harm, and not wounded much at all — shall not we walk freely, as we said? But adorned with philosophy and taking suitable pride in her gifts, we thus run rejoicing, we thus enter into you, lovely nourisher of our youth, since you received us from the start when we fell to earth from our mothers, and brought us up like a mother, and cared for us like a nurse, and have given us illustrious beauty. In gratitude we bring you this speech in return, and by accepting it, brilliant city, you will leave us not without a share of your grandeur of spirit. But we are sure to have a share in all your blessings, so that we may be bound, in our most happy homecomings to you from the fields of victory, to bring you the praises of greatest reputation; and dedicating our victories to you for ever, may in exchange, with glory, draw victory from you.

Commentary on Laskaris

The remarks which follow have two main objects: to provide a running summary of the speech, part by part, so that its contents may become more intelligible, and to comment on points of interest, primarily historical and topographical. The text itself will not form part of the discussion, since it will hopefully be published with a full critical apparatus by Sophie Georgiopoulou. Her text is reproduced here, with a few modifications in which, generally, the readings of Bachmann ("B"; see the bibliography) have been preferred to those of Georgiopoulou ("G"). Words absent from the Thesaurus or the lexica of Ducange, Liddell and Scott, Sophocles, or Lampe are indicated, but words whose meanings, however unusual, appear in the dictionaries, have not normally been annotated. Biblical passages or reminiscences have been noted, though many no doubt have escaped detection.

1. The excellence of Nicaea in every respect, especially in its practice of reason.

Laskaris opens with an unconventional exordium, not stressing the greatness of the matter at hand or his own weakness before it, or even, as is usual, establishing his relation to the subject. He touches only rapidly on the elements which form the normal base of an encomium. Among these are the fortifications, the greatest ornament of Nicaea.

3. περὶ κύκλωσε B and the late MSS; περικυκλώσεως G. Note that Laskaris uses κύκλωσε in the same sense in 9.12.

5. θέσεως: this topic, the site, is usually the first to be discussed in an encomium of a city.

8. οὐσιωδῶν: the philosophical language which is frequent in the speech is no doubt best left to specialists.

9. Καθ' ἑκάστην, with ellipsis of ἡμέρα, to mean "daily" is common in Byzantine as it is in modern Greek; cf 4. 19, and Metochites 19.12.

11. ἀσυγκρίτων B; ἀσύγκριτον G and MSS.

— queen: the notion of the capital as queen is a commonplace in encomia; see Fenster (1968) *passim.*

2. *Many cities have wealth and fame, but lack the true glory which comes from learning.*

Here, Laskaris begins his stress on Nicaea as a centre of education, as it indeed was in his day; see above 67-71. This section follows the precepts of the handbooks that the defects of other cities should be mentioned to the advantage of the subject. It opens with a list of topics which usually merit praise; the novelty of the speech again becomes evident, for Laskaris reduces the usual qualities of cities to something insignificant beside the learning displayed at Nicaea.

4. ἐπιδόσεσιν B; ἐπιδόσεων MSS and G.

10f. The comparison with Babylon is another commonplace, that with India far less usual. It is conceivable that Laskaris heard of such places from merchants, for goods from Egypt and India were reported to be available in the markets of Magnesia, the effective capital of Vatatzes: Skoutariotes *ap.* Acropolites 286. In fact, the cities of India being built at this time by the Sultans of Delhi were indeed rich, and on scale to dwarf Nicaea.

11. περικείμεναι B; παρακείμεναι MSS and G.

15-22. Note the play on the two meanings of κόσμος, "world" and "decoration"; these are a common feature of the speech.

20-2. The strong image of wealth decorating a corpse is an unexpected turn, showing once again the departure from convention.

3. *Such a city as Nicaea brings glory to its inhabitants.*

3. ἐρυθρῷ means of course "red," but we have translated here as "purple" since red in this period was the color of the imperial majesty, as purple had long been. See, for example, Psellos, *Chronographia* 1.27 and Pachymeres I.185 (red shoes as symbols of imperial power), Anna Komnena 10.ix.6 (red clothes of an emperor), 13.i.1 (imperial red tent) and 13.xii.3 (imperial red ink).

11-15. Laskaris here introduces the notion of the city as a mother to its inhabitants, to which he will return in the peroration.

Commentary on Laskaris

4. The city is like a divine mind which contains citizens whose learning makes them resemble pure thoughts, the harmony of city and inhabitants resembles that of a well-formed body.

2. πολίτας B; πολιστὰς MSS and G.

8. The reference is to Iliad 8.19 where Zeus tells the gods to hang a golden chain from heaven if they wish to test his strength; all of them together would not avail to pull him down.

13-16. This comparison reveals the interest in anatomy and medicine most forcefully expressed in sec. 15.

17. λογιότητι; Bachmann emended to λογηκότητι which, strictly speaking, is correct, for "rationality" is better suited to the context than "eloquence," and would conform to the previous use of this word in 1.13 and 2.17. On the other hand, it is not evident that late Byzantine writers made much distinction between the two easily confused words, especially since λογιότης had come to take on the meaning of "intelligence"; see *TGL ad locc.*

5. Athens was once famed for its learning, but is inferior to Nicaea because it was pagan.

Comparison with Athens is virtually *de rigeur* in these speeches; Menander frequently prescribed it and a host of writers on Constantinople duly included it (Fenster [1968] index).

The novelty of Byzantine encomia is apparent in this passage, for the Christian piety of Nicaea here first mentioned becomes a major motif of the speech, combined with the normal elements of praise derived from the pagan tradition.

The section begins with a favorite device of Laskaris for changing the subject, the introduction of an imaginary interlocutor who objects to the train of thought.

7. ὁ δὴ λέξαι τις; ὃ δὴ λέξαι τις MSS and G.

9. ἀκοντισθήσονται B; ἀκουτισθήσονται MSS and G.

10f. The play on Νίκαια and νίκη "victory" occurs frequently in the speech, as do many others which will not be systematically noted.

17-19. The complex play on λόγος and its derivatives cannot be reproduced in the translation.

> 6. *The Nicaeans excel in all kinds of learning, especially in philosophy and rhetoric.*

The whole passage is of importance for presenting the synthesis of pagan and Christian learning to produce a kind of Christian humanism: see Hunger (1959) 136f.

1. λαμπρόπολις: the word is attested only here and in 17.12.

7. The inclusion of Hermogenes among the great writers of antiquity, however incongruous it may seem, is a true proof of the importance of his works for the Byzantines.

8. μένος πνείουσι, a variation of the Homeric phrase μένεα πνείοντες.

> 7. *Nicaea also excels in theology, which it generously pours forth like waters from a spring.*

5. μετακεντρίζοντες: this sense of the verb seems to appear only here; it is attested once elsewhere in the sense 'transplant'. The present meaning is guaranteed by the passage from which this is derived, Romans 11:24 where, however, Saint Paul uses ἐγκεντρίζω.

6. αἰχμαλωτίζοντες . . . . Χριστόν: taken from II Corinthians 10:5.

11. ἀκρώρεια, "mountain peak"; on this meaning, see Renehan (1975) l9f.

> 8. *I have been praising the citizens and their learning, which are indeed basic, rather than the city itself.*

Here, Laskaris recalls the normal subject of an encomium, and gradually returns to it, at least for a moment.

4. ἐγκώμια. It was evidently clear to the author that he was writing an encomium (the term also appears at 13.18 and 17.16), however far the speech is removed from the classical models.

> 9. *Introduction continued: if the audience wishes to hear about the city, I could travel through the whole universe and not find a better place.*

Once again, an imaginary dialogue (this time, a rude interruption) introduces a change of subject: cf. secs. 5 and 12.

1. ἀγροικῇ μοι βοήσει B and, with some variants, MSS; G prints ἄγροι[κος ἐ]μοὶ βοήσει, which seems to introduce an inappropriately concrete interlocutor.

5f. The brief praise of Magnesia by Skoutariotes (507; *ap*. Acropolites 286) contains an almost identical phrase; both indicate that the idea is a commonplace in such speeches:

ἐν δὲ τῇ κατὰ Λυδίαν Μαγνησίᾳ...τί τίς ἂν ἐζήτησεν ἀφ' ὧν ἄνθρωποι χρῄζομεν, καὶ οὐκ εὑρὼν ἐκπληρώσατο τὴν ἀπόλαυσιν, οὐ τῶν ἐν τοῖς ἡμετέροις τόποις εὑρισκομένων ἀλλὰ καὶ ὅσα ἐνιαχοῦ τῆς οἰκουμένης...

10. *The city is so rich in vegetation that it appears to be a grove; its buildings, especially its churches and monasteries, inspire reflection.*

The speech here finally arrives at the point where many encomia begin, a description of the city. Although vague and rhetorical, these passages are important because they show the vivid impression made by crops and trees, thus indicating that large parts of the city within the walls were uninhabited; cf. Metochites sec. 11.

8-9. τὰς ποικιλίας...τὰς ἰδέας...τὰς...εὐπρεπείας B; ταῖς...ποικιλίαις...ταῖς...ἰδέαις...ταῖς...εὐπρεπείαις MSS and G.

8. θεάτρων ἰδέας: the meaning of this phrase is far from clear, especially since the ancient theatre, long ruined and probably unrecognisable, was then being used as a graveyard and dumping ground.

11. *Nicaea, as capital, has received an outer ring of walls, rendering its defences to those of other cities.*

4-9. This convoluted language almost conceals the simple fact that Vatatzes erected a second, outer wall around the city, doubling its defensive strength. This fact is the most important piece of new information to come from the speech. For this wall, see Schneider (1938) 16-19, 27ff, with excellent plans and illustrations; cf. Foss and Winfield (1985) 83, 97, 103.

12. The crops and water supply are exceptionally abundant; citizens and countrymen have close relations.

Another imaginary interruption introduces a new subject.

10. φύσις: this is one of the two main headings (with θέσις) for treating the site of a city, here barely sketched.

10-13. This passage apparently conflates two kinds of water: the streams "easy to cross" of the surrounding country, among which the waters of the moat "in a circle" may be counted; and the city water supply, brought by the aqueduct through the walls (but not actually carried on them), and thus reaching the inhabitants "above the level of their heads" (this novelty also struck Metochites: 11.10). The course of the aqueduct within the city has not been determined. The fountains of the houses could have been fed from the aqueduct or, perhaps more probably, from wells. Ibn Battuta (p. 453), who visited Nicaea a century later, in 1335, remarked on the wells within the town.

14. ὕδασιν MSS and B; ὕδατος G.

15-17. It appears from this that visitors from the country would camp under the rich growth of trees in the city.

20-22. The image of water finally turns into a metaphor for education, further emphasising the close relations between the urban and rural population; cf. the springs of piety of 7.7-13 which water other cities from Nicaea. With this praise of water, the short section of the speech, 10-12, which deals with the actual physical aspect of the city, comes to an end.

13. Address to Nicaea: you have saved the empire by being its refuge when Constantinople was taken, and by resisting all enemy assaults.

As the speech draws near its end, the emotional tone rises. Note especially the long rhetorical period connected by subordinate participles (9-16) which culminates in the three concrete verbs (17). This section summarizes what for contemporaries was the greatest role of the city.

6. μὲν B; νῦν MSS and G.

14. (Continuation of 13): You alone have defeated the Latins, and held off the Turks, under both Laskaris and Vatatzes; you deserve the highest praise.

1-20. Another long, emotional, and carefully constructed period with only one finite verb, ἀνάγει, at the end. The sentence thus culminates on an optimistic note with the actions of Vatatzes. The city is also stressed: it appears, halfway through in the nominative σύ, after a long series of genitive absolutes; its primacy in the action is stressed as the period leads toward the deeds of the Emperor.

4. μύστιδος: the image is of someone with special knowledge, who is therefore set apart from the rest – that is, although Constantinople had a privileged position, she neglected the cities entrusted to her care.

8. μισθωτοῦ: the reference is to the hired shepherd of John 10:12 who runs away and abandons the sheep when a wolf approaches.

10f: σηπεδόνα...ἁλυκότητι. This curious image is one of salt preserving meat, and thus defeating the rot.

13. Persia: the conventional Byzantine designation for enemies from the east, in this case the Turks.

15-18: A remarkable collocation of sesquipedalian adjectives, some attested only here, most of them peculiar to the twelfth and thirteenth century, a period when such bombast was at its height. A similarly elevated vocabulary adorns (or deforms) the works of many contemporary writers, notably Mesarites.

16. ἀετοδρόμου: attested only here.

17. γενναιόφρων: only here and in Eustathios of Thessalonica, a writer of the twelfth century.

17. βριαρόχειρ: attested only in this period. The word appears in a similar context in an inscription of 1225 *(CIG* 8750) on the walls of Durazzo, where it is used to describe their builder Theodore Angelos of Epiros. In a more humble context Mesarites, *Reisebericht* 37, employs it to describe soldiers in especially inflated language, perhaps intended as amusing. It also appears in Eustathios.

18. Δούκας: the official family name of Vatatzes.

18. χαριτώνυμος: by this, Laskaris alludes to the name of the emperor, John, which in Hebrew means "God is gracious." John Komnenos is described in the same way in an inscription of the church of the Pantokrator which he built in Constantinople: *CIG* 8722.

22. νόμος: there seems to be nothing corresponding to this in the Byzantine laws of the sea which, on the contrary, make careful provision for the owners of ships and goods that survive a storm or shipwreck: see the full discussion of Ashburner (1909) ccli-ccxciii.

27. φερωνυμίαν: reference to the name of Nicaea, ultimately derived from νίκη: see above 5.10.

15. *At that time, you acted like the heart, which draws the blood in, warms it, and sends it back to revivify the body; so you revived and strengthened the Empire.*

This complex metaphor is to be understood in the light of the medical doctrine of innate heat, widely accepted in Byzantine times. According to it, the body had a natural warmth whose centre was the heart, which distributed it to the members. This heat was natural to living creatures; its absence meant death. See the helpful discussions of Harris (1973) 137-139, 374-379 and May (1968) 50-53. My thanks to Professor Robert Renehan for these references and his comments.

Here, the image is of a diseased body regaining its strength; the disease was the Latin conquest and occupation of Constantinople.

The metaphor is expressed in another complex period, with a series of participial phrases which build up to the main verb, ἐχρῆν. This in turn introduces a series of dependent infinitives.

16. *Because of her achievements, Nicaea is led by the Empire as a bride to the Emperor, who will produce from her a victorious generation.*

The image of the first part is so vivid and specific as to give the impression of reflecting an actual painting.

6. γεννήματα ἐχιδνῶν...ὀργῆς: adapted from Matthew 3:7 (= Luke 3:7) which typically uses more direct language in μελλούσῃ ὀργῇ.

11. ἀετῷ: this continues the imperial image of 17.14 where it was applied to Theodore Laskaris.

16, 18. θησαυρός: metaphorical, for the actual treasury of the empire at this time was in Magnesia: Skoutariotes 507 *(ap.* Acropolites 286); Pachymeres I.97, 101f (=68,71 B).

17. *Peroration: Our speech is brought to Nicaea with the gratitude felt toward a kindly nurse.*

This ending, although it reflects the common feeling of gratitude of a speaker toward a city, presents it with a characteristically emotional tone designed to leave a strong last impression on the audience who would no doubt have been moved by the effective metaphor: see above, 148 n.23.

15f. ἐγκώμια, νίκας: The speech ends with a reference to its own nature, and the usual pun on the name of the city.

Θεοδώρου Μετοχίτου
Νικαεύς

1. Εἶχον μὲν τέως ἐπὶ τῇδε τῇ πόλει ὡς σιγῇ μόνον θαυμάζειν καὶ μὴ πλέον φιλόκαλος εἶναι πειρᾶσθαι, ὥστε καὶ λόγους ἀξιοῦν εἰσφέρειν καὶ τὴν νομιζομένην χαρίζεσθαι τοῖς καλοῖς εὐφημίαν, ἐπειδή μοι καὶ ἐργῶδες ἐπιεικῶς εἶναι δοκεῖ, τῶν
5 αὐτῇ προσόντων ἀγαθῶν ἀντιλαβέσθαι μὴ ἀγεννῶς, καὶ ὅσοις πολλή τις ἡ περιουσία τοῦ λέγειν καὶ τὸ ἐν τούτοις κράτος μεγάλων ἀξιοῦται πραγμάτων, καὶ ἅμα ὃ προσέστι νῦν, ὅτι καὶ πρὸς παρόντας καὶ ὁρῶντας τοὺς ἀκούοντας γίγνοιντ' ἂν οἱ λόγοι, καὶ τοῖς φαινομένοις, εἰμή τι πλέον, ἔστι προσ-
10 μαρτυρεῖν, καὶ πολλὴ πάντως ἡ αἰσχύνη μὴ μόνον ὑπερσχεῖν τοῖς ἐγκωμίοις, ἢ τό γε δεύτερον παραθεῖναι τοῖς πράγμασι τὸν λόγον, ἀλλ' ἔτι καὶ πολὺ τῶν ὄντων ἀπολειφθῆναι ἐν εἰδόσι τοῖς ἀκροωμένοις σπουδάζοντα· ὁ μὲν γὰρ ἀγνοῶν τάχ' ἂν ἀποχρώντως ἔχειν οἰηθείη τὴν ἀγωνίαν καὶ ἀγαπήσοι τῷ
15 προστυχόντι, πῶς δ' ἄν τις καὶ διαγένοιτο περὶ μεγάλων καθιστάμενος καὶ συνιεὶς ἧττον ἔχων, ὁπόταν ὁ κριτὴς εὐθὺς μεταφέρῃ καὶ προσαρμόζῃ τοὺς λόγους τῷ συνεῖναι τοῖς πράγμασιν;

Theodore Metochites
Nicene Oration

1. My conduct towards this city until now has been simply to admire her in silence, and not try to be so much a lover of beauty as to think right to bring words into the matter, and bestow on her that praise which is usual for noble things; for it seems to me laborious work to apprehend her good qualities in a not unworthy fashion, even for those who have great excellence in speaking and whose powers are judged worthy of great affairs; and then also, in this case, the speech is to be before auditors who are present and see the subject of it, and who can, if nothing more, testify to what is visible. And great is the shame if one makes one's effort before an informed audience, when one not only does not exceed in a speech of praise nor bring what one says up to a level with the facts but falls short of the reality. An unknowing man might easily think the endeavour sufficient and be satisfied with whatever he found. But how could anyone succeed, having set himself such a great task and knowing that he is unequal to it, when his judge may at once compare and measure his words against his own familiarity with the facts?

2. Οὐ μὴν ἀλλ' ὃ μάλιστα τὴν δυσχέρειαν ἐδόκει τῷ λόγῳ ποιεῖν, τοῦτό με δὴ πρὸς τὸ ἐναντίον ἅπαν, ἐπιβαλεῖν ἐπέρρωσε τῇ παρούσῃ σπουδῇ καὶ θαρρῆσαι κατέστησε τοὺς ὑπὲρ τῆς πόλεως ὡς ἔξεστι λόγους· μάλιστα μὲν γὰρ ὅστις μετὰ
5 τῶν πραγμάτων ἀκούει, ἅμα τε ἂν ἔχοι γνῶναι ὅπῃ τῶν λόγων μακρὰν ἐλαύνοι καὶ συγγνῶναι πάντως, καλῶς διαιτήσας· ὡς τὸ μὲν ἐνδεῶς τῶν ὄντων ἐρεῖν τοῦ μεγέθους ὂν τῶν πραγμάτων, τὴν δὲ περὶ τὰ κρείττω προθυμίαν, οὐκ ἀδόκιμον οὖσαν, οὐδ' αἰτίας ἴσως ἀξίαν· καὶ τοσούτῳ μᾶλλον
10 ὅσῳ περ ἄν, ὡς περὶ μεγάλων φρονῇ τῶν πραγμάτων, καὶ τοὺς ἄλλους βούλοιτ' ἂν οὕτω λογίζεσθαι· ἔπειτα δ' οὐδὲ τοῦτο δεινὸν οὐδέν, ἀλλὰ καὶ μᾶλλον καθ' ἡδονὴν τοῖς διακειμένοις οὕτω τῶν ἀκουόντων, καὶ τῷ λέγχοντι δὲ οὐ ἧττον, ἐλλεῖψαι τοῖς οὖσι καὶ τὴν ὑπερβολὴν ἐντεῦθεν παρα-
15 στῆσαι τῶν ἔργων, οἷς ἐνεχείρησε. Τούτοις ἐγὼ τοῖς λόγοις ἔδωκα τῇ παρούσῃ σπουδῇ, καὶ εἰσήχθην εἰς ἀνάγκην ταύτην δοκοῦσαν αὐθαίρετον. Οὐ μὴν ἀλλὰ πατρίς μοι ἡ καλλίστη πόλις αὕτη, τὸ μέρος, καὶ τῇ πατρίδι τι πάντως εἰσφέρειν ἐκ τῶν ἐνόντων ὀφείλεται.

3. Ἔθος δὲ ὂν τοῖς ἐπὶ ταῦτα καθισταμένοις, οὐ μόνον τοῖς παροῦσι χρῆσθαι καὶ φαινομένοις, ἀλλ' ἔτι καὶ ἀνατρέχειν καὶ πόρρω τῶν προτέρων χρόνων ἐπιχειρεῖν, τὰ ἀρχαῖα σεμνύνοντας τοῖς εὐφημουμένοις. Εἰ μὲν ᾤμην οἷός τε ὢν ἀμφο-
5 τέροις ἀρκέσαι, οὐδὲν ἂν ἦν ἴσως πρᾶγμα πλέον τοῦ προχείρου διατρίβειν, καὶ τοῖς παλαιοῖς τῆς πόλεως φιλοτιμεῖσθαι τοὺς λόγους· νῦν δέ, τί ἄν τις περὶ ταῦτα φιλονεικῇ, ἐνδεῶς ἔχων, ἢ ὡς τῶν ὁρωμένων περιγενέσθαι; καὶ πολλῷ μᾶλλον ἀναγκαίων προσάγειν, ἐπεὶ βουλομένῳ περιττὰ φρονεῖν, πολ-
10 λὴν ἀφθονίαν, τά τε παλαιὰ σεμνὰ Βιθυνῶν ἀρχαιολογοῦντα πολυπραγμονεῖν, καὶ ἔτι τὸ κλέος ὅσον ἀρχῆθεν ἥκει τῇ πόλει, καὶ ὡς οὐ προσβραχὺ τὰ κατ' αὐτήν, οὐδ' ὀλίγοις ἐσπουδάσθη, ἀλλ' ἄλλοις τε τῶν πάλαι γενναίων σκοπὸς γέ-

2. And yet this very thing, which seemed to constitute the greatest obstacle to this composition has, quite to the contrary, strengthened me to undertake my present effort, and has made me take confidence and speak as best I can about this city. For he who listens while surrounded by the subject will be able to tell how far he is going in the speech, and to forgive altogether, being well disposed to judge that what is inadequate to the reality is owing to the greatness of the subject, and that enthusiasm over good things, which is no disgrace, is not, perhaps, to be blamed. All the more so when he thinks highly of the subject himself, and would wish others to consider it likewise. Furthermore it is nothing terrible, but rather likely to please those of the audience who are thus minded and to please the speaker no less, to fall short of the reality, and by so doing to bring to mind the superiority of the subject he has undertaken. To these reasons I have yielded in making my present effort and have been led into this necessity, which might appear self-chosen. And then besides this fairest of cities is my country in a sense; and one always owes to one's country, to contribute to her something of what is in oneself.

3. It is a custom with those who undertake such things not only to deal with what is present and visible, but to go further back and discuss earlier times, honouring antiquity with their praises. If I thought I were able to suffice for both, it might have been no trouble to spend more time than is available, and to dignify my speech with the ancient history of the city; but now, why should a man be ambitious of that, when he has not the strength to succeed with what he sees before him, and which it is much more necessary that he describe? Since, if one wishes to entertain lofty ideas, there is plenty of opportunity to do so by busying oneself in investigating that grand ancient history of the Bithynians, and how great is the fame that the city has had from the beginning; and how its reputation was not narrow, nor were its admirers few, but it was an

γονε φιλοτιμίας· καὶ δὴ καὶ Τραϊανὸς αὐτός ὕστερον Ῥω-
15 μαίων αὐτοκράτωρ, οὗ πολλὰς μὲν τὰς κατὰ γνώμην καὶ
τὸ ἦθος εὐδοκιμήσεις, πολλὰς δὲ καὶ τὰς κατὰ χεῖρα μεγαλουργίας οὐκ ὀκνεῖ παραπέμπων εἰς ἡμᾶς ὁ χρόνος, οὐκ ἠδέ-
σθη μᾶλλον κατὰ τῆς ἑτέρων φιλοκάλου σπουδῆς ἐπεξιέναι
καὶ διατρίβειν, ἀλλὰ τοῖς ἀγαθοῖς τῶν ἔργων ὀρέγειν χεῖρα
20 δεῖν ἐγνωκὼς καὶ εἰς ὅσον δύναιτο προάγειν, μετὰ τῶν ἄλλων
καὶ Νίκαιαν τήνδε τὴν πόλιν, ὡς ἔχοι νῦν, ὑπόμνημα καὶ
στήλην τῆς αὐτοῦ μεγαλοψυχίας ἵστησιν· ὥστε τὴν αὐτὴν
ἐξεῖναι παλαιάν τε ὁμοῦ καὶ νέαν ὁρᾶν· καὶ εἰδήτω σεμνὸν
ἡ ἀρχαιότης καὶ τοῦτο μετὰ τῆς πόλεως, καὶ εἰδήτω σοφὸς
25 ὁ χρόνος τὰ κρείττω γνωρίζων ἀεί, καὶ τοῦτο πρόσεστιν αὖθις
τῇ πόλει· ἀλλ' ὅπερ ἔλεγον οὔ μοι σχολὴ περὶ τὰ τοιαῦτα
πολυπραγμονεῖν, καὶ τὴν σπουδὴν ἀναλίσκειν.

4. Ὅτι δὲ θέσεως ἡ πόλις ἔλαχεν εὐφυῶς καὶ τῆς γῆς ἐπικαίρως ἵδρυται, τοῦτο καὶ πάρεστιν ὁρᾶν, κἀνταῦθα τῷ λόγῳ
πειρᾶσθαι δεικνῦναι προσῆκον· ἔχει γὰρ οὕτω δεξιῶς, ὡς μήτε
πρὸς ἀσφάλειαν, μήτε πρὸς χάριν ἐνδεῖν· ἀλλ' ἀμφότερα
5 ἱκανῶς εἶναι, ὡς οὐκ ἔστιν εὑρεῖν ὑπερβολήν· θαλάσσῃ μὲν
γὰρ ἔοικεν, οὐ μάλα τοι πιστεύειν· διὸ δήπου μηδὲ συνάπτειν
μηδὲ συνοικεῖν ἔγνω· ἀλλ' εἰς τοσοῦτον ἀναχωρεῖ, ὡς τῶν
μὲν ἀπ' αὐτῆς πάντων ἀγαθῶν οὐ δυσχερῶς ἀπολαύειν ἐξεῖναι, εἰ δέ τί που δύσνουν ἐκεῖθεν, οἷα δήπου τὰ ἐκ θαλάσσης
10 ἀφανῶς ὑφέρπει, μακρὰν ἀπῳκίσθαι καὶ μηδὲν ἐντεῦθεν εἶναι
δεινόν· καὶ ἔστι τοῦτο ἡδύ τε ἅμα καὶ καινὸν ἐκτόπως θαυ-
μάσαι, μὴ μετέχειν οἷα δὴ δοκεῖ, πᾶσα ἀνάγκη, τῶν ἐκ τοῦ
αὐτοῦ ἐναντίων, ἀλλὰ τὴν μὲν τῶν ἐκεῖθεν καλῶν ἀπόλαυσιν, καθ' αἵρεσιν ἄφθονον εἶναι· καὶ γὰρ δὴ καὶ φιλότιμος
15 ἔλαχεν ἡ γείτων οὖσα· πᾶν δὲ τὸ ἀπ' αὐτῆς δυσχερὲς ἀργὸν
ἐπέχεσθαι καὶ ἀμήχανον ἐγχειρεῖν· καὶ τοῦτο οὐ λόγον μόνον
ἔστιν ἀκούειν, ἀλλὰ καὶ ὁ προλαβὼν ἅπας χρόνος πάρεστιν

object of emulation even to those others who were great in olden times. Not less afterwards was that same Trajan, emperor of the Romans — time is not yet weary of transmitting to us many favourable testimonies of his mind and character and many splendid works of his hand — ashamed to give his time and effort to what others' zeal for beauty had created; but being resolved to set his hand to good works already existing and to advance them as much as he could, among other things he established this city Nicaea, as it is now, to be a reminder and a monument of his greatness of mind. As a result, this same city may be regarded as both old and new. And let Antiquity adjudge this honor also to the city; and let wise Time who always determines right adjudge it also; and this also the city possesses. But, as I said, I have no time to busy myself with such things, and so to waste my efforts.

4. That the city has a fine situation and is seated advantageously on the earth, this is at hand to see, and then it is right to try to show it by words. She is so rightly placed as to lack neither security, nor charm, but to have both so sufficiently that it is not possible to find more of them anywhere. For she seems first to rely on the sea, and yet not greatly so; she has therefore resolved neither to adjoin nor to live together with it, but withdraws inland so far that, while able to enjoy without difficulty all the good that comes from it, yet, if anything hostile come from thence — such things as creep upon one unseen from the sea — she is settled far away, and nothing from there is to be feared. And what one may extremely admire as both pleasing and novel is that she does not share, as seems altogether inevitable, the opposite aspects of the same thing, but the enjoyment of the good from there is as plentiful as she may wish — and this neighbor is a generous one — while all its disadvantadges are feeble and incapable of taking effect. And this is not only to be heard in words, but the whole past age is ready here to bring forward the proofs of it: an

ἐνταῦθα, τὰς πίστεις εἰς μέσον ἄγων· ἐν ᾧ πολλάκις παρά-
λιαι μέν ἐκεῖναι τόσαι πόλεις τῶν καθ' ἡμᾶς, αἱ μὲν μακρὰν
αἱ δὲ καὶ ἔγγιστα ταύτῃ εὐδαιμονοῦσαι, ἠλλάξαντο τὰ τῆς
τύχης καὶ κακῶς ἀπηλλάγησαν τῶν πρὸς τὴν θάλασσαν συν-
θηκῶν· τῇ δὲ περιῆν ὁ βίος ἀκύμων, καὶ ἅμα προσῆν τὸ καὶ
ταῖς ἄλλαις ὡς ἀπὸ ναυαγίων εἰς λιμένα γίγνεσθαι· ἀλλὰ
τοῦτο μὲν ἐκ τοῦ παρήκοντος οὕτως εἰσήχθη· ὅπερ δὲ ἀρτίως
ὁ λόγος ἐσπούδαζεν, ὅτι θαλάττῃ μὲν μὴ μάλα τοι θαρρεῖν
ἐπιγνοῦσα, διὰ τὸ κρυψίνουν ὡς τὰ πολλὰ καὶ ἀφανὲς τῶν
ἀπ' αὐτῆς ἐπιχειρήσεων, ἐν ἀσφαλεῖ τῆς γῆς ἡ πόλις
ὑποχωρεῖ· ὥσπερ δέ τις ἐφ' ἑαυτῷ τὸ καθ' ἡδονὴν ῥᾴδιον
ἔχον ἀνύειν ἢ μή, τὴν θάλασσαν ἐκ τοῦ προχείρου δαψιλῶς
ἄττα πρὸς χρείαν ὑπηρετοῦσαν ἔχει· καὶ πάρεστιν ἐνταῦθα
τὰ ἐκείνης ἄφθονα τρυφᾶν οὐδὲν ἧττον ἢ ταῖς παροικούσαις
τῶν πόλεων.

5. Καὶ οὔπω προσέθηκα τὴν ἐκ τῆς πόλεως ταύτης φέρουσαν
θάλατταν· διειδὲς μὲν ὕδωρ ὀφθαλμοῖς χρήσασθαι, ἡδὺ δὲ
προσενεγκεῖν καὶ ἅμα ἀφορμὴν τοῖς σώμασιν ὑγιαίνειν, ὡς
οὐκ οἶδ' εἴ τι τῶν ἁπάντων ἔστιν εἰσφέρειν, θεῖον οὕτω καλόν,
εὐπόριστον καὶ πρόχειρον ἰατρεῖον· καὶ μὴν ἔτι μῆκος, ὅσον
τῶν ἄλλων οὐδὲ μιᾶς ἑτέρας λίμνης ἱκανὸν παραθεῖναι, ὡς
τοῖς ἀκριβῶς εἰδόσιν ἀναγκαῖον θαρρεῖν· καὶ πρόσεστι παντοίων ὄψων θησαυρός, τοῦτο μὲν εἰς ἀνάγκης χρείαν, τοῦτο
δὲ εἰς τρυφὴν ὑπηρετῶν τῇ βουλήσει· οὐ μόνον δὲ ἀλλὰ καὶ
τὰ ἐκ ποταμῶν ἔγγιστα παραρρεῖ, ὥστε ἐξεῖναι, καὶ εἰ μὴ
φίλα πρὸς τὴν θάλατταν ᾖ, αὐτὴν ἐφ' ἑαυτῆς ἔχειν τὴν πόλιν, καὶ τοῖς οἰκείοις ἀνενδεῶς χρῆσθαι· ὅση δὲ ἄλλως ἡ ρᾳ-
στώνη ταῖς ὄψεσιν ἐφίσταται τρυφᾶν ἐξ αὐτῆς πόλεως καθο-
ρῶντι τὴν λίμνην ἐπειγομένην, καὶ ποῖ μὲν τῶν ὑποκειμέ-
νων ἀπολαύουσαν πεδίων, ποῖ δὲ συνεχομένην ταῖς δυσχω-
ρίαις καὶ εἴκουσαν, εἰ καὶ τέως ἀντεῖχε τῆς ἐλευθερίας ἐφ'
ἱκανὸν ἀντιποιουμένη· καί σοι οὐδ' ἡ ἐφ' ἑκάτερα ταύτης μετὰ
τῶν ὀρῶν συμπλοκὴ δόξειεν ἂν ἄχαρι, οὔθ' ὡς ἂν ἔτυχε συμ-

age in which all those cities which in our time are on the sea — some far and some very near to this one in prosperity — have often changed their fortune, and come off badly from their contract made with the sea; but the life of this one remained calm, and it became in addition a harbour as it were for the shipwreck of the rest. But this has been brought in by the way. My speech was just about to say that, having resolved not to trust too much in the sea because of the usual secrecy and invisibility of the attacks that come from there, the city was withdrawn into a safe part of the land. Like one who has it easily in his power to do or not to do whatever he pleases, she has the sea available to provide plentifully whatever is of use; and one may there enjoy the luxury of the abundance the sea gives, no less than in the cities that dwell beside it.

5. And I have not even added the sea that begins from this city: a water transparent to the sight of the eyes, sweet to carry to the lips, and as well a source of health to the body, so much so that I do not know if anything else can be mentioned that is such a marvellous remedy, so lovely, so easily obtained, and so available; and then its size, so great as not to be compared with that of any other lake, as those with accurate knowledge must be confidently sure; and besides it is a storehouse of every kind of delicacy, serving them up at one's wish, both for the use of necessity and for luxury. Not only this, but the produce of the rivers flows very nearby, so that the city can, even if there is hostility from the sea, make use of its own resources without deficiency. And then what ease may the eyes enjoy, when one looks down from the very city onto the lake pressing closely upon it: in one direction having the enjoyment of the adjacent plains, and in another adjoining the rough ground and giving way to it, as if at that point it had enough of resisting and defending its liberty. And then the enfolding of it between the mountains on both sides might seem to you not

βαίνειν, ἀλλ' οἷον ἐναρμονίως, καὶ ὁμαλῶς, καὶ σκοπὸν εἶναι
ταύτην, ὥσπερ ἀποχαρακοῦσθαι καὶ ἐγκλείεσθαι τῇ πόλει·
οὐκ οἶδ' εἴτε χάριτος ἀσχολίαν καὶ τρυφῆς ὁρᾶν τε καὶ
χρῆσθαι, ὅπῃ ἂν δοκῇ, καθάπερ ἀμέλει τὰ χειροποίητα σπου-
δάσματα, εἴτε θαλάσσης εἰκόνα δοθεῖσαν τῇ πόλει· καὶ γὰρ
δὴ καὶ πρόεισιν εἰς μήκιστον, φεύγουσα τὸν θεατήν, ἀφορμὴν
ἐρωτικοῦ πάθους· οὐ γὰρ ὀλίγον δέος μή που βασκήνασα ἡ
γείτων ἐλλοχήσει θάλασσα καὶ ὑφέληται δόλῳ· ἀλλ' ἀσφαλῶς τε ἴεται, καὶ διὰ πολλοῦ πομπεύει τὰ ἑαυτῆς ἐπιδεικνῦσα,
ἐγγὺς ὅτι μάλιστα ταύτῃ· καὶ διαγενομένη τῶν ἐκεῖθεν ἐπι-
βουλῶν, ἔπειτα μέμνηται τῶν πρὸς τὴν πόλιν συνθηκῶν, καὶ
ἀσμένως ἐπανάγουσα ἑαυτῆς γίνεται. Ἀλλὰ ταῦτα μὲν ἅλις
ἂν ἴσως ὁ λόγος ἔχει.

6. Ἃ δὲ κατ' ἤπειρον, πολλὴ μὲν ἡ χάρις, πεδιάδες τόσαι
πρὸς τὴν πόλιν πάντοθεν ἀπαντῶσαι καὶ ἀλλήλαις σὺν ὥρᾳ
καὶ τῇ πόλει συμφυόμεναι· πολλὴ δὲ ὄνησις, τὸ ἀπ' αὐτῶν
γόνιμον, ὡς ἔρρωται παντοίαν φοράν· οὐ γάρ ἐστιν ἐφ' ὅτῳ
μᾶλλον φέρειν πέφυκεν, ἀλλὰ τοῦτό γε δὴ πάντων κομιδῇ
δυσχερέστατον συνιδεῖν, ὅποι τῶν γινομένων ἑαυτῆς ἡ πόλις
ἥττηται· ταῖς μὲν γὰρ ἄλλαις οὐ πάντα ἀρκεῖ τὸ φιλότιμον,
ἀλλ' ἔστιν οὗ τῶν ὄντων ἐλλείπει· καὶ τοῦτ' ἔστιν εὖ πράττειν, μὴ τῶν ἀναγκαίων ἐλλείπειν· ἐνταῦθα δὲ ὁμοῦ μὲν ὅσα
τε ἀνάγκη παρεῖναι, ὁμοῦ δὲ καὶ ὅσα ποικίλλεται τρυφῇ πάντων ἀπολαύειν ἄφθονον ἡ γῆ ταμεῖον. καὶ μόνῃ ταύτῃ σχεδὸν τῇ πόλει ἔξεστιν ἀπόνως τρυφᾶν· δαψιλεῖς μὲν αἱ τῶν
παντοίων καρπῶν ἀναδόσεις· ἄμπελοι δὲ θαυμαστὸν γέ τοι
τὸ χρῆμα, πάρεστιν ὁρᾶν τὸ πλῆθός τε καὶ τὴν γινομένην
ἀρετήν· καὶ οὔπω προσέθηκα τὰ ἐκ φυτῶν ὡραῖα, ὧν εἰ πα-
ρήσω τὸ πλῆθος, τοσαύτη γε μὴν ἡ φιλοκαλία καὶ τὸ περὶ
ταῦτα τῆς φύσεως εὐμήχανον, ὡς καὶ ἀποφοιτᾶν πόρρω τῆς
ἐνεγκούσης, εἰς ὅσον ἂν ἐξικνεῖσθαι δέδοται, ὥσπερ ἃ εἴωθεν
ἐξ ἀλλοδαπῶν περιοδεύειν τεράστια φύσεως· ἤδη δέ τισιν
ἐσπουδάσθη, καὶ τὴν οἰκείαν ἐκ τῆς ἐνταῦθα εὐκαρπίας εὐερ-

unpleasing, not like something that happened by chance but, as it were, by arrangement and with regularity, and that the aim was as if to fence off and bar this water in for the city — I know not whether as an occupation of pleasure and enjoyment, to look at and to turn on every side one wishes, as we often do with the admirable works of men's hands; or as an image of the sea granted to the city; for indeed it goes on to an extreme distance, escaping the viewer, and rousing the passion of desire, for no small fear arises that from jealousy the neighbouring sea may lie in wait for and capture it by a trick. But it travels safely and carries all it brings through great distance as near as can be to this place; and, having survived the plots from there, remembers its contract with our city, and gladly brings itself back. But of this perhaps enough is said.

6. As for the land, it has great charms: so many plains meeting the city from every side, and joining gracefully with one another and with the town. And the usefulness of what they bear is great, so vigorous is the land in every kind of crop. Since there is no one thing that it bears better, what is most difficult of all to discover is, in which of its productions is the city inferior to itself? The ambition of other towns is not sufficient in every respect, but there is a point at which it falls short of reality, it is this, that for them prospering means not falling short of necessities. But here the earth provides a plentiful storehouse, both of necessities and of all by which luxury is adorned. And this city, almost alone, can have luxury without labour, for all kinds of crops grow in abundance. As for the vines — a marvellous thing — it is easy to see their number and their innate excellence. And I have not yet added the fruits of the plants, for which — though I leave aside their number — so great is the love of beauty and ingenuity applied to this part of nature that they go beyond the earth that bore them as far as it is granted them to reach, like the marvels of nature usually brought here from foreign countries. And some have

γετῆσαι καὶ ἀναγκάσαι πράττειν εὖ, τῆς ἐντεῦθεν βλάστης ἀφορμὴν ἐνθεῖσι δημιουργεῖν παραπλήσια.

7. Καὶ ταῦτα μὲν μέτρια τῶν ὄντων ἐκ τῶν ἔξωθέν ἐστιν εἰσφέρειν τῇ πόλει· ὁ δ' οὖν οἰκεῖος αὐτῇ στέφανος καὶ ὁ διὰ πάντων, οὐκ οἶδ' εἴτε τελευταῖος εἴτε πρῶτος, νικᾷ λέγειν, τῆς εὐδαιμονίας ὅρος ὄντως ἀσάλευτος· τίς ἂν ἰδὼν οὐκ ἀγασθείη
5 τείχη ταῦτα περὶ αὐτὴν τοσοῦτον ἔχοντα τὸ ἀπὸ τῆς τέχνης θάρρος, ὡς μηδὲν εἶναι πρᾶγμα παντοίαν πρὸς αὐτὰ μηχανημάτων φιλονεικίαν, ἀλλ' ἀνόνητον ἄλλως κατὰ τῶν ἀδυνάτων διατριβήν; Σχῆμα μὲν δὴ τῇ πόλει κυκλικὸν τῶν ὄντων τὸ πολυχώρητον· περιφρονεῖ δὲ πᾶσαν ἀνισότητα παρακει-
10 μένην καὶ ἀποσεμνύνεται συνάπτειν, οἷα δὴ κλέπτουσιν αἱ πολλαὶ τὰς δυσχωρίας, καὶ τὸ ἐρυμνὸν ἐπίτηδες σοφίζονται· φιλανθρώπως δὲ ἔχουσα καὶ ὁμαλῶς κεχυμένη ἑαυτῇ πιστεύει καὶ τοῖς ἔξωθεν περιβλήμασιν, οὕτω τοι καλῶς ἠσκημένοις, ὡς ἡδονήν τε ἅμα εἶναι καὶ θαῦμα προσβλέπειν προμήθειαν
15 ἀκλόνητον, κάλλος ἄμαχον ὅσον, δεσμὸν εὐπρεπῆ· οἷα μὲν γὰρ ἡ τῆς ὅλης δημιουργίας, ἡρμοσμένης τῆς ὕλης, ἀπαθὴς ἀνάγκη, οἷα δὲ τὰ ἐν τῷ μέσῳ πυργώματα, τοῦτο μὲν εἰς ὕψος ἐπείγεται, ταῖς ἕδραις θαρροῦντα, τοῦτο δὲ κάτωθεν προεξίστανται τῆς συνεχείας τοῦ παντὸς συνασπισμοῦ, καὶ
20 ἀπαντῶσι τοῖς ἐναντίοις ἄπονοι καὶ ἀκίνητοι πρόμαχοι· τὸ δὲ πρὸς ἄλληλα τούτων φιλικὸν καὶ μὴ προσολίγον ἐθέλειν ἀφίστασθαι, χορείαν σοι τινὰ ταύτην ἂν δόξῃ περιελίττειν, εὐαρμόνιον μὲν καὶ ἡδίστην ἐντὸς τῇ πόλει τρυφᾶν, ἔνοπλον δὲ εἴ τις ἔξωθεν ἐναντίοις προσπελάζει καὶ ἀκοινώνητον συγ-
25 γενέσθαι. Οὕτω δὲ περὶ ταῦτα μεγαλοφύχως ἡ πόλις ἔχει, ὥστε σοι καὶ ἕτερον μικρῷ πρόσθεν περίβολον ἵστησιν· ὃ δὴ κἂν ἑτέραις ἴσως ἤρκεσε μόνον, προσλαβὸν καί τινα τοπικὴν δυσχέρειαν σύμμαχον, οἷα δὴ τὰ πολλὰ μηχανᾶσθαι εἰώθασι·

already attempted to benefit their own cultivation from the excellence of ours and to make it prosper by taking shoots of this country as a starting point to produce something almost as good.

7. And we may introduce this moderate number of things from the outside into our discussion of the city. But what is her own proper crown, and in all ways, I know not whether it is better to say the last or the first, unshakable boundary of her prosperity — who would not be astounded to look upon these walls around her, which draw so much confidence from their construction that the effort of every kind of engine against them is of no use but a wholly vain spending of time on the impossible? The form of the city is circular, the most capacious that exists. She disdains every inequality lying near her and makes it a point of honour to join them together; not the way most towns cheat at the rough ground and take advantage of its steepness. But she, well disposed toward mankind and regularly built, relies on herself and her external circuits, so finely constructed that it is at once a pleasure and a marvel to behold their undeceived foresight, their great unconquerable beauty, their splendid barrier. Such is the unyielding strength of the whole construction from the arrangement of its materials and such are the towers in it: they strive upward, trusting in their foundations; below, they stand forward from the continuous line of defense, and meet the enemy as champions unwearied and unmoved. And their friendliness to one another and unwillingness to stand far apart might look to you like some surrounding circle of dancers, orderly and very pleasing for the city to enjoy from within, yet armed, if an enemy approach them from outside, and unsociable for him to meet with. So generous is the city in these matters that, as you can see, it also places another circuit a little in front of the first; this by itself might have been enough for other towns, taking some difficult ground as an ally, as they devise in most cases. But

τῇ δὲ οὐδ' οὕτως ἀπέχρησεν ἡ περὶ τὸ ἀσφαλὲς περιουσία,
30 οὐ μὴν οὐδ' ἐνέλειφεν εἰς τοῦτο καινοτομεῖν· ἀλλ' ἔτι σοι
πρὸ τούτου τάφρος ὑποτείνει βαθεῖα, ἰλύος πλέως, ἣν σοφιζομένη τὴν αἴσθησιν ὑποκρύπτει καὶ θησαυρίζει τοῖς ἀπροό-
πτως ἐμπίπτουσιν.

8. Ἀλλὰ τί ταῦθ' ὁ λόγος ἔξωθεν ἔτι τῆς πόλεως διατρίβει
καὶ οὐκ εἰσχωρεῖ; Οἷα δὴ παραχρῆμα ταῦτα πάντοθεν προσ-
βάλλει θαυμάζειν, μῆκος τοσοῦτον ὅσον ταῖς πρώταις τῶν
πόλεων ἀρκεῖν, τῷ συνεχεῖ τῶν ἐπικειμένων οἰκοδομημά-
5 των ἐνδεέστερον ἔχειν ἑαυτοῦ δοκοῦν, ὧν τὰ πλείω καὶ πρὸς
τὸν ἀέρα φιλονεικεῖ καὶ τὴν περιουσίαν τῆς τέχνης ἐπίδειξιν
ἐκ μετεώρου ποιεῖται, περιττῶς ἠσκημένα· ἀλλὰ μὴν καὶ βα-
λανείων ἄφθονος ἀπόλαυσις, καὶ πρόσεστιν ἡ χάρις προστιθεῖσα τῇ χρείᾳ τὸ τρυφᾶν· ἃ δὲ τῆς κρείττονος ὄντως πολι-
10 τείας ἐνταῦθα πρόσεστιν, ᾗ που πολὺς μὲν ὁ κόσμος, μείζων
δὲ ἡ ὄνησις· ταῦτα δὴ ταῦτα λέγω τὰ τῶν καμνόντων ἐν
νόσοις μετὰ τῆς πενίας κοινὰ καταγώγια, ὧν οὐ μᾶλλον τὸ
κάλλος τῶν οἰκοδομημάτων ἔστι θαυμάζειν ἢ τὴν ὁμολο-
γίαν τῆς φυσικῆς ἀσθενείας αἰδεῖσθαι καὶ τὴν συναίσθησιν,
15 καὶ τὴν κατ' ἄμφω τοῦ γένους φιλανθρωπίαν, τήν τε ἐπὶ τῇ
νόσῳ παρὰ τῆς τέχνης ἐπικουρίαν καὶ τὴν τῆς πενίας παρα-
μυθίαν, καὶ ταύτην δίχα νενεμημένην τοῖς τε ὑπὸ τῆς ἱερᾶς
νόσου πάντα τὸν βίον ἑαυτῶν ἀπογνοῦσι, καὶ τὸ μόνον κοινὸν
ἰατρεῖον τῆς φυσικῆς ἡμῶν οὐκ οἶδ' εἴτε ἀσθενείας εἴτε κου-
20 φότητος χρὴ λέγειν, ἀπολέσασι τὰς ἐλπίδας, καὶ τοῖς μετ'
αὐτῶν ἔτι σὺν ἀπορίᾳ κάμνουσι, τῶν τε ξένων καὶ ὅστις ἐγχώ-
ριος· κατ' ἀμφότερα γὰρ ἡ βασιλικὴ φιλανθρωπία τὸν οἶκτον
μερίζει, καὶ νικᾷ τῇ μεγαλοψυχίᾳ τὴν χρείαν, τά τε ἄλλα
τιμῶσα τὴν πόλιν τοῖς γιγνομένοις καὶ ἔτι ὑπόμνησιν ἑαυτῶν
25 εἶναι, καὶ μηδὲν πλέον τῆς σωματικῆς ταπεινώσεως φρονεῖν.

as for her, the excellent care taken for security is not thus satisfied nor has she failed to innovate in this, but even in front of this, as you see, stretches a deep ditch filled with mud, which, cleverly contrived, she hides from sight and treasures up for those who unexpectedly fall in.

8. But why is my speech still spending time outside the city and not coming in? Since the city offers at once, on every side, objects to be admired—a size so great as to suffice for the first among cities, yet which seems to be inadequate for its own self from the continuity with which the buildings join one another, the greatest number of them striving upwards into the air and making display from on high of the superiority of their art, being most excellently wrought. There is also plentiful enjoyment of baths, with a charm that adds luxury to utility. And what a truly excellent government has added is of great beauty and greater use. This, this I mean—the common shelters for those who are suffering in illness joined to poverty; we ought not to marvel more at the fineness of their buildings than to respect their confession of our natural weakness, their understanding, and their charity in both kinds: in the assistance given to illness by art and in the consolation of poverty. This help is provided separately to those who have entirely despaired of their own lives under the effects of the sacred disease, and have lost that only universal remedy—I know not whether one ought to say for the weakness or the lightness of our nature—their hopes, and even to those along with them who are suffering from poverty, both strangers and natives: for to both does the royal charity grant a share in its compassion. And it excels the necessary in its generosity, and in other ways honours the city by what is done in it and further reminds us of ourselves that we not lift our thoughts above the humility of our bodily state.

9. Τὰ δὲ δὴ σεμνὰ ταῦτα τοῦ κάλλους ἀγάλματα, αἱ περιφανεῖς στῆλαι τῆς καθ' ἡμᾶς φιλοσοφίας, οἱ ταύτης καρποί, τὰ λαμπρὰ καὶ φιλότιμα τέλη, τὰ ἱερὰ φροντιστήρια τῶν ἑλομένων τῆς ὕλης ἀναχωρεῖν καὶ μόνῳ σχολάζειν θεῷ, τίνος ἂν ἑτέρας εἴη πόλεως τοσαῦτα ἢ οὕτως ἔχοντα παραθεῖναι; τοῦτο μὲν ἀνδρῶν, τοῦτο δὲ καὶ τῆς ἑτέρας μερίδος, μεγαλοψύχως τὴν αὐτὴν ἀνελομένων σπουδήν, ὧν τὸ περὶ τὴν αἵρεσιν φιλόπονον, καὶ ὅση τις ἡ περὶ αὐτήν, τοῖς μὲν ἁπαλοῖς ἔτι καὶ τῶν καιρῶν ἐνδεῶς ἔχουσιν ἡ παρασκευή, τοῖς δὲ τῶν χρόνων ἀπολαύσασιν ἡ τελείωσις· μεγάλη μὲν ἡ τῆς δόξης αὕτη προσθήκη τῇ πόλει καὶ μείζων ἴσως τῶν ὄντων· οὐ μὴν ἀλλ' οὐκ ἐμὸν ταῦτα προφέρειν καὶ ἱστοροῦντα διατρίβειν· ὡς ἐγὼ δέδοικα μὲν σφόδρα ἧττον ἔχων, ἢ ὡς τῶν ὄντων ἐγγὺς γενέσθαι, αἰσχύνομαι δὲ γέλωτα ὀφλῆσαι τοῖς συνεσομένοις, οὕτως ἔχων, ἔπειτα τοῖς τοιούτοις ἐπιχειρῶν προσάγειν τὸν λόγον· ὅτι δὲ καὶ πλῆθος ὅσον οὐκ ἄλλῃ τῶν τε οὕτω βιοῦν ᾑρημένων καὶ αὐτῶν δὴ τῶν θείων οἴκων, ἐν οἷς ἡ μεγαλόφρων αἵρεσις αὕτη φιλοσοφεῖται, καὶ κάλλος τῶν πλειόνων οἷον ἀμήχανον ἐρεῖν, πολλή τε τρυφὴ τοῖς ὀφθαλμοῖς ὁρᾶν, καὶ τῷ λόγῳ πάντως περὶ ταῦτ' ἔχειν ἀκίνδυνον.

10. Αὐτίκα πολλὴ μὲν ἡ περὶ τοὺς θείους νεὼς εὐμήχανος παρὰ τῆς δημιουργίας ἀσφάλεια, πολλὴ δὲ ἡ ἐπανθοῦσα χάρις· ὄροφος μὲν ἄνωθεν ἁβρῶς ἠσκημένος, χρυσοῦ τε αὐγαῖς καὶ τοῖς ἐκ βαφῶν ἄνθεσι, τὴν πᾶσαν ποικιλίαν ἐνταῦθα δαπανώσης τῆς τέχνης· ταῦτα δ' ἐπὶ πολὺ κάτεισιν ἐφ' ἑκάτερα· διαδέχεται δὲ ποικίλης λίθου διαύγεια, πρὸς τὴν ἄνω χάριν ἐπειγομένη τῇ παντοίᾳ τῆς χρόας ἑτερότητι, συνεργούσης τῆς τέχνης καὶ σοφιζομένης τὴν ἀναλογίαν τῆς ἁρμονίας· τὸ δ' αὐτὸ κάτωθεν καὶ τὸ ἔδαφος ταῖς αὐταῖς ποικιλίαις ὑφαίνεται· ἔδει γὰρ εἶναι πάντα τοῖς ἄνω τὰ ἐντεῦ-

9. And then, these reverend treasures of beauty, the illustrious monuments of the wisdom of our times, the fruits of it, its brilliant and superb rites, the holy places of meditation for those who have chosen to withdraw from material things and to give their time only to God; what other city could compare in having so many or such kinds of them? Some are of men and some of the other part of mankind, both having generously taken up the same endeavour; whose chosen life is a laborious one, in proportion to the work of preparation required of those yet tender who have not yet fulfilled much time, and to the perfection of those who have had the enjoyment of their years. This is a great addition to the reputation of the city, greater, perhaps, than any other. But it is not for me to bring these things forward and go on discussing them, since I fear being much too weak to come close to their reality, and am ashamed to provoke the laughter of those who shall be with me, when I, being such as I am, shall then attempt to direct my speech to such subjects. But, that there is such a number here as nowhere else of those who have chosen to live thus, and of the holy dwellings themselves in which this same high-minded choice of life is meditated; and that the beauty of most of them is such as is impossible to describe; that is a great pleasure for the eyes to see, and there can be no danger for a speech in dwelling upon it.

10. Turning now at once to the holy churches, great is the ingenious security they derive from their workmanship, and great is the beauty that blossoms upon them. The ceiling is delicately worked above, with gleams of gold and the flowers of pigment — art has expended there its every ornament; and this same decoration descends far on each side, It is succeeded by the brilliancy of variegated stones, closely rivalling the beauty above by the multiplicity of color; skill cooperates with this, making use of the regularity of arrangement; and likewise below, the floor also is woven with the same diversity; for it

θεν ἐφάμιλλα· στοαὶ δὲ ὑπαλάττουσι, ταῖς ὑφισταμέναις κίοσιν ἔχουσαι τὸ θαρρεῖν, καὶ προαρπάζειν φιλονεικοῦσαι τὴν ἕδραν, τὴν ἐντυγχάνουσαν ἀπαντῶσιν ὄψιν· κίονές τε ἀνατείνουσιν ἐν μέσῳ, αἱ μὲν τὸν ὄγκον αἱ δὲ τὴν ἔνδειαν παρεχόμεναι
15 θαυμάζειν, τὸ μὲν φυσικῆς περιουσίας, τὸ δὲ τεχνικῆς οἰκονομίας ἐπίδειξιν· κορυφαὶ τούτων καὶ βάσεις μυρίαν ὑπέχουσαι τὴν ἀπὸ τῆς τέχνης τομήν· καὶ ὁ διὰ πλοῦτον κάλλους πάντα τυραννούμενος χρυσός, κἀνταῦθα ὠθούμενος, πάντα φαιδρά, πάντα ἀλλήλοις ἀναλογεῖ. Καὶ οὔπω προσέθηκα θείων
20 εἰκόνων λαμπρότητας, κἀνταῦθα τῶν πολυτελῶν λίθων τιμίαν ὄντως τὴν χρείαν, καὶ τὸν χρυσὸν αὖθις εἰς κόσμον βιαζόμενον· καὶ σεπτῶν ἀναθημάτων εὐσέβειαν, πολυτάλαντα σκεύη, καὶ βίβλων ἱερῶν θησαυρούς.

11. Ἃ δὲ ἐξιόντι τοῦ νεὼ παραχρῆμα ἀπαντᾷ, ᾗ που πολλὴ χάρις, ὁρᾶν ἔνθεν μὲν λειμῶνας κεχυμένους, ἔνθεν δὲ φυτῶν εὐκαρπίαν τε ὁμοῦ καὶ πολυκαρπίαν, καὶ ἔτι τὴν ἐνίων ἀγονίαν ἐνταῦθα εἰσφέρουσαν· καὶ γὰρ ἄκαρπον μὲν ἀλλ' ἰθυτενὲς
5 ἡ κυπάριττος καὶ εἰς οὐρανοὺς ἀναχωροῦν, ἐμοὶ δοκεῖν ἀτεχνῶς ὑποδεικνύει τοῖς ἐκεῖ φιλοσοφοῦσιν, ὅποι δεῖ τρέχειν καὶ ἀνατείνεσθαι, μετὰ τῆς ἀνόδου καταβραχὺ τὰ περιττὰ τῆς ὕλης ἀποτιθεμένους καὶ στενουμένους πρὸς τὴν ἀνάβασιν. Πάρεστι δὲ καὶ ὑδάτων θαυμάζειν ἐπιρροίας, ὅσας τε
10 δαψιλῶς ἡ γῆ χορηγεῖ, καὶ ὅσας ἐπὶ τῇ φύσει μηχανᾶται τέχνη, τὰς ἀναδόσεις ἐκ μετεώρου σοφιζομένη. Καὶ σιγῆσαί μοι τὰ πλείω δοκῶ, ὅσα τοῖς ἐνοικοῦσιν ἐγγίνεται τῆς φυσικῆς ἀσθενείας ἀναψυχή, καὶ τῷ κατὰ τὴν ἔφεσιν ἀλόγῳ τῆς ψυχῆς ἐνδίδωσι τρυφῇ σχολάζειν καθαρωτέρα, τοῦ λογισμοῦ κά-
15 μνοντος καὶ προσβραχὺ τῶν πόνων μεθιεμένου. Καὶ ταῦτα μὲν μέτρια πάνυ τῶν ὑπαρχόντων.

was right that everything there should rival what is above. And the colonnades then follow, drawing their security from the columns under them, and, jealously seizing the advantage of position, deceive the sight that encounters them. And columns stretch upward in the middle as well, some offering their mass, others their slenderness to be admired—the one displaying the richness of nature, the other the economy of art—with their capitals and bases presenting the endless varieties of carving that are found in art. And gold, that usurps the sovereignty over all things by its wealth of beauty, being there inlaid, makes all things brilliant, and all like to one another. And I have not yet added the splendours of the divine images, and the truly honorable use there made of precious stones, and again gold compelled to serve for decoration; and the pious respect evidenced by the holy offerings, and the precious vessels, and the stores of sacred books.

11. And what meets one on leaving the church, and a very pleasant thing it is, is to see on one side meadows spread out and on another an excellent and a rich growth of trees; and to see even the unproductiveness of some there make its contribution. For an unfruitful thing, yet a straight-standing one, is the cypress, which in rising even to the skies, as it seems to me, proclaims without artifice to those who meditate there the way in which they are to walk and strive upward, laying aside gradually as they go up the excess of their material part and growing thinner as they rise. And one may there admire streams of water, both those that the earth plentifully supplies and those that art has added to nature, inventing the means of making them spring forth from above. And I seem to myself to be leaving untold the greatest part of all that those who dwell there possess by way of relief from the weakness of nature, and of giving to the speechless desires of the soul the chance to pass the time in a purer kind of enjoyment, when reason falls sick and gradually gives way from its toil. And this is a very moderate part of what is there.

12. Παρῆκα δὲ τῶν ἄλλων ναῶν πλήθη καὶ κόσμους, οἳ διὰ πάσης τῆς πόλεως ἵστανται, κάλλους περιουσία, ὑπόμνησις ἀρετῆς, τῆς κοινῆς εὐσεβείας ἀρραγεῖς σύνδεσμοι, ὧν εἴ μοι βουλομένῳ σχολὴ προσῆν ἕνα τῶν πάντων τῷ λόγῳ προθεῖ-
5 ναι σπουδῆς ὑπόθεσιν, καὶ εἰ βούλει τοῦτον δὴ τὸν ἐπὶ τῇ κλήσει φρονοῦντα τοῦ γενναίου τὴν ἄθλησιν Τρύφωνος, ὅπως μὲν μεγέθους, ὅπως δὲ ὥρας ἔχει, μέγιστον ἔργον ἂν ἦν διαγενέσθαι καὶ τῶν ὄντων μὴ πάνυ τοι ἐνδεῶς ἀνῦσαι. Καί τοι τί τοῦτο παρελθεῖν ὁ λόγος ἐπείγεται; τέρας ἡδονῇ σύμμικτον
10 καὶ ἅμα δόξης ἀφορμὴν τῇ πόλει, οὐκ οἶδ' ὡς εἴ τι τῶν ἄλλων, ὅπως ἔτους ἑκάστου τῷ καιρῷ τῆς μνήμης, ἐκ τῶν ἄνω λειμώνων ὁ μάρτυς μετὰ τῶν ἀνθέων ἐνταῦθα γίνεται, καὶ προβάλλεται θαυμάζειν αὐτόματα ὡραῖα, λειμώνων ἀερίας, μᾶλλον δὲ ἄνευ λειμώνων ἄνθη, ἄνευ ῥίζης καρπούς· καὶ
15 τοῦτο δεῖγμα μὲν τῆς περὶ τὴν πόλιν σπουδῆς τοῦ μάρτυρος, δεῖγμα δὲ εὐσεβείας αὐτῷ, δι' ἣν ἡ σπουδή· τοῖς μὲν γὰρ ἐνταῦθα τὴν τῶν ἔργων ἐπίδειξιν ποιουμένοις, ἔνθα ἢ πατρίς, ἢ χρονία διατριβή, ἢ τὸ τελευταῖον τοῦτο, τοῦ μακαρίου τέλους ἐπιτυχία πρόσεστιν ἕλκουσα, κἂν ἀνάγκην εἶναι
20 τῇ φιλοτιμίᾳ φαίη τις τὴν παλαιὰν κοινωνίαν, κἂν ἀντίδοσιν ταῦτα τῆς ἡγησαμένης τύχης τῇ μεγαλοψυχίᾳ νικῶσαν· ὅταν δὲ πάντα ἀπῇ, καθάπερ ἀμέλει νῦν ἔχει τῷ μάρτυρι καὶ τῇ πόλει, τί τις ἂν λέγοι ἢ ὅτι χάριτος εἶναι μόνον, καὶ χάριτος τῇ εὐσεβείᾳ πάντως προσμαρτυρούσης;

13. Ἀλλ' ἐπειδήπερ εὐσεβείας ἐμνήσθην, τίς οὐκ οἶδε καὶ τῶν πάντα ἀμαθῶς ἐχόντων, ὅτι τοσοῦτον περίεστιν ἐνταῦθα τῇ πόλει φρονεῖν, ὡς ἐντεῦθεν οὖσαν τοῖς ἄλλοις ἅπασι τὴν πηγὴν τῶν τῆς ἀληθείας δογμάτων, καὶ τὴν ἀρχὴν καὶ τὴν
5 ὑπόθεσιν ὅπως ἄρα ἔχει περὶ τῶν θείων ὀρθῶς νομίζειν; καὶ πάρεστιν ἡ δεῖξις ἐγγὺς αὕτη, ὅτι πρῶτος συνασπισμὸς ἐπὶ

12. And I have passed by the number and the ornaments of the other churches which stand through all the city — a wealth of beauty, a reminder of virtue, the unbreakable bonds of public piety. If, as I wish, I had the time to bring forward in this speech one out of all of them as an object of our attention — and, if you like, this one which by its name recalls Tryphon, noble in his sufferings — how great and how beautiful it is — it would have been a very great work to get through it and not to treat it in a way which falls entirely short of reality. And why does my speech haste to pass this by? This miracle, at once infused with pleasure, and such a source of reputation to the city as I do not know what other, how every year, on the occasion of the commemoration, the martyr comes here with his flowers from the meadows above and offers to our admiration self-growing fruits of meadows in the air; or rather flowers without meadows, and fruits without root. And this is a sign of the martyr's care for the city, and a sign of the reverence for him which is the cause of his care. Of those who display their works in a place to which their birth, their long stay, or finally their presence at the time of their blessed demise draws them, one might say their long association requires of them these ambitious efforts, and that these efforts are a repayment, exceeding in generosity the benefit they think they have received. But when all this is wanting, as it certainly now is in the case of the martyr and this city, what should one say, but that it comes of grace only, and of a grace that testifies to the piety of those who receive it?

13. But since I have mentioned piety, who is there, even of the wholly ignorant, who does not know that this city possesses great ground for pride in this, that the spring of the dogmas of the truth has flowed from here to all the rest of mankind, and the beginning and the foundation for how one may rightly think of divinity? And the proof is near at hand, in that the

γῆς κατὰ τῶν ἀποστατῶν τοῦ Χριστοῦ, πρώτη παράταξις ἀληθείας κατὰ τῶν τοῦ ψεύδους προμάχων, ἐνταῦθα συνέστη, καὶ τὸ ἀλλότριον ἅπαν καὶ δύσνουν ἐξέτεμε τῇ μαχαίρᾳ τοῦ
10 πνεύματος· τῆς γὰρ Ἀρείου δυσσεβείας τὸ θράσος ἀπ' Αἰγύπτου μὲν τὴν ἀρχήν, κατὰ πάσης ἐπανέστη τῆς οἰκουμένης, καὶ ὥσπερ τι νόσημα δεινὸν ὑφέρπον, περιλαβεῖν ἤδη τὸ καλὸν ἐφιλονείκει σῶμα τῆς ἐκκλησίας· ἐνταῦθα δὲ ἔστη, καὶ ἤλεγκται τῇ πόλει, ἧττον ἔχον ἢ περιγενέσθαι καὶ πάντα
15 ἄρδην ἀνατρέψαι τὰ καλῶς κείμενα· ὁ γὰρ δὴ μέγας ἐκεῖνος τῆς εὐσεβείας, οὐκ οἶδα εἴτε διδάσκαλος εἴτε ὑπηρέτης χρὴ λέγειν, ὁ βασιλεύσας πρῶτος μετὰ Χριστοῦ, ἔγνωκέ τινα συμμαχίαν καταστῆσαι ταῖς αὐτὸς αὑτοῦ πράξεσι, καὶ πάντοθεν εἰς ἓν ἀγαγὼν τοὺς τοῦ θείου πνεύματος ὑποφήτας, μίαν δὴ
20 ταύτην ἀγωνίαν ἀναγκαίαν εἰς μέσον προθεῖναι, τῇ τε ἐκκλησίᾳ τὴν ἀσφάλειαν ἀποδοῦναι τῆς περὶ θεοῦ δόξης, καὶ τὸ ἐπίβουλον ἅπαν καὶ νόθον, ἐπισχεῖν τε καὶ ἀποθέσθαι· μόνην δὲ ἀρκοῦσαν τῷ σκοπῷ καὶ τῇ χρείᾳ τήνδε τὴν πόλιν ᾠήθη, καὶ μόνην ἀξίαν χωρῆσαι τόν τε ὄγκον τῆς παρούσης σπου-
25 δῆς καὶ τῆς ἐσομένης ἐντεῦθεν τὸν ἑξῆς πάντα χρόνον ἀγαθῆς τύχης· καὶ οὐκ ἴσχυσαν ἀνθελέσθαι τὴν κρίσιν τόσαι μὲν ἐπὶ τῆς γῆς πόλεις, τόσαι δὲ ἐπ' αὐτῆς μάλιστα τῆς θαλάττης τῆς τῶν Ῥωμαίων ἡγεμονίας, τῷ τῆς οἰκουμένης σχεδὸν μήκει τηνικαῦτα συμμετρουμένης· καὶ οὐκ ἔγνω μὲν οὕτω
30 περὶ ταύτης μεγαλοψύχως, οὐκ ἐπέθηκε δὲ παραχρῆμα τὸ τέλος, ἀλλ' εὐθὺς πάντα ἠρευνᾶτο καὶ πάντα εἰσέφερε καὶ συνετέλει τῇ πόλει τὸν καλὸν τοῦτον ἔρανον.

14. Ἐν ἐκείνοις τοίνυν τοῖς χρόνοις ἐπεστάτει μὲν τῆς οἰκουμένης ἡ πόλις καὶ θειοτέραν ὄντως ἐπιστασίαν, προσεῖχον δὲ πᾶσαι καὶ ἅμα ἔπεμπον εὐσεβείας συνθήματα δέχεσθαι· ἐπεὶ δὲ ὁ Φαραὼ τὸν ἄξιον ὄλεθρον ὑπέστη τοῦ θράσους, καὶ ἡ ἀκρό-
5 τομος ἐρράγη καὶ ἀνέδωκεν ἀφθόνους τὰς τῆς ἀληθείας ῥοάς, καὶ ἡ κιβωτὸς οὐκέτι συνέκρυψε τὰς πλάκας, ἀλλ' ἠνοίγη

first gathering in arms on earth against those who rebelled from Christ, the first marshalling of truth against the champions of falsehood, was here assembled, and here cut away every alien and hostile element with the sword of the spirit. For the daring impiety of Arius had its beginning from Egypt, and it rose up over all the world, and, like some dreadful disease creeping upon it, already struggled to seize the lovely body of the church. Here it came to a stand and was convicted by this city, being too weak to overcome it and totally overturn what had been rightly established. For that great man of piety—I do not know if he should be called teacher or servant—he that first was emperor with Christ, resolved to form a kind of alliance of the church with his own affairs, and, bringing together from all parts the interpreters of the divine spirit, set before them this one necessary object of their efforts, to restore to the church the security of its opinion concerning God, and to grasp and remove everything that was hostile or spurious. And he judged this city alone capable of meeting his aim and the need, and alone able to bear the weight of the effort he then made, and of the good effect that was to come of it for all future time. And all the cities of the Roman empire, which at that time was nearly equal in extent to the inhabited world, had not strength to contend against this judgment, whether those in the land or still more those on the sea itself. He did not make this judgment of her from generosity nor bring it suddenly to completion, but at once investigated everything, and brought everything together, and contributed this splendid feast to the city.

14. In those times, indeed, this city presided over the world and with a truly divine presidency, while all others attended her and sent to her to receive the agreed teachings of religion. And when Pharaoh underwent the destruction his boldness had deserved; and the cliff was split, and poured out plentifully the streams of truth; and the ark no longer concealed the tables,

καὶ προέθετο παρρησίᾳ τοὺς θείους νόμους, καὶ ὁ ταμίας τῆς
ἁρμονίας ὑπέκρουσεν ἀρχὴν ἐμμελοῦς συμφωνίας, τηνικαῦτα ἦν ὁμοῦ πάντα χρήματα, πρόχειρος μὲν ἀπόλαυσις
10 τῶν ἐντεῦθεν τῆς εὐσεβείας ῥευμάτων, ὅστις βούλεται χρῆσθαι, πανταχοῦ δὲ ἀνακήρυξις καὶ διάδοσις τῶν θείων τῆς
ἀληθείας ὅρων· καὶ τέλος ἡ παγκόσμιος αὕτη λύρα μετὰ τὴν
ἐντεῦθεν ἀφορμὴν καὶ κίνησιν πρώτην, πάντα ἁρμοζομένη
καλῶς καὶ πρὸς τὴν ἀσφαλῆ περὶ θεοῦ δόξαν ἐμμελῶς συμ-
15 φωνοῦσα· αὕτη τῶν ὅλων τῆς ἐκκλησίας δογμάτων ἀρχὴ καὶ
κατάστασις πρώτη, τοῦτο τῆς καθ' ἡμᾶς εὐσεβείας τὸ στή-
ριγμα· ἐπὶ ταύταις ταῖς ὑποθέσεσιν, ἐπὶ ταύτῃ τῇ βάσει τῶν
ἑξῆς ἡ δημιουργία, καὶ ἡ πρὸς τοὺς κατὰ καιροὺς ἀποστά-
τας τῆς ἀληθείας ἀντικατάστασις.

15. Τοῖς μὲν οὖν πολλοῖς ἴσως ἂν ἔδοξεν, ἐνταῦθα εἶναι τὸ
πέρας τῶν ἀγαθῶν, καὶ ἀποχρώντως ἔχειν τῇ τε πόλει τῆς
περὶ ταῦτα φιλοτιμίας τῶν ἔργων, καὶ τῷ λόγῳ τῆς ἱστορίας,
ὡς οὐκ ἄδηλον ὂν τὴν πᾶσαν ἑξῆς ἀκολουθίαν τῆς εὐσεβείας
5 εἶναι τῆς ἐνταῦθα τῇ πόλει δεδομένης ἀρχῆς· καὶ γὰρ ἱκανῶς
ἔχειν τοῖς τε ἄλλοις οὕτω λογίζεσθαι καὶ κρίνειν, καὶ ἔτι τῷ
λόγῳ νῦν πρὸς τοῖς ἄλλοις· ἀλλ' ἡ πόλις οὕτω τοι παρῆλθε
τῇ μεγαλοψυχίᾳ καὶ διὰ πάντων ἐγένετο σαφῶς ἑαυτῆς ποιου-
μένη τε καὶ συνάπτουσα, ὥστε καὶ τὰ δεύτερα κρείττω πάσης
10 ἐπιθεῖναι προσδοκίας, καὶ τὸ τέλος τῆς ὅλης κατὰ τῶν αἱρε-
τικῶν ἀγωνίας καὶ μάχης ἐπαγαγεῖν. Ἐπεὶ γὰρ ἔδει καὶ τὴν
τελευταίαν ταύτην ἀκολουθῆσαι ταῖς προλαβούσαις ἓξ τῶν
ἱερῶν διδασκάλων σύστασιν, ποῦ μᾶλλον ἔδει ἢ ἔνθα τὸ τῆς
εὐσεβείας ἀσφαλὲς ταμεῖον, ἔνθα ἡ πρώτη τῆς ὑγιαινούσης
15 πίστεως πῆξις; καὶ μέντοι σύνοιδε τὸ δέον ὁ χρόνος καὶ προσα-
πέδοτο τῇ πόλει καὶ ταύτην, μᾶλλον δὲ τῇ ἐκκλησίᾳ καὶ ταύτην ἡ πόλις ἀπέδοτο· καὶ ὑπέθετο μὲν τέως τὴν βάσιν καὶ
τὴν ἀρχὴν τῆς ὅλης περὶ ταῦτα κινήσεως, ἐπήνεγκε δὲ τὴν
ἐπὶ πᾶσι κορυφήν, καὶ τελευταίαν συνοχὴν καὶ ἀσφάλειαν·
20 καὶ εἰ δή τις μέγα οἴεται, πάντως δὲ μέγιστον, τὴν πρώτην

but was opened, and freely gave forth the divine laws; and the steward of harmony first conducted the melodious agreement of voices; then there were all good things at once, first, the ready enjoyment of the streams of piety that flowed from here, for whoever wanted to use them; and everywhere the proclamation and transmission of the divine definitions of truth; and finally this universal lyre, which had from here its beginning and first movement, arranged everything well, and sounded in beautiful unison towards the safe and sure belief concerning God. This was the beginning and first settlement of the whole dogma of the church, this is the support of religion in our times. On these premises, on this base, stands the workmanship of those who came after and their defence against those who at times have rebelled against the truth.

15. To most people it might have seemed that the limit of good things was here, and that the town had enough of the pride of such achievements, and that my speech had history enough, since it was evident that the whole succession of religion in after times came from the start given here by this city; for there was enough to make other people reason and judge thus, as well as for the present speech in addition. But this city has so far exceeded in greatness of spirit, and has altogether visibly acted and continued to act like herself, as to have added a second prize, greater than all expectation, and to put an end to the whole conflict and battle against the heretics. Since this last assembly was destined to follow the six preceding ones of the holy teachers, where rather than here should the safe storehouse of religion have been placed, the site of the first fixing of our salutary faith? Indeed time is conscious of what is right, and gave this assembly also to the city — or rather, the city gave this also to the church. And, as it laid the base and the beginning of the whole movement in this matter, so it added what is in every way its finishing touch, and its final bond of union and security. And so, if one thinks it a great thing

τῆς ἀληθείας φανέρωσιν παρέσχεν ἡ πόλις· καὶ εἴ τις τὴν ὑστέ-
ραν αὖθις σφραγῖδα καὶ διὰ τὸ πάντων κῦρος, καὶ τοῦτο μετὰ
τῆς πόλεως.

16. Τοῖς δὲ παλαιοῖς κομιδῇ καὶ τὰ νέα συμβαίνει· τῶν γὰρ
δὴ προτέρων χρόνων, ὅτε καὶ τὰ Ῥωμαίων τῆς ἐπὶ θάτερα
ῥοπῆς ᾔσθετο καὶ μετέβαλε τῆς πρῴην εὐδαιμονίας, καὶ πόλις
μὲν ἐκείνη προϊσταμένη καὶ τῶν ἄλλων τὸ κράτος ἔχουσα
5 δουλεύειν ἔγνω τῇ τύχῃ, ἐτράπη δὲ ἡ τῆς ὅλης ἡγεμονίας
παραχρῆμα εὐκληρία, κἀντεῦθεν ἐνόσει, τὰ μὲν εἴχετο, τὰ
δὲ ἐκινδύνευε, τὰ δὲ προσεδοκᾶτο· πάντα ἦν ὁμοῦ τὰ δεινά·
στάσεις τῶν οἰκείων, τῶν κύκλῳ βαρβάρων ἐπιθέσεις μετὰ
τοῦ καιροῦ, καὶ ἔτι πρὸ πάντων κίνησις αὕτη δὴ μεγίστη τῶν
10 ἐπὶ παντὸς τοῦ κόσμου πραγμάτων ἐδόκει γίγνεσθαι· καὶ ἅμα
δέος οὐ βραχὺ τὴν κρείττω καὶ σεμνοτέραν τῶν ἐπὶ γῆς ἀρχὴν
ἄρδην ἀνάρπαστον γενέσθαι καὶ ἀνῃρῆσθαι· ἆρ' οὐκ ἔδεισεν
ἂν τηνικαῦτα περὶ τῇδε τῇ πόλει, μήπου τι καὶ αὕτη μετὰ
τῶν πραγμάτων γένηται καὶ τῆς κοινῆς σὺν ταῖς ἄλλαις
15 αἴσθηται τύχης· ἡ δὲ οὕτω γενναίως ἀντέσχε τῇ δυσχερεῖ
φορᾷ, μᾶλλον δὲ ὑπερέσχε καὶ διεγένετο, ὥστε μὴ μόνον ἀντὶ
ἀκροπόλεως κατέστη τοῖς ὅλοις τῶν Ῥωμαίων πράγμασιν,
ἀσμένως ὑποδεξαμένη προσχωρήσασαν τὴν βασιλικὴν ἐπι-
στασίαν· καὶ τέως μὲν συστῆναι χαρισαμένη, τὰ δ' ἑξῆς καὶ
20 τοῖς οἰκείοις ἐπεξελθεῖν, ἀλλὰ καὶ ἔτι προστιθεῖσα τῆς εὐποιΐας, ἐδέξατο μὲν τὴν τῆς εὐσεβείας ἕδραν, τὸ τῆς ἐκκλησίας
εὔκοσμον σύνταγμα, τὴν πρώτην καὶ τελεωτέραν ὄντως τῶν
καθ' ἡμᾶς πραγμάτων ἀσφάλειαν καὶ συνοχήν, ἐδέξατο δὲ
τοὺς λόγους αὐτοὺς μετὰ τῶν ἄλλων πλανωμένους καὶ κινδυ-
25 νεύοντας.

17. Καί τοι πῶς ἂν ἔδειξε μᾶλλον ἡ πόλις ἑαυτῆς οὖσα, καὶ
τοῦ πάλαι περὶ ταῦτα φρονήματος; ἢ πῶς ἂν μᾶλλον τοῖς τε
οἰκείοις ἐνέπνευσέ τι φρονεῖν ἑαυτῶν ἄξιον, καὶ τοῖς ἐναντίοις

— as really it is the greatest — this city produced the first manifestation of truth; and if one thinks its later renewed sealing and complete confirmation great, this too belongs to the city.

16. With the old, the new wholly corresponds. Since in that time past, when the Roman state felt the balance swing to the other side, and was changed from its earlier prosperity; and when that city which stood in the front and had power over all others resolved to submit to its fate; and the happiness of the whole empire was at once turned aside and thence fell sick with some parts being taken, others endangered, and others expecting to be, terrible things were everywhere at once: civil wars, assaults of the surrounding barbarians at the advantageous moment, and above all else, this greatest revolution of the affairs of the whole world seemed to be happening, and at the same time there was no small fear that the empire, greater and more august than all those on earth, would be wholly taken and destroyed. Would one not then have feared for this our city, that she too might be involved in the events, and feel the common fate together with the others? But she so nobly resisted the tide of evil, or rather overcame and survived it, that she not only was set as a citadel for the whole Roman state, gladly welcoming the imperial presence which had come to her and giving it first the chance to survive and afterward to pursue its own affairs but, adding further to her benefactions, she received the seat of religion, the well-ordered assembly of the church, truly the first and most complete security and bond of union of the affairs of our time; and she received learning itself, which, like everything else, was wandering and in danger.

17. And how could the city better have shown that she was worthy of herself and of her former pride? Or how better have inspired her countrymen to thoughts worthy of themselves, and

ἐνέκοψε τὴν ἄσχετον τοῦ θράσους ὁρμήν, ὡς οὐδὲν ὂν
Ῥωμαίοις δυσχερές, οὐδ' οἷον ἐλλείπειν τῆς πρώτης εὐδαιμονίας, μέχρις ἂν ἡ Νικαέων ὑποδέχηται πόλις, ἢ τοιαῦτα
ἑλομένη καὶ ἀνύσασα, ἐξ ὧν οὐ μόνον ἐστὶν ὅπερ ἔφην, πάντα
ἀσφαλῶς ἔχεσθαι, ἀλλὰ καὶ ἔτι πρόσεστιν αὕτη δόξα, μόνων
εἶναι τῶν πλέον τοῦ μετρίου καὶ αὐτάρκους ὄντων περὶ ταῦτα
μεγαλοψύχως σχολάζειν· τοῦτο τὸ ἔργον ἔθραυσε μὲν τέως
τὰς ἀκρατεῖς τῶν ἐχθρῶν ἐλπίδας, ἐπέσχε δὲ τὸν παντελῆ
τῆς ἀρχῆς ὄλεθρον, διέσωσε δὲ ὑστέρας ἀναβιώσεως σπέρμα-
τα, καὶ γέγονεν ἡ πόλις ὥσπερ ὀπὸς τῇ πάσῃ τῶν Ῥωμαίων
ἡγεμονίᾳ διαλελυμένῃ, καὶ συνῆξεν αὖθις καὶ συνεστήσατο·
τοῦτο τὸ ἔργον ἐμοὶ δοκεῖν οὐχ ὁποίας βούλει τῶν ἐπὶ τῇ
γείτονι θαλάσσῃ φρονουσῶν πόλεων ἀνῦσαι, ὥσπερ δῆτα παρέσχεν ἐπικαίρως εὐεργετῆσαι τὴν σωτηρίαν ἡ ἀνήμερος τὴν
ἀσφάλειαν αὕτη πόλις καὶ μὴ τρυφῶσα τὰ ἐκ θαλάττης.

18. Ἀλλ' ἐπειδὴ χρόνοις ὕστερον Ῥωμαίοις ἐπανῆλθε τὰ
πράγματα, καὶ ἡ κατεσκαμμένη τέως σκηνὴ τοῦ Δαυῒδ αὖθις
συνεπήγνυτο καὶ συνίστατο, καὶ ὁ νόθος καὶ ὑβριστὴς ἡττήθη
καὶ ὑπεχώρησε, καὶ ἡ κιβωτὸς ἐπανῆλθε τῷ Ἰσραήλ, καὶ
ὁ χρόνος φέρων ἀπέδωκε τὸ χρέος οἷς ὤφειλε, τὸν κάλλιστον
κόσμον τῆς ὅλης ἀρχῆς τὴν βασιλίδα τῶν πόλεων, τηνικαῦτα
δὲ καὶ ἡ πόλις, ὥσπερ μήτηρ ἐν καιρῷ χρείας περιποιησαμέ-
νη καὶ συντηρήσασα, ἀπεδίδου μὲν τῇ φιλτάτῃ τὴν καλὴν παρακαταθήκην, τὸν κόσμον τῆς ἐκκλησίας, καὶ προσετίμησε
φιλοτίμως ἐκ τῶν οἰκείων· ἐξέπεμπε δὲ τοὺς λόγους αὐτούς,
ἐξέπεμπε δὲ τὰς καλὰς ἀποικίας, ἀφορμὴν βιοτῆς δευτέρας,
παρέσχε δὲ τεχνῶν χρείαν ἄφθονον, τὰς μὲν συνεκπέμψασα,
τὰς δὲ παρ' αὐτῇ κατασχοῦσα, ὧν ἐνταῦθα μόνον ἡ τῆς ἀσκή-
σεως τελειότης ὑπόμνησιν ἔρωτος ἴσως, καὶ ἅμα χάριν τῆς
τῶν ὅλων εὐποιΐας εἰδέναι· οὐ μὴν ἀλλὰ καὶ τούτων συνεχ-

cut off the irresistible thrust of the boldness of the enemy; as if there was nothing really difficult for the Romans, nor such as to make them fall short of their earlier prosperity, as long as the city of the Nicaeans was their refuge; she who had undertaken and accomplished such things, from which not only was it possible for everything to be safe, as I have said, but also added to that is the reputation that is only for those who are above mere mediocrity and self-sufficiency to give their time generously to such actions. This achievement overthrew the unbridled hopes of the enemy, held back the total ruin of the empire, preserved the seeds of later revival, and the city became, as it were, the life-giving sap to the whole dissolved empire of the Romans, and gathered it together again and assembled it. This work, it seems to me, was not one to be done by any you may wish to name of those cities that are proud of their neighbour the sea; just as indeed it was this city, untamed in its security, and not enervated by what comes from the sea, which opportunely provided the benefit of safety.

18. But when in later times the affairs of the Romans rose again, and the tabernacle of David, till then dismantled, was again fitted together and assembled, and the usurping and violent power was beaten and withdrew, and the ark returned into Israel, and Time brought the fairest ornament of the whole empire, the queen of cities, and paid it back as a debt to those it owed; then this city, having preserved and watched over them like a mother in time of need, restored to her dearly beloved that splendid deposit, the glory of the church, and generously added to it from her own possessions: she sent forth learning itself; she sent forth those splendid colonies, the starting point of renewed life; and she provided a plentiful supply of the arts, sending some along, and keeping others whose perfection is found only here for herself — perhaps as a reminder of affection, and at the same time to show gratitude for all the benefits received — yet even of these she sends the useful products,

πέμπει τὴν χρείαν, καὶ διὰ τῆς ἐνταῦθα μόνον καλλίστης
ἱστουργικῆς κοσμεῖ τὰ βασίλεια· καὶ σιωπῆσαί γε τὰ πλείω
δεῖν ᾠήθην, καὶ τῇ τῆς πόλεως χρήσασθαι μεγαλοψυχίᾳ.
Πάντων δὲ οὕτω μεταδοῦσα, πάντων ὅμως εὐπορεῖ, καὶ οὐδε-
20 μιᾶς ἐνδεῖ τῶν πρώτων ἐν πόλεσιν· ἀλλὰ τὰς μὲν τῷ τῆς
θέσεως ἐπικαίρῳ παρέρχεται, τὰς δὲ τῇ φύσει τῆς γῆς καὶ
τῇ παντοίᾳ τοῦ ἐντεῦθεν φορᾷ, τὰς δὲ τῷ μήκει τοῦ περιβό-
λου, τὰς δὲ τῷ θάρρει, καὶ ἅμα πρόσεστιν ἡ χάρις, τὰς δὲ
τοῖς ἐντὸς κάλλεσι, τὰς δὲ τῷ κοινωφελεῖ τῶν ἐν αὐτῇ πα-
25 λαιῶν τε καὶ νέων φιλανθρώπων ἔργων· πᾶσα δὲ πᾶσι καὶ
ἰδίᾳ ἑκάστῳ τινὶ καὶ πᾶσιν ὁμοῦ.

19. Τὸ δὲ δὴ σὸν τοῦτο, κράτιστε βασιλεῦ, πῶς ἄν τις καὶ
παρέλθοι σιγῇ; μάλιστα μέν, ὅτι σὲ καὶ δεσπότην καὶ κηδεμό-
να πλουτεῖ, καὶ τῆς ἐκ θεοῦ τοσαύτης εὐκληρίας ἀπολαύει
μετὰ τῶν ἄλλων καὶ συνίσταται καὶ προάγεται, καὶ ἔτι ταῖς
5 ἐλπίσιν ἀεὶ τὰ κρείττω θαρρεῖ· ἔπειτα οὐδὲ τοῦτο βραχύ· πῶς
γὰρ οὔ; μέγα μὲν οὖν καὶ πάντων μέγιστον τοῦ κάλλους μαρ-
τύριον ἡ σὴ περὶ τὴν πόλιν σπουδή, ὁ φιλότιμος πόθος, ὁ
ἐκ τῶν λόγων κόσμος ἐπὶ τοῖς ἔργοις. Καὶ ὅτι μὲν τὰ παρόντα
τρυφᾷς καὶ πλείω βούλεσθαι κατάδηλος εἶ· ὅτι δὲ δύνῃ πάντα
10 προστίθης ἑξῆς· τεκμήριον δέ, ἐπιδημεῖς τῇ πόλει, καὶ θερ-
μαίνει μὲν τὸν πόθον ἡ τῶν καλῶν ἔντευξις, προσφέρειν δὲ
νομίζεις καὶ χαρίζεσθαι δῶρα ὁπόσα τοῖς ἐκ γειτόνων ὀχλη-
ροῖς πρόσεστι, καὶ μετάγεις ἐκεῖθεν λείαν φησὶν ὁ λόγος Μυ-
σῶν, ἀνθρώπων μὲν οὐκ εὐαρίθμητον θεραπείαν, μυρίαν δὲ
15 ἵππον, μυρίαν δὲ βοῦν, βοσκήματα δὲ ἄλλα πάντα τόσα καὶ
τόσα, καὶ προσάγεις τῇ πόλει τῶν μεγάλων ἐλπίδων ἐχέγ-
γυα· οὕτω νικᾷς μὲν ἀεὶ τοὺς ἐχθρούς, νικᾷς δὲ τοὺς πρὸ
σοῦ πάντας ἐπὶ τῶν πραγμάτων στάντας, νικᾷς δὲ τὸ μεῖζον

and decorates the imperial palace by the art of weaving, which here only is at its finest. And I have thought right to leave the great part unsaid, and show the same generosity as the city. Having thus shared everything, she is yet well provided of all, and no way falls short of the first among the cities. But she exceeds some of her advantageous site, others by the nature of the land and the crops of all kinds that it bears, others by the length of her circuit, others by its defensive strength — and yet it is attractive as well — others by the beauties she contains, and others by the common utility of the philanthropic establishment she possesses, both old and new — she, as a whole, exceeds in all things, both separately in each one, and in all together.

19. And as for this work of yours, most mighty emperor, how could anyone pass over it in silence? Particularly since she is rich in having you for her lord and protector, and enjoys this so great blessing from God among others, and is established and brought forward, and still grows ever more confident in her hopes. And then this is no small thing — how could it be? It is a great, indeed the greatest of all testimonies of beauty — your own zeal for this city, your generous affection, your adding to your deeds the ornament of speech; and that while you enjoy what there is, you obviously wish it were more, and, since everything is in your power, you make the addition at once. The proof is, that you spend time in the city; the presence of beautiful objects warms the desire for them, and you are accustomed to bring and offer as gifts all that is possessed by our troublesome neighbours. You transport from there, as the saying goes, the plunder of the Mysians — a number of slaves not easy to be counted, innumerable horses, innumerable cattle, and flocks of every other kind in the same quantity — and you bring them to the city as a pledge of great hopes. Thus you ever outdo your enemies, you outdo all those who before you have stood at the head of affairs, and greatest of all you

σαυτόν, ταῖς καθεκάστην ἐπιδόσεσι κρείττων φαινόμενος,
μόνων δὲ τῶν καλῶν γίνῃ, κἀνταῦθα ἁλίσκῃ ὁ πάντα ἀνά-
λωτος, καὶ οὐδὲν οὕτως ἔχει σε τῶν πάντων, ὡς ὁ τῶν ἀγαθῶν ἔρως, ἡ περὶ τὰ κρείττω σπουδή· ἐπεὶ δὲ μετὰ τῶν ἄλλων
καὶ λόγους νικᾷς, καὶ πάντες ἐπίσης καὶ μικροὶ καὶ μείζους
τῶν σῶν ἀπολιμπάνονται πράξεων, τί χρὴ πλείω διατρίβειν
ἐν τούτοις; μόνον εἴης ἐνταῦθα μνημονευθεὶς ὕστερος ἐπὶ πᾶσι
κόσμος τῇ πόλει καὶ τῷ λόγῳ.

outdo yourself, appearing greater every day in your gifts. You belong only to noble actions, and there you, always unconquered, are overcome, and nothing of all things so possesses you as love of the good and eagerness for the better. And since you exceed words, as you do all else, and as all of these, both small and great, are equally left behind by your deeds, why should I spend more time in them? May you only be remembered here as a final glory, added to the rest, for the city and for my speech.

Commentary on Metochites

1. *Excellence of the subject and inadequacy of the speaker.*
The conventional opening for an encomium; compare the introduction to Libanios' *Oration on Antioch* 1, where he remarks that so far he has been silent about the city that bore him. He goes on to say, however (6), that it is the common custom of writers to claim that their talent falls short of the subject. Libanios disclaims such false or real modesty.

11. ἐγκωμίοις: Metochites makes the nature of his speech clear from the beginning.

2. *A speech given in a city before auditors who know it well may be judged with indulgence.*
18. τὸ μέρος: for the meaning of this phrase see Sevcenko (1962) 269ff., with evidence that Metochites was born not in Nicaea as had been supposed from this passage, but in Constantinople.

3. *It is such an enormous task to praise the city adequately that I have no time to treat its earlier history.*
The origin and history of a city normally occupy a large part of an encomium; see Menander 46-58 and Libanios, *Antioch* 12, where he announces his intention to discuss the history as well as the modern greatness of the city and 44-130, about a third of the whole, where he does so. Abridgement of the history is a novelty of this speech.

2. φαινομένοις is an obvious and necessary correction for the φαινόμενος of the printed edition.

14. Although Trajan did not found or rebuild Nicaea, his name was associated with it in Byzantine times. The apocryphal life of Saint Andrew (*Acta Andreae* 323) attributed the walls and adornment of the city to him, and the life of Saint Neophytos 246 mentions a bridge which he built in the vicinity. Neither the historical nor archaeological record suggests that Trajan was a major

benefactor of Nicaea, but the attribution of the walls to him may help to explain the association. Much of Nicaea was destroyed in an earthquake in 123; the city was restored by Hadrian who was honoured as its second founder. His name consequently appears in two prominent inscriptions over the eastern gate, dedications to the Emperor Trajan Hadrian, son of the divine Trajan. It is possible that these inscriptions, which would certainly have been visible in the Middle Ages, were misunderstood and taken to refer not to Hadrian, but to Trajan, after whom he was officially named. It is also possible that the theatre and gymnasium which Pliny mentioned in his letters to Trajan as being in a state of collapse were completed by the emperor and bore dedications to him; if so, they have not survived.

4. The city has a fine site, neither too close to the sea nor too far from it. It has been spared the dangers which afflicted coastal cities in recent times, but still benefits from maritime trade

1. θέσεως: this section corresponds exactly with the precept of Menander 33f. that the site should be the first topic for the encomiast. Libanios, *Antioch* 13-14 likewise began with the site, noting also, 35-41, the advantages of not being directly on the sea.

4. ἀσφάλειαν ... χάριν: Menander specifically ordained (30, 32, 36) that the speaker never lose sight of the twin aspects of pleasure and utility. Metochites faithfully follows the advice.

5. θαλάσσῃ: Relation with the sea is an important part of the description of a site. See Menander 36 on continental and maritime cities, and those which possess the advantages (and have escaped the disadvantages) of land and sea.

18-23. This refers to the time when Nicaea, unconquered, acted as capital of the empire while other cities were taken by the Latins who, of course, came by sea.

5. Size and wealth of the lake and rivers; fine situation of the city in a plain between lake and mountains.

1-12. The water supply, with springs, rivers, and lakes, is the next subject for a standard encomium: Menander 38.

1. οὔπω προσέθηκα: A pedestrian way of introducing a new subject, repeated at 6.15 and 10.19.

9f. ἀνάγκης ... τρυφήν: see above 4.4.

12-31. This involved passage is really an *ekphrasis* within the encomium, giving a visual image of the relation between city, land, and mountains. The description reflects reality: Nicaea stands on the edge of the lake in a relatively small but fertile plain surrounded by mountains on the other sides. See the extremely effective panorama in Schneider (1938) facing p. 56.

In this section, the speech turns to the nature of the site, on which see Menander 40f., 105f.

25-31. This means that the lake is so long that it disappears from sight, allowing a worried imagination to conceive of it stretching as far as the sea, which might swallow it up from jealousy.

6. *The land and its products: its crops are so superior to those of other places that they seek to copy them.*

This continues the discussion of nature: Menander 28. The products of a city may be considered as part of its nature, as here (Menander 28), or under the heading of climate (Menander 34); but much licence was allowed (Menander 106).

1, 3. χάρις ... ὄνησις: See on 4.4.

10. ἀνάγκη ... τρυφή: terms repeated from 5.9.

13. ἄμπελοι: Laskaris 12.9 also remarks on the vineyards around the city. His rare deviation into the material forms the most striking contrast with the abundant descriptions of Metochites.

19-21. It appears that some (unspecified) local crops were so excellent that they were transplanted elsewhere.

7. *The crowning glory of the city is her walls, with their close-set towers, outer circuit, and moat.*

The speech now approaches the city, as ordained, pausing to consider the fortifications: see Menander 49f. on citadels. Because of their importance and outstanding strength, the walls were also praised by Laskaris, sec. 11.

3. Τελευταῖος εἴτε πρῶτος νικᾷ: a reminiscence of Aeschylus, Agamemnon 314: νικᾷ δ' ὁ πρῶτος καὶ τελευταῖος δραμών. This enigmatic phrase later became a proverb, and it is probably that rather than a direct quotation from the playwright that Metochites is using. See the commentary of Fraenkel 166-169.

6-8. The walls, in fact, were so strong that the city only fell once to direct assault, during the First Crusade.

8. σχῆμα: the plan of the city is not really circular, but forms an irregular pentagon.

9-11. περιφρονεῖ: This means that the fortifications are built in a plain, a site more difficult to defend, in contrast to those of other cities which take advantage of steep hilltops, a notion repeated below 26f. Most cities of the time, e.g., Nicomedia, Magnesia, Smyrna, etc., stood on hilltops or had an acropolis which acted as the main fortification.

14. ἡδονήν: after discussing the practical aspect, Metochites turns to the pleasing in a vivid passage which constitutes another short *ekphrasis* (16-33).

14. θαῦμα: the notion of a building as a marvel is already common in texts and inscriptions of Late Antiquity: see Robert (1948) 66ff.

20. πρόμαχοι: Saint Neophytos is likewise called a πρόμαχος because of his church situated between the walls and the lake: *Vita Neophyti* 250f.; so also is Saint Tryphon, the patron Saint of the city in the passage quoted above, 118.

8. The city has magnificent buildings, especially its works of imperial charity, the hospital, and poorhouse.

Praise of buildings, although not specified by Menander, is certainly part of the tradition: see pseudo-Dionysius of Halicarnassus, *Art of Panegyric* 257 where various kinds of buildings are enumerated, notable among them the temples of the gods, and note the example of Libanios, who devotes a long section in his speech on Antioch, 196-248, to the buildings of city and suburbs.

5-7. This description is reminiscent of the *Expositio totius orbis* of the fourth century; see above, 9.

8. χάρις was a natural attribute of baths in antiquity because of their association with the Graces; the word is thus frequent in late antique epigrams: Robert (1948) 28ff. Metochites may here be making a classical allusion (which would be unusual in this speech; cf. above on 7.3) but more probably is simply employing the term in contrast to χρεία in the next line; cf. 4.4.

10f. κόσμος ... ὄνησις: the inevitable reference to pleasure and utility; see above, 4.4.

11f. The hospital and poorhouse were major charitable establishments of the city, singled out also by Blemmydes 113, and thus probably of Laskarid date. On their nature and role in imperial philanthropy, see Constantelos (1968) 152-84, 257-69.

17. ἱερᾶς νόσου: epilepsy. Special accommodation existed for its victims in Constantinople: Constantelos (1968) 179.

9. *The city has great and numerous monasteries, such as I can barely describe.*

For the monasteries, see above, 97-117 *passim*.

10. *Its churches are richly adorned.*

This passage is discussed at length above, 115-117.

11. *The groves and streams around the church provide a healthy and pleasant place for meditation.*

1-3. Laskaris 12 also dwells on the greenery around the city, and the waters.

4-9. The cypress, which grows narrower the top, is a model for ascetics to put aside the material as they rise toward the spiritual. For Laskaris (sec. 11), the straight trunks of cypresses were a simile for the towers of the walls.

11. ἐκ μετεώρου: reference is to the waters of the aqueduct: cf. Laskaris 12.12.

12. *The miracle effected in the church of Saint Trypho is a sign of the spontaneous grace of the martyr toward the city.*

9. τέρας: the miracle, when the lilies of Saint Tryphon bloomed out of season, was the great event in the local ecclesiastical year: see above, 104-107.

16-21. The passage means that martyrs worked miracles (τὴν τῶν ἔργων ἐπίδειξιν) in other cities because of some obligation, but Saint Tryphon's favor to Nicaea came from his generosity alone. The premise is actually false, for the Saint suffered martyrdom in Nicaea and thus enters into one of the categories mentioned here: see above, p. 6.

13. *The city may take great pride in its piety manifested when Constantine chose it above all others as the site of the Council which established orthodoxy.*

The speech here turns to the accomplishments, ἐπιτηδεύσεις, among which piety has a prominent place: Menander 62f.

3-4. The image of the springs of truth appears in Laskaris 7.8-11 and is perhaps taken from there. It is likely in any case that Metochites knew and used the speech of Laskaris, with which his own had many points in common despite their great differences of style and content.

9. μαχαίρα τοῦ πνεύματος: the phrase is taken from Ephesians 6:17, where it is defined as the Word of God. It is also used in the brief praise of the council by Nikephoros Choumnos, above, 83.

14. *The council of Nicaea (embellished with metaphor) laid the basis for those who followed.*

4. ἀκρότομος: cf Deuteronomy 8:15: ἐκ πέτρας ἀκροτόμου πηγὴν ὕδατος, referring to Moses splitting the rock to produce water for the thirsting Israelites: cf. Exodus 17.

15. *The First Council might have brought sufficient glory, but Nicaea was also the site of the Seventh Council where the dogmas of the church were perfected*

16. *In recent times, when the empire was in danger of collapsing altogether, Nicaea alone resisted to become the seat of emperor, church and learning.*

The speech continues to treat the accomplishments of the city, which in this case would fit into the category of bravery: Menander 68.

Although this paragraph could be construed as one sentence in the Greek, its construction with a series of correlate finite verbs is far less elaborate than the corresponding periods of Laskaris 14 and 15.

17. *The achievement of the city in preserving the empire was indeed exceptional.*

15-18. Metochites returns to the advantages of the city's position, neither on the sea nor far from it: see sec. 4. In this context, the two familiar contrasts reappear: 20: ἀσφάλειαν ... τρυφῶσα.

18. *When the empire was restored, Nicaea returned the glories it had guarded, yet still remains a great city with outstanding qualities.*

Most of this section again consists of one long period, comparable with those of Laskaris, yet differing in its structure, preferring

Commentary on Metochites

finite verbs to a long string of dependent participles; cf. 16. The appearance of these long and complex sentences near the end of both speeches is intended to build up the feelings of the audience as the peroration approached,

2. σκηνή: the phrase derives from Acts 15:16 where Saint Luke is quoting Amos 5:11: ἀναστήσω τὴν σκηνὴν Δαβίδ... καὶ τὰ κατασκευαμμένα αὐτῆς.

8. καλὴν παρακαταθήκην: taken from 2 Timothy 1.14; for the legal significance of the phrase, see Hunger (1959) 135.

17. ἰστουργικῆς: this is the only attestation of what was apparently an important local craft.

20-25. Metochites here summarizes the standard qualities of a city which he has already treated. Note θέσεως and φύσει (21), the two characteristics of a place and the typical apposition of χάρις and κοινωφελεῖ (23,24).

19. *Peroration: praise of the emperor who from his base in Nicaea defeats the enemy and brings added glory to the city.*

13-15. These campaigns are treated in the (unpublished) *Imperial Orations* of Metochites, briefly summarised in Laiou (1972) 77ff.

APPENDIX

The Seljuk "Palace"

It is often supposed that the Seljuk Sultan Suleyman built a palace in Nicaea on the basis of Anna Komnena III.vi who, referring to his occupation of the city, adds: οὗ καὶ σουλτανίκιον ἦν ὅπερ ἂν ἡμεῖς βασίλειον ὀνομάσαιμεν. This may at first sight seem to refer to a palace – though that is more commonly expressed by the plural βασιλεία – but parallel passages in the same text show that σουλτανίκιον must mean "royal power" or here, more specifically, "capital." In XV.i, in describing Alexios' planned march against Iconium, Anna writes: κεῖθι γὰρ τὸ σουλτανίκιον τῷ Κλιτζιασθλὰν ἀπομεμέριστο. This plainly refers to a territory, not a building. A third mention, VI.x, merely states again that the σουλτανίκιον was in Nicaea The word has another sense which illuminates its meaning in VI.ix, VI.x and VI.xii, ἡ τοῦ σουλτανικίου ἀξία is used to designate the office of Sultan. In the fifteenth century, the word βασίλεια (here in the plural) appears in contexts where it clearly means "capital city." Chalcocondyles 7, referring to the Byzantines fleeing to Nicaea after 1204, writes: τὰ βασίλεια ἐν αὐτῇ ποιουμένους· and on p. 20 he describes Osman as setting out on campaign from Prousa, ἐν ᾗ τὰ βασίλεια ἐπεποίητο. These usages make it clear that the words used by Anna in reference to Nicaea can have an abstract meaning, "royal power," or refer specifically to a "capital city," but do not denote a particular building. The Seljuk palace of Nicaea, therefore, if it existed, is not attested by any surviving text.

ABBREVIATIONS

AASS: *Acta Sanctorum*. Antwerp 1643–.
ACO: *Acta conciliorum oecumenicorum*, ed. E. Schwartz, Berlin 1924-1940
BGA: *Bibliotheca geographorum arabicorum*, ed. M. J. de Goeje. Leyden 1889.
CIG: *Corpus inscriptionum graecarum.*
CJust: *Codex Iustinianus*, ed. P. Krueger. Berlin 1929.
CodTh: *Codex Theodosianus*, ed. T. Mommsen and P. Meyer. Berlin 1905; tr. C. Pharr, *The Theodosian Code*. Princeton 1952.
DACL: *Dictionnaire d'archéologie chrétienne et de liturgie.*
EO: *Echos d'Orient.*
INikaia: S. Sahin, *Katalog der antiken Inschriften des Museums von Iznik (Nikaia)*. Bonn 1979-1983.
Kazi: Kazi Sonoçlari Toplantisi. Ankara 1979-1991.
AS: *Anatolian Studies.*
PG: J. P. Migne, *Patrologiae cursus completus*, Series graecolatina. Paris 1857–.
RHC: *Recueil des Historiens des Croisades*. Paris 1841-1906.
SynaxCP: *Synaxarium ecclesiae constantinopolitanae (Propylaeum ed Acta Sanctorum Novembris),* ed. H. Delehaye. Brussels 1902.

BIBLIOGRAPHY

SOURCES

Acropolites, ed. A. Heisenberg. Leipzig 1903.
Acta Andreae Apostoli, ed. M. Bonnet in *AB* 13 (1894) 309-378.
Aeschylus, *Agamemnon,* edited with a commentary by E. Fraenkel. Oxford 1950.
Albert of Aix, *Liber Christianae Expeditionis,* in *RHC Occ. 4.*
Ammianus Marcellinus, ed. and tr. J. Rolfe. London 1935.
Amphilochius, *Opera,* ed. F. Combefis. Paris 1644.
Anna Comnena, *Alexiad,* ed. B. Leib. Paris 1945.
Arculf: *Adamnani de locis sanctis,* in P. Geyer, *Itinera hierosolymitana.* Vienna 1898. 219-297.
Asikpasazade, ed. Ali. Istanbul 1332 H.
Attaliates, Michael, ed. I. Bekker. Bonn 1853.
Basil, Saint, *Letters,* ed. R. Deferrari. London 1926.
Baudri of Dol, *Historia Jerosolimitana,* in *RHC Occ.* 4. 1-111.
Blemmydes, Nikephoros, *Curriculum vitae et carmina,* ed. A. Heisenberg. Leipzig 1896.
Bryennios, Nikephoros, *Historiae,* ed. P. Gautier. Paris 1975.
Cantacuzene, John, *Historiae,* ed. L. Schopen. Bonn 1828.
Cedrenus, George, ed. I. Bekker. Bonn 1838.
Chalcocondyles, ed. E. Darkó. Budapest 1922.
Choniates, Nicetas, *Historia,* ed. J. van Dieten. Berlin 1975.
—*Orationes et epistulae,* ed. J. van Dieten. Berlin 1972.
Choumnos, Nikephoros, Ἐπιτάφιος εἰς Θεόληπτον, in *Anecdota graeca,* V. 183-239, ed. J. Boissonade. Paris 1833.
Chronica Breviora: P. Schreiner, *Die byzantinischen Kleinchroniken.* Vienna 1975-79.
Chronicon Paschale, ed. L. Dindorf. Bonn 1832.
Constantine Porphyrogenitus, *de Ceremoniis,* ed. I. Reiske. Bonn 1829.
—*de Thematibus,* ed. A. Pertusi. Vatican 1952.
Cramer, J. A., *Anecdota graeca.* Oxford 1835-1841.
Dionysius of Halicarnassus, *Rhetorica,* ed. A. Usener and L. Rademacher. Leipzig 1904.

Dölger, F., *Regesten der Kaiserurkunden des oströmischen Reiches.* Munich 1924-1965.
Eusebius, *Vita Constantini,* ed. F. Winkelmann. Berlin 1975.
Evagrius, *Historia ecclesiastica,* ed. J. Bidez and L. Parmentier. London 1898.
Expositio totius mundi et gentium, ed. J. Rougé. Paris 1966.
Fulcher of Chartres, *Historia Hierosolymitana,* in *RHC Occ.* III. 313-485.
Genesius, ed. C. Lachmann. Bonn 1834.
Gesta francorum, ed. L. Brehier. Paris 1924.
Golubovich, F., *Bibliotheca bio-bibliographica della Terra Santa.* Quatroccci 1906.
Gregory of Nazianzus, *Oratio* VII, *PG.* 35.
Gregoras, Nicephorus, ed. I. Bekker. Bonn 1855.
Gregory (George) of Cyprus, *Autobiography,* ed. W. Lameere, in *La tradition manuscrite de la correspondence de Grégoire de Chypre.* Brussels 1937.
Ibn Battuta: *The Travels of Ibn Battuta,* tr. H. A. R. Gibb. Cambridge 1962.
Idrisi: *Opus geographicum,* ed. A. Bombaci. Naples 1970-; *Géographie d'Idrisi,* tr. A. Jaubert. Paris 1850.
Ioannou, Th., Μνημεῖα ἁγιολογικά. Venice 1884.
Lascaris, Theodore, *Epistulae,* ed. N. Festa. Florence 1898.
—*In laudem Nicaeae urbis oratio,* ed. L. Bachmann. Rostock 1847.
Laurent, V., *Les régestes des actes du patriarcat de Constantinople* I.4: *Les régestes de 1208 a 1309.* Paris 1971.
Leo of Synnada, *Correspondence,* ed. M. Vinson. Washington 1985.
Libanius, ed. R. Foerster. Leipzig 1903-1927.
—Oratio I: *The Autobiography of Libanius,* ed. A. Norman.
—Oratio XI: G. Downey, "Libanius' Oration in Praise of Antioch," *Proceedings of the American Philosophical Society* 103 (1959) 652-686.
Malchus of Philadelphia, ed. C. Müller, in *Fragmenta historicorum graecorum IV.* 111-132. Paris 1851.
Mansi, J. D., *Sacrorum conciliorum nova et amplissima collectio.* Florence 1769.
Marcellinus Comes, ed. Th. Mommsen in *MGH, Auctores antiquissimi XI* (1894) 37-108.
Menander Rhetor, ed. D.A. Russell and N.G. Wilson. Oxford 1981.
Mesarites, Nicholas, *Bericht:* A. Heisenberg, "Neue Quellen zur Geschichte des lateinischen Kaisertums und der Kirchenunion III: Der Bericht des Nikolaos Mesarites über die politischen und kirchlichen Ereignisse des Jahres 1214," *Sitzungsberichte der bayerischen Akademie der Wissenschaften* Phil.-phil Klasse, 1923.3.
— *Reisebericht:* "Neue Quellen...II. Reisebericht des Nikolaos Mesarites an die Mönche des Euergetisklosters in Konstantinopel," *SB bayer. Akad.* 1923. 2.35-46.

Bibliography

Metochites, Theodore, *Nikaieus*, ed. F. Sathas in Μεσαιωνικὴ Βιβλιοθήκη I (Venice 1872) 139-153.

Miklosich, F. and J. Müller, *Acta et diplomata graeca medii aevi*. Vienna 1860-1890.

Nicephorus Callistus, *Migne, PG* 145-147.

Nicephorus Patriarcha, *Opuscula historica*, ed. C. de Boor. Leipzig 1880.

Nicholas, Patriarch of Constantinople, *Letters*, ed. R.J.H. Jenkins and L.G. Westerink. Washington 19~3.

Νουθεσία γέροντος περὶ τῶν ἁγίων εἰκόνων, in B. Melioransky, *Georgii Kipriyanin i Ioann Ierusalimyanin*, Saint Petersburg 1901.

Odo of Deuil, *De profectione Ludovici VII in orientem*, ed. and tr. V. Berry. New York 1958.

Pachymeres, George, ed. I. Bekker. Bonn 1835. (When reference is made to this edition, page numbers are preceded by 'B').

—*Relations historiques*, ed. A. Failler and V. Laurent. Paris 1984. (Vol. I only).

Palaeologus, Michael, *De vita sua*, ed. and tr. H. Grégoire, *Byzantion* 29/30 (1959/60) 447-476.

Palamas: "La captivité de Palamas chez les turcs: dossier et commentaire," ed. A. Philippidis-Braat, *Travaux et Mémoires* 7 (1979) 109-221.

Philostorgius, *Historia ecclesiatica*, Migne, *PG* 86. 165-228.

Procopius, *de Aedificiis*, ed. J. Haury. Berlin 1913.

Psellus, Michael, *Opera minora*, ed. E. Kurtz and F. Drexl. Rome 1936-1941.

Raymond of Aguilers, *Historia francorum qui ceperunt Iherusalem, RHC Occ.* III. 233-369.

Scriptores originum constantinopolitanarum, ed. F. Preger. Leipzig 1907.

Skoutariotes, Theodore, Σύνοψις χρονική, in K. Sathas, Μεσαιωνικὴ Βιβλιοθήκη, VII (Venice 1894) 1-556. Relevant excerpts in Acropolites, ed. Heisenberg.

Scylitzes Continuatus, ed. E. Tsolakes. Thessalonica 1968.

Socrates, *Historia ecclesiastica*, Migne, *PG* 67.

Sozomen, *Historia ecclesiastica*, ed. J. Bidez and G. Hausen. Berlin 1960.

Stephen of Blois, *Epistolae, RHC Occ.* III. 885-890.

Synaxarium ecclesiae constantinopolitanae (Propylaeum ed Acta Sanctorum Novembris), ed. H. Delehaye. Brussels 1902.

Theodore Lector, *Excerpta ex ecclesiastica historia*, Migne, *PG* 86. 165-228.

Theodore of Studium, *Opera*, Migne, *PG 99*.

Theophanes, *Chronographia*, ed. C. de Boor. Leipzig 1883.

Theophanes Continuatus, ed. I. Bekker. Bonn 1838.

Theophylact Simocatta, *Historia*, ed. C. de Boor. Leipzig 1887.

Villehardouin, *La conquête de Constantinople,* ed. and tr. E. Faral. Paris 1961.
Vita Constantini olim Iudaei, AASS Nov. IV. 627-656.
Vita Ioannicii, AASS Nov. III. 311-435.
Vita Neophyti, in Ioannou, Μνημεῖα, 239-251.
Vita Nicephori, in Nicephorus, *Opuscula,* 139-217.
Vita Petri Atroae: La vie merveilleuse de Pierre d 'Atroa, ed. V. Laurent (=*Subsidia Hagiographica* 29). Brussels 1956.
Vita Symeonis Stylitae: La vie ancienne de S. Simeon Stylite le Jeune, ed. P. v.d. Ven (=*Subsidia Hagiographica* 32). Brussels 1962.
Vita Theodori Syceotae: Vie de Théodore de Sykéon, ed. A.-J. Festugière (*Subsidia Hagiographica* 48) Brussels 1970.
Vita Theophanis et Theodori Grapti, ed. J. Papadopoulos-Kerameus, Ἀνάλεκτα Ἱεροσολυμιτικῆς Σταχυολογίας (St. Petersburg 1891-98) 4, 185-225.
Vita Tryphonis, AASS Nov. IV, 318-383.
William of Tyre, *Historia rerum in partibus transmarinis gestarum, RHC Occ.* I; tr. E. A. Babcock and A. C. Krey, *History of Deeds Done beyond the Sea,* New York 1943.
Willibald, *Hodeoporicon,* and *Itinerarium* in T. Tobler, *Descriptiones terrae sanctae.* Leipzig 1874.
Zepos, J. and P., *Ius greco-romanum.* Athens 1931.
Zosimus, *Historia nova,* ed. L. Mendelssohn. Leipzig 1887.

MODERN WORKS

Alpatoff, M. (1926): "Les fresques de Sainte Sophie de Nicée," *EO* 29: 42-45.
Angold, M. (1975): *A Byzantine Government in Exile.* Oxford.
Arnakis, G. (1947): Οἱ πρώτοι Ὀθωμανοί. Athens.
Ashburner, W. (1909): *The Rhodian Sea Law.* Oxford.
Barnes, T. (1981): *Constantine and Eusebius.* Cambridge, Mass.
Batiffol P. (1925): "Les sources de l'histoire du Concile de Nicée," *EO* 24: 385-402.
Beck, H. G. (1959): *Kirche und theologische Literatur im byzantinischen Reich.* Munich.
Beldiceanu, N. (1973): *Recherches sur la ville ottomane au XVe siècle.* Paris.
Bloch, H. (1985): *Monte Cassino in the Middle Ages.* Rome.
Brounoff, N. (1925): "L'église de Sainte Sophie de Nicée," *EO* 28: 471-481.
Bryer, A. (1971): "Nicaea, Byzantine City," *History Today* 21: 22-31.
Bryer, A. and D. Winfield (1985): *The Byzantine Monuments and Topography of the Pontos.* Washington.
Buchwald, H. (1979): "Laskarid Architecture," *JOB* 28: 261-296.
Cahen, V. (1948): "La première pénétration turque en Asie Mineure," *Byzantion* 18: 5-67.
Clark, D. (1957): *Rhetoric in Greco-Roman Education.* New York.
Constantelos, D. (1968): *Byzantine Philanthropy and Social Welfare.* New Brunswick, N.J.
Corbo, V. (1960): "Scavo archeologico a ridosso della basilica dell'Ascensione," *Liber annuus studii biblici franciscani* 10 (1959160): 205-248.
Dagron, G. (1984): *Constantinople imaginaire.* Paris.
Darrouzès, J. (1949): "Les catalogues récents de manuscrits grecs," *REB* 7: 56-68.
—(1960): *Epistoliers byzantins du Xe siècle.* Paris.
Delehaye, H. (1926): "S. Bassus évêque martyre honoré à Nicée," *AB* 50: 295-310.
—(1937): "Sainte Théodote de Nicée," *AB* 5: 201-225.
Devedjian, K. (1926): *Pêches et pêcheries en Turquie.* Constantinople.
Dmitrievskii, A. *Euchologia.* Kiev 1901.
Dräseke, J.H. (1894): "Theodoros Laskaris," *BZ* 3: 498-515.
Dvornik, F. (1958): *The Idea of Apostolicity in Byzantium and the Legend of the Apostle Andrew.* Cambridge, Mass.

Eyice, S. (1949): "Iznikte bir Bizans kilisesi," *Belleten* 13: 37-51.

—(1963a): "Two Mosaic Pavements from Bithynia," *DOP* 17: 373-383.

—(1963b): "Bursa' da Osman ve Orhan Gazi Türbeleri," *Vakıflar Dergisi* 5: 131-147.

—(1983): "Die byzantinische Kirche in der Nähe des Yenisehir-Tores zu Iznik." *Materialia Turcica* 7/8 (1981|82): 152-167.

—(1988) *Iznik.* Istanbul.

Featherstone, J. (1980): "The Praise of Theodore Graptus by Theophanes of Caesarea," *AB* 98: 93-152.

Feld, O. (1970): "Mittelbyzantinischen Sarkophage," *Römische Quartalschrift* 65: 158-184.

Fenster, E. (1968): *Laudes constantinopolitanae.* Munich.

Firatli, N. (1974): "An Early Byzantine Hypogaeum Discovered at Iznik," *Mélagnes Mansel* 919-932. Ankara.

Foss, C. (1996): *Survey of Medieval Castles of Anatolia II: Nicomedia.* Ankara.

Foss, C. (1987): "Saint Autonomus and his Church in Bithynia," *DOP* 41: 187-198.

Foss, C. and D. Winfield (1985): *Byzantine Fortifications, an Introduction.* Pretoria.

Gardner, A. (1912): *The Laskarids of Nicaea.* London.

Geanakoplos, D. (1959): *Emperor Michael Palaeologus and the West.* Cambridge, Mass.

Gibbon, Edward: *The Decline and Fall of the Roman Empire* (numerous editions).

Golubovich, H. (1919): "Disputatio latinorum et graecorum," *Archivum franciscanum historicum* 12: 412-470.

Grégoire, H. (1930): "Encore le monastère d'Hyacinthe à Nicée," *Byzantion* 5 (1929/30) 287-293.

Hadzipsaltes, K. (1964): " Ἡ ἐκκλησία τῆς Κύπρου καὶ τὸ ἐν Νικαίᾳ οἰκουμενικὸν πατριαρχεῖον", *Κυπριακαὶ Σπουδαί.* 28: 141-168.

Halkin, F., (1975): "La passion inédite des saints Eustathe, Thespesius et Anatole," *AB* 93: 287-311.

Harris, C., (1973): *The Heart and the Vascular System in Ancient Greek Medicine.* Oxford.

Hefele, C., *Histoire des Conciles,* tr. and ed. C. Leclercq. Paris 1907-1910.

Heisenberg, A. (1920): "Aus der Geschichte und Literatur der Palaiologenzeit," *Sitzungsberichte der bayerischen Akademie der Wissenschaften,* Phil.-phil. Klasse, Abh. 10. Munich.

Hendy, M. (1969): *Coinage and Money in the Byzantine Empire 1081-1261.* Washington.

—(1985): *Studies in the Byzantine Monetary Economy.* Cambridge.

Hunger, H. (1959): "Von Wissenschaften und kunst der frühen Palaiologenzeit," *JÖBG* 8: 123-155.
—(1978): *Die Hochsprachliche Profane Literatur der Byzantiner.* Munich.
Iznik (1973): *Iznik (Tarih ve Müze Komitesi Yayini).* Istanbul.
Janin, R. (1975): *Les églises et les monastères des grands centres byzantins.* Paris.
Johnson, G. (1984): *Roman Bithynia and Christianity to the Mid-Fourth Century.* University of Michigan Dissertation.
Jones, A. H. M. (1964): *The Later Roman Empire.* Oxford.
Karlsson, G. (1962): *Idéologie et cérémonial dans l'epistolographie byzantine.* Uppsala.
Kennedy, G. (1983): *Greek Rhetoric under Christian Emperors.* Princeton.
Krautheimer, R. (1979): *Early Christian and Byzantine Architecture.* Baltimore.
Kurtz, E. (1906): "Tri synodalnykh gramoty mitropolita Efesskago Nikolaya Mesarita," VV 12: 99-111.
Kustas, G. (1970): "The Function and Evolution of Byzantine Rhetoric," *Viator* 1: 55-73.
—(1973): *Studies in Byzantine Rhetoric.* Thessalonica.
Laiou, A. (1972): *Constantinople and the Latins.* Cambridge, Mass.
Laurent, V. (1958): "L'embleme du lys dans la numismatique byzantine," *Centennial Publication of the American Numismatic Society,* 417-428. New York.
—(1969): "La chronologie des patriarches de Constantinople au XIIIe siècle," *REB* 27: 129-150.
Lindner, R. (1983): *Nomads and Ottomans in Medieval Anatolia.* Bloomington, Indiana.
Lipshits, E. (1964): "Navkratii i nikeiskii mozaiki," *ZRVI* 8: 241-246.
Mango, Cyril (1959): "The Date of the Narthex Mosaics of the Church of the Dormition in Nicaea," *DOP* 13: 245-252.
—(1973): "Eudocia Ingerina, the Normans and the Macedonian Dynasty," *ZRVI* 14/15: 17-27.
—(1976): *Byzantine Architecture.* New York.
—(1981): "Observations on the Correspondence of Ignatius Metropolitan of Nicaea," *Überlieferungsgeschichtliche Untersuchungen=Texte und Untersuchungen* 125. Berlin.
—(1994): Notes d' épigraphie et d'archéologie: Constantinople, Nicée, *Travaux et Mémoires* 12: 343-357.
Mansel, A. (1963): *Die Ruinen von Side.* Berlin.
May, M. (1968): *Galen, On the Usefulness of the Parts of the Body.* Ithaca.
Meliarakis, A. (1868): Ἱστορία τοῦ βασιλείου τῆς Νικαίας. Athens.
Mélikoff-Sayar, I. (1960): *La geste de Melik Danismend.* Paris.
Merkelbach, R. (1987): *Nikäa in der römischen Kaiserzeit.* Opladen.

Möllers, C. (1987): "Beobachtungen zur Hagia Sophia in Iznik/Nikaia," *AA* (1987) 689-693.

Ostrogorsky, G. (1932): "Löhne und Preise in Byzanz," *BZ* 32: 293-333.

Papadopoulos, J. (1952): "Ὁ ἐν Νικαίᾳ τῆς Βιθυνίας ναὸς τοῦ ἁγίου Τρύφωνος," *EEBS* 22: 110-113.

Papadopoulos, J. (1908): *Théodore II Lascaris.* Paris.

Peschlow, U. (1972): "Neue Beobachtungen zur Architektur und Ausstattung der Koimesiskirche in Iznik," *IstMitt* 26: 145-187.

Polemis, D. (1973): "The Speech of Constantine Acropolites on St. John Merciful the Young," *AB 91:* 31-54.

Raby, J. (1976): "A Seventeenth Century Description of Iznik-Nicaea," *IstMitt* 26: 149-188.

Renehan, R. (1975): *Greek Lexicographical Notes.* Göttingen.

Robert, Louis (1948): *Epigrammes du Bas-empire =Hellenica* 4.

—(1961): "Les Kordakia de Nicée, le combustible de Synnada et les poissons-scies. Sur des lettres d'un métropolite de Phrygie au Xe siècle I." *Journal des Savants.* 1961: 97-166.

—(1977): "Le titulature de Nicée et de Nicomédie: la gloire et la haine," *HSCP* 81: 1-39.

Ruge, W. (1936): "Nikaia 7" in Pauly-Wissowa-Kroll, *Realenzyclopädie der Classischen Altertumswissenschaft* 33: 226-243.

Runciman, S. (1950): *A History of the Crusades.* Campridge.

Schmit, T. (1927): *Die Koimesis-Kirche von Nikaia.* Berlin.

Schneider, A. M. (1938): *Die Stadtmauer von Iznik (Nicaea) (= Istanbuler Forschungen 9).* Berlin.

—(1943): *Die römischen und byzantinischen Denkmaler von Iznik-Nicaea (=Istanbuler Forschungen* 16). Berlin.

Seeck, O. (1906): *Die Briefe von Libanius.* Leipzig.

Sevcenko, I. (1962): *Etudes sur la polemique entre Théodore Metochite et Nicéphore Choumnos.* Brussels.

—(1975): "Theodore Metochites, the Chora, and the Intellectual Trends of his Time," in P.A. Underwood, ed., *The Kariye Djami* 4, 19-91. Princeton.

Sharf, A. (1980): "Jews under the Laskarids and in Epirus," *Actes du XVe Congrès international d' études byzantines,* 283-290. Athens.

Sinogowitz, B. (1952): "Über das byzantinische Kaisertum nach dem vierten Kreuzzüge," *BZ* 45: 345-356.

Ulbert, T. (1969): *Studien zur dekorativen Reliefplastik des östlichen Mittelmeerraumes.* Munich.

—(1970): "Untersuchungen zu den Reliefplatten des 6. bis 8. Jahrhunderts," *IstMitt* 19/10 (1969/70). 339-357.

Underwood, P. (1959): "The Evidence of Restorations in the Sanctuary Mosaic of the Church of the Dormition at Nicaea," *DOP* 13: 235-243.

van Dieten, J. (1971): *Niketas Choniates. Erlaüterungen zu den Reden und Briefen nebst einer Biographie.* Berlin.

—(1985): "Manuel Prinkips: Welcher Manuel in welcher Kirche zu Nikaia?," *BZ* 78: 63-91.

Vincent, H. and M. Abel (1914): *Jérusalem* II: *Jérusalem nouvelle.* Paris.

von Hammer, J. (1818): *Umblick auf einer Reise von Constantinopel nach Brussa.* Pesth.

Vryonis, S. (1971): *The Decline of Medieval Hellenism in Asia Minor.* Los Angeles.

Westerink, L. (1966): "Trois textes inédites sur Saint Diomède de Nicée," *AB* 84: 161-227.

Wilson, N. (1983): *Scholars of Byzantium.* Baltimore.

Wulff, O. (1903): *Die Koimesiskirche in Nicäa und ihre Mosaiken.* Strassburg.

Yalman, B. (1979): "Iznikteki kilise altyapisi kazisi," *VIII. Türk Tarih Kongresi* I. 457-466. Ankara.

—(1981-1991): annual reports, all entitled "Iznik Tiyatro Kazısı," as follows:

(1981) in *3.Kazı,* 31-34

(1982) in *4.Kazı,* 229-235

(1983) in *5.Kazı,* 215-220

(1984) in *6.Kazı,* 459-467

(1985) in *7.Kazı,* 579-595

(1986) in *8.Kazı,* 2.233-257

(1987) in *9.Kazı,* 2.299-326

(1988) in *10.Kazı,* 2.339-379

(1989) in *11.Kazı,* 2.301-324

(1990) in *12.Kazı,* 2.379-404

(1991) in *13.Kazı,* 2.377-402

Zacos, G. (1984): *Byzantine Lead Seals* II, ed. J. Nesbitt. Berne.

Zacos, G. and A. Veglery (1982): *Byzantine Lead Seals.* Basel.

Index

A

Abraham ben Meier 71
Abul Qasim 42-3
Adramyttion 58
Aeschylus 199
Agalmates 75, 80-3, 108, 110
akritai 77
Akropolites, George 63, 66, 69, 81
Akropolites, Constantine 81-2
Alexander, bishop 29, 115
Alexios I Komnenos 37, 41-3, 49, 51-2, 92-3, 98, 204
Alexios III 60-1, 98
Alexios Angelos 55, 57-8
Amorion 25
Amphilochios 114
Anastasios 12-3
Andrew, apostle 2, 22-3, 197
Andronikos I Komnenos 54-5
Andronikos II 80-1, 95, 123, 128
Andronikos III 84
Angelos, John 79
Ankyra 7, 11-2, 25, 91
Anna Komnena 31, 41, 45-6, 48, 156, 204
Anna, empress 79
Ano Lakkous 59
Antigonos 1
Antioch on the Maeander 61
Antonia 7
Aphthonios 59, 124,126
Apollo 2, 22
apotheke 24
aqueduct 13, 159, 201
Arabs 17-8, 23, 25, 30, 90-1, 112, 114

archaeology 13, 37, 71, 92
archers, archery 36, 45, 47, 76-7, 84
arches 1-2, 10, 14, 89
archon 68
Arculf 113
Arians 7-8, 11, 14, 114
Aristainetos 8-9
aristocracy 8, 15, 24, 68-9, 77
Aristotle 139
Arius 7-8, 21-2, 34, 112, 185
Armatos 13
army 14, 30
Arsenios 69-71, 75-6, 83, 107, 110
Artavasdos 18-9, 91
Artemios 17, 90
Athens 129, 137, 139, 157
Attaliates 30
Attikos 12
Augustus 1
Axouch 49

B

Babylon 135
Bachmann, L. 155
Baldwin 57
ballistas 46, 94
bandits 22, 60
Bapheus 80
baptistery 115
Bardas Phokas 31
Bardas Skleros 30-1, 48, 92
Basil I 29
Basil of Adrianople 79
Basil, St. 10-1, 114

Basileia 37
Basilinopolis 12, 16n
Basiliskos 13
Bassos 7
baths 13, 177, 200
battering rams 47, 54
beauty 125
Bekkos, John 77, 79
Biblical references 158, 160, 162, 202-3.
Bithynia 1-2, 10, 15, 21-2, 33-4, 36-7, 41, 54, 81, 167
Blemmydes, Nikephoros 58, 66-9, 72n, 119, 128, 201
bombast 128, 161
Boutoumites 49
bridge 13, 32
Brounoff, N. 103
Bulgars 17, 58, 69, 78
Bursuk 42
Buzan 43

C

catapults 47, 54
cathedral 11, 57, 101, 110-1, 114
cattle 193
cemetery 93
Chair of Constantine 111
Chaka 43
Chalcedon 11-2, 36, 59
charity 12, 30, 177
Choniates 55, 58
Chosroes 15
Choumnos, Nikephoros 83, 202
Chrysostom, John 7, 12
Church B 108-9, 117
Church C 108-9, 117
Church of Christ *tou Bolenou* 59, 110
Church of Hagia Sophia (Constantinople) 57, 59, 67, 99

Church of Hagia Sophia (Nicaea) 1, 13, 20, 35, 101-4, 109, 111-2, 114, 117, 120, 128
Church of Roufinaous 30
Church of St. Anthony 109, 117, 120
Church of St. Diomedes 114, 119
Church of St. Tryphon 70, 82-3, 104-9, 114, 116, 120, 122, 128, 201
Church of the Archangel Michael 70, 110
Church of the Ascension (Jerusalem) 113
Church of the Dormition: see Monastery of Hyacinth
Church of the Fathers 18, 35, 110-114
Church of the Holy Trinity 80, 110
Church of the Virgin Kyriotissa 110
church property 25, 30, 67
churches 145, 183
Cilicia 41
cities 124-6, 156
Civetot 45-6; see also Kibotos, Helenopolis
Claudius Gothicus 5, 89
coinage 71, 105
Constance 65
Constantine 2, 7-8, 110, 149, 201
Constantine V 19, 90, 101
Constantine VII Porphyrogennetos 24, 30
Constantine X Doukas 35, 101
Constantine Laskaris 57, 110
Constantine the Jew, St. 29, 97
Constantinople 5, 10, 13, 17-20, 30, 57-62, 66, 70-1, 76-9, 89, 95, 126-9, 157, 160-1, 197, 200
Consul of the Philosophers 67
Council, First Ecumenical 7-8, 15, 19, 34, 66, 111-2, 117, 129, 202

Council, Seventh Ecumenical 19-21, 25, 101, 127, 202
council (1209) 61
crops 143, 159, 173, 199
Crusade, First 43-9, 53, 92, 96, 200
Crusade, Second 52
Crusade, Fourth 51, 55, 57
Cyprus 29-30, 61

D

Daukomis 23
David of Paphlagonia 58
Decius 6
Dekte 35
Demosthenes 139
Despot 58
Didymoteichon 59
Dio Chrysostom 2
Diocletian 5, 10, 125
Diomedes, St. 7, 11
Dionysius of Halicarnassus 125, 200
ditch 89, 177; see also moat
Dorylaion 52, 55
Doukas See John III Vatatzes
Doukas, Constantine 35-6
Doukas, John 54
Drakon, river 41, 46, 75
Drakontios, bishop 23
Durazzo 37, 161

E

earthquakes 1, 10, 13, 19, 35, 38, 93, 101, 104, 112
education 67-71, 123, 126, 128, 133, 135, 137, 139, 141, 147, 160
Egypt 156, 185
Eirenikos, Nicholas 65
ekphrasis 124
encomium 104-5, 123-4, 126-7, 155
English 66
Ennaton 79

Entrechios 9
eparch 24
Ephesos 22, 26, 59, 62-3, 67-9
epilepsy 200
Epiphanios of Catana 20
Erotikos, Manuel 30-1
Eunomios 12
Eusebios 7-8, 111
Eustathios, St. 6
Eustathios of Thessalonica 161
Eustratios, bishop 52
Expositio totius orbis 9, 127, 200

F

fish 25, 31-3, 38n, 59
Florentius 11
Fort Saint George 37, 42, 48-9, 51, 60, 67, 76, 109
Franciscans 65
Franks 42
Frederick II 65
French 52, 66
frescoes 14, 104, 108-9, 119

G

Galata 76-7
Gallienus 5, 89
gates 82
gate: Istanbul 90, 107-8, 110, 114
gate: South Lake 91
gate: Yenishehir 108
Georgiopulou, S. 123, 155
Germanos II, patriarch 59, 65-6, 110
Germans 14, 45-6, 52
Gerontion 8
Ghiyath ed-Din Kaykhosraw 57, 61
Gibbon, Edward 123, 130
Gonatas tower 48, 92
Goths 5, 89-90
Graces 143, 145
grammar 70, 124

graves 108
gravestones 93
graveyard 71, 110
Greek fire 17, 30
Gregory, abbot 101
Gregory, bishop 29
Gregory, bishop 31
Gregory of Cyprus 70
Gregory of Tours 22
Gregory the Theologian 10
grove 117, 143, 158
Gulf of Nicomedia 6, 76
gymnasium 1-2, 198

H
Hades 35
Hadrian 1-2, 89, 197-8
heat, innate 151, 162
Helenopolis 11, 37, 45, 76; see also Kibetos, Civetot
helepoleis 31
Herakleia 62
Herakleion 67
Hermogenes 59, 124-6, 139, 158
Hexapterygos, Theodore 69, 72
highway 1, 12-4; see also roads
Himerius 126
Holobolos, Manuel 78, 98
Homer 59, 69, 137, 157
hospice 30
hospital 200
houses 145
Hyacinth (monk (VII c.) 97-8
Hyacinth (monk, XIII c.) 70-1, 110

I
Ibn Battuta 84, 159
Ibn Khordadbeh 23, 53
iconoclasm 17-20, 25, 100, 112
icons 17-8, 99-100
Idrisi 32, 53
Ignatios, bishop 25, 31

Ikonion 51-2
Iliad 156
Illos 13
images 17-9, 66, 112, 116, 181
India 135, 156
Inger, bishop 25
inscriptions 2, 18, 73n, 90, 92-3, 98, 100, 113, 161
Ioannikios 25
Irene 19, 21-2
Isaak Angelos 54
Isaak Komnenos 34-5
Islam 85
Italians 149
Iznik 84-5, 115

J
Jerusalem 112-4
Jews 14-5, 22-3, 29, 71
John II Komnenos 49, 52, 161
John III Vatatzes 65-9, 71, 76, 83, 93-5, 98, 104, 109, 123, 128, 160-1
John IV Laskaris 75, 77, 89, 95
John VI Kantakouzenos 84
John the Geometer 34, 127
John the Merciful the Younger, St. 82-3, 107-8, 110
John, *protovestiarios* 37
Joseph, abbot 25, 115
Jovian 10
Julian 9-10, 12
Justinian 6, 13, 117-8

K
Kaisarios 10
Kalliopios 12
Kamateros, John 59
Kamytzes 51
Kantakouzenos, Theodore 54-5
Karacakaya 23
Karykes, Demetrios 68
Katzapos 22

Kekaumenos 35
Kibotos 45, 51, 79; see also Civetot, Helenopolis
Kilich Arslan 43
Kios 42, 47, 81
Klemantios 8
kommerkiarios 24
Kotyaion 35, 55
Kyzikos 11

L

lake 1, 7, 22-5, 31-4, 46-8, 53, 171, 198
Latins 52, 57-8, 60-3, 66-7, 71, 110, 198
laws 161
learning 139, 156-7, 189
Leo of Synnada 31
Leo III 17-9, 26, 90-1, 112
Leo VI 5
Libanios 8-9, 197, 200
lilies 6, 105-6, 201
Lochous 22
Longinus 13
Lopadion 51-2, 54, 80
Luke, St. 202
luxury 135, 143, 145
Lysimachos 1

M

Macrianus 5, 89
Magnesia 61, 65, 156, 158, 162, 199
Malik Shah 42-3
Manichaeans 68
Manouelites, Nicholas 77
Mansur 36
Manuel Komnenos 49, 52, 93
Manuel of Thessalonica 74
Manuel *prinkips* 98
manuscripts 70, 110
Manzikert 35

Marcellus 11
Marcian 12-3
mathematics 139
Maximos, patriarch 59, 63
meadows 181
Medes 137
medicine 139, 157
medicines 33
Menander the Rhetor 125-6, 128, 157, 197-202
merchants 60
Mesarites 59-60, 62-3, 94, 161
mesazon 70
Methodios, abbot 66
Methodios, patriarch 98
Metochites, George 128
Metochites, Theodore 70, 80, 85, 89, 95, 97, 104, 115-20, 122n, 123, 127-30, 164-203
Michael III 26, 91-2, 94, 103, 122n
Michael VII 35-6
Michael VIII Palaiologos 67, 70, 75-80, 110
Michael Autorianos, patriarch 59, 62, 98, 111
mills 33
mint 10, 39, 61
miracle 6, 29, 106-7, 183, 201
missiles 46
moat 54, 84, 159, 199; see also ditch
monasteries 145, 201
Monastery of Agalma 110
Monastery of Ano Lakkous 108
Monastery of Christ the Saviour *tou Kophou* 110
Monastery of Hyacinth 29, 61, 65-6, 78, 85, 97-101, 108-111, 116-7
Monastery "of the Potters" 25, 115
Monastery of Phlouboute 29
Monastery of Tornikios 80, 109, 117

Mongols 77-8, 81
monograms 97, 99, 102
mortar 47, 103, 108
mosaics 97, 99-101, 104, 107-9, 112, 116-7
Mosque of Orhan 102
Mount of Olives 19, 112
Mouzalon, George 75
Mouzalon, Theodore 80, 109
Muawiya 18
mule train 60

N
Naukratios 100-101
Neakomis 59
necropolis 3, 110
Neokastra 93
Neophytos, St. 6, 32-3, 115, 127, 197, 200
Nicholas, bishop 55
Nicholas Mesarites 59-60, 62-4
Nicholas Mystikos 30
Nicomedia 2, 5-10, 12, 17, 36, 41-2, 45-6, 51, 57-60, 67-8, 79-81, 199
Nikephoros Botaniates 35-7
Nikephoros Melissenos 36-7
Nikephoros, *hetairiarch* 100
Nikephoros, patriarch 19, 25, 112
Nikephoros II, patriarch 76
Niketas, bishop 52
nomads 78
Normans 37, 41, 45, 46, 52
Novatians 8, 14
nunnery 14, 115
Nymphaion 61, 65-6, 68, 75-6, 80

O
obelisk 3
obscurity 128-9
olives 33, 38, 67, 76, 109
Olympos, Mount 6, 22, 29-30, 82

Opsikion 19-20, 23, 30, 35, 90
opus sectile 100, 104, 107-9, 116
Orhan 84, 102
Osman 80, 81, 84, 114, 204
outer wall: see *proteichisma*

P
Pachymeres 80
pagans 9, 15, 22-3
paintings 116
palace 8, 14, 66, 193, 204
Palaiologos, George 37
Palamas, Gregory 85, 98, 117
panic 77
paraphylax 24
Paschasios 75
patriarch 59, 62-3, 101
patriarchate 57, 61, 66, 110-4
Paulicians 26
Pelekanon 46
peraequator 11
Persians 90, 113
Peter, bishop 25
Peter of Atroa 24-5
Peter the Hermit 45-6, 49
Petroa 35
Pharmoutios river 32
Philadelphia 75
Philokrene 84
philosophy 135, 139, 141, 153
Phokas 15
Phrangopoulos, Andronikos 69
pirates 62
Plato 139
Pliny 1-3, 198
poetics 67, 69-70
Polemon 35
poorhouse 200
population 12, 54
post 7, 13
pottery 38, 71, 108
Poulchas 43

Prainetos 36, 38n, 42
prison 77
Prokopios 11, 90, 117
progymnasmata 70, 124
prokathemenos 77-8
proteichisma 89
protokentarchos 24
Prusa 54-5, 57-9, 79, 81
Psellos, Michael 35
Pylai 36, 60, 62
Pythia 79

Q

Quietus 5, 89
Quintilian 125

R

reason 133, 135, 137, 139, 141, 143
referendarios 59
refugees 58, 61
rhetoric 29, 59, 67, 69-70, 123-4, 129
roads 13, 16n, 60; see also highway
Rome 1, 9, 62
rotunda 111, 113, 117
Rufinianai 59

S

Sangarios 36, 62, 76, 79-80
sappers 47
Sardis 62
Schneider, A.M. 103-4
school 70, 107
seals 24
Seleucia 10
Seljuks 41, 77-8, 93, 95, 204
Sennacherim, Michael 69-70, 76
Serenianus 11
Sinope 42
skeletons 71
Skoutariotes 70, 107, 158

slaves 193
Smyrna 59, 61, 67, 91, 199
Socrates 139
Solomon 145
spring 115
Strabo 1, 89
Strategopoulos 76
Suleyman 35-7, 41-2, 204
Sultan 41-2, 45-8
supply 159
Svetoslav 78
Synnada 29
synod, permanent 68
synods 61-3
synthronon 102

T

Tatikios 42
taxes 25, 35
temple 2, 23
Terter 78
tetrapylon 10
theatre 1-2, 18, 38, 71-2, 85, 91, 145, 159, 198
Themistius 126
Theodore, bishop 30
Theodore, patriarch 63
Theodore I Laskaris 57-63, 67, 93-4, 98, 109
Theodore II Laskaris 6, 69-71, 75-6, 104-5, 107, 118-20, 123, 127-30, 133-53, 155-63, 201-2
Theodore Angelos 161
Theodore Eirenikos 62, 67
Theodore *graptos* 25
Theodore of Studios 25, 115
Theodore of Sykeon 15
Theodosios III 17
Theodosios, son of Maurice 15
Theodote, St. 6, 115
Theognis 8
Theoleptos of Philadelphia 78, 83

Theophanes 114
Theophanes, bishop 79
Theophanes *graptos*, bishop 25
Theophilos 25
Theophilos, St. 18
tombs 14, 23, 100-1
tombstones 2, 14, 44, 71
Tornikios, Demetrios 109
Tower of Babel 94
tower of Gonatas 48, 92
towers 46-8, 60, 89-96, 133, 137, 145, 175, 199
Trajan 2, 22-3, 32, 169, 197-8
treasury 10
treaty 61
trebuchet 95
Trikokkia 76
Tryphon, St. 6, 82-3, 104-6, 115, 183, 200-1
Turks 34-7, 41-3, 45-9, 51-2, 54, 61, 77-81, 83-5, 93, 95, 98, 101, 115, 160

U-V
Ulu Cami 102
Union of churches 78
Valens 11-2, 114
Valentinian 11-2, 117
Valerian 5
Vatatzes: see John III
Vespasian 1-2, 89
vines, vineyards 33-4, 77, 147, 173

W
walls 5, 18, 26, 31, 33, 35, 43, 45-9, 53-5, 58, 80, 84, 89-96, 133, 137, 145, 147, 159, 198
water 147

weaving 193
William of Tyre 53, 127
Willibald 18, 112-3

X-Z
xenodocheion 30, 118
Xerigordos 45, 49n
Xiphilinos, Theodore 77
Zeno 13

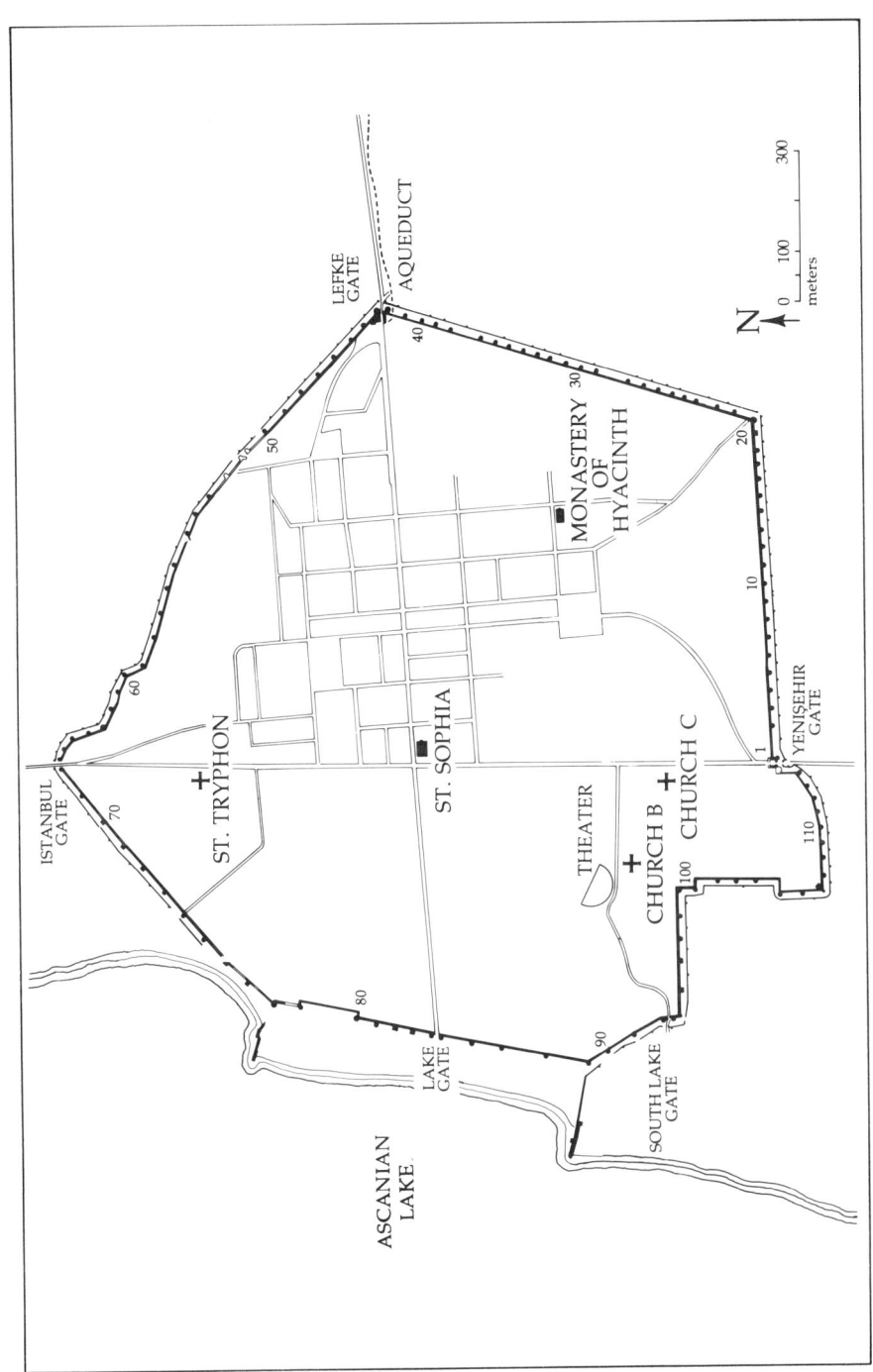

Fig. 1: Plan of Nicaea, showing Byzantine walls and churches.

Fig. 2 (above). Wall and tower 108, of the third century, with added balustrade of Leo III on wall.

Fig. 3 (left). New facing of reused material added to tower 71 by Leo III.

Fig. 4. Inscription of Leo III and Artavasdus on tower 71.

Fig. 5. Tower 9, added to the southeast wall by Michael III.

Fig. 6 above. Tower 97 of Michael III (note original crenellations preserved when the tower was raised in the thirteenth century) and adjacent wall with elaborate Lascarid brickwork.

Fig. 7 left. Corner bastion 106B added to corner of south wall by Alexius Comnenus.

Fig. 8 left. Seljuk tombstone reused in bastion of Alexius I.

Fig. 9 below. Tower 37, with recessed brick of the eleventh century.

Fig. 10. Decorative brickwork of Manuel Comnenus on wall facing the lake.

Fig. 11. Tall SE tower 20 of Theodore Lascaris.

Fig. 12. Tower of outer wall built by John Vatatzes adjacent to the south (Yenisehir) gate of the city.

Fig. 13. Outer wall of Vatatzes; tower 7 of inner wall in background.

Fig. 14. Tower 88, probably built by Andronicus II in 1290.

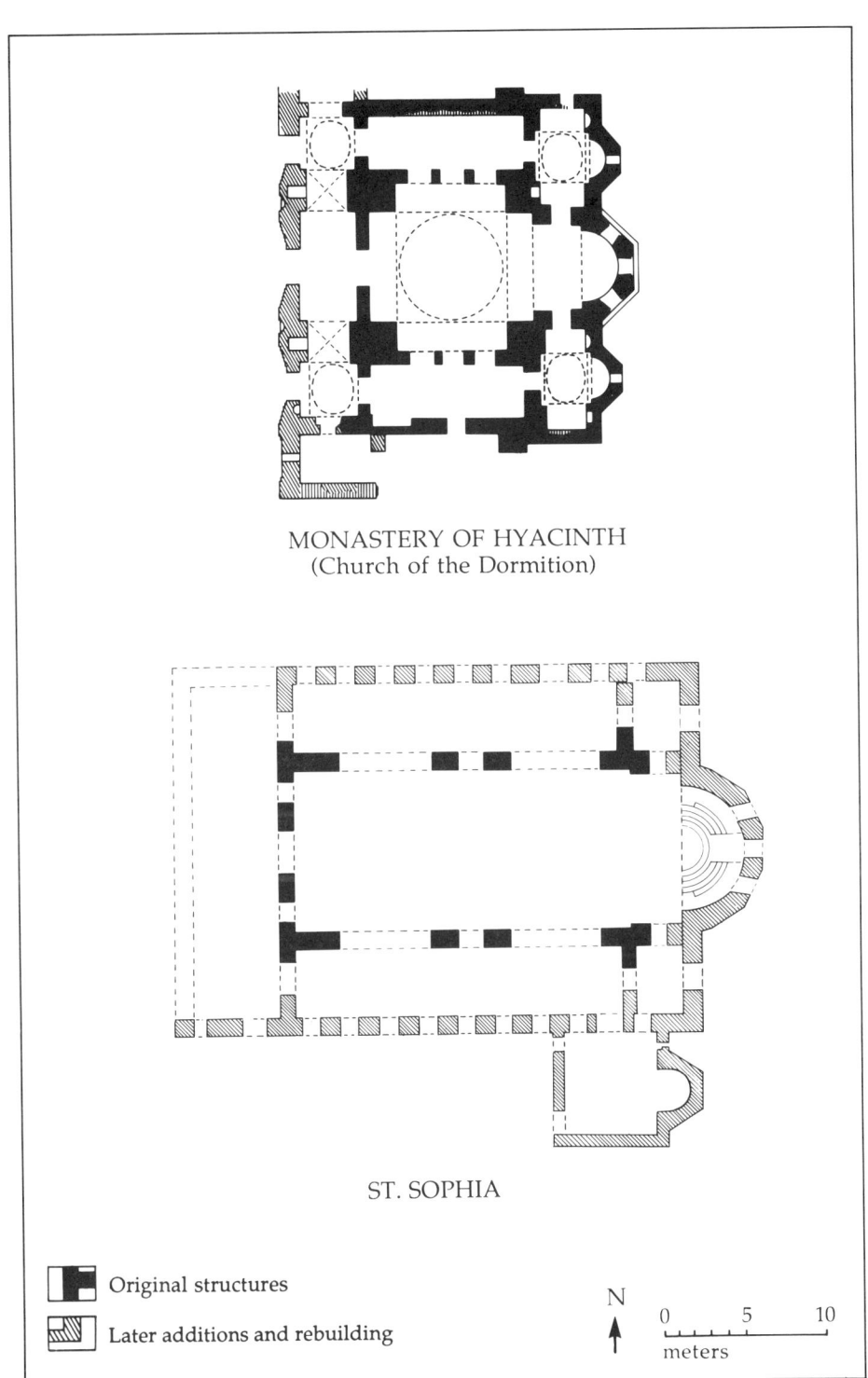

Fig. 15. Plan of surviving churches of Nicaea.

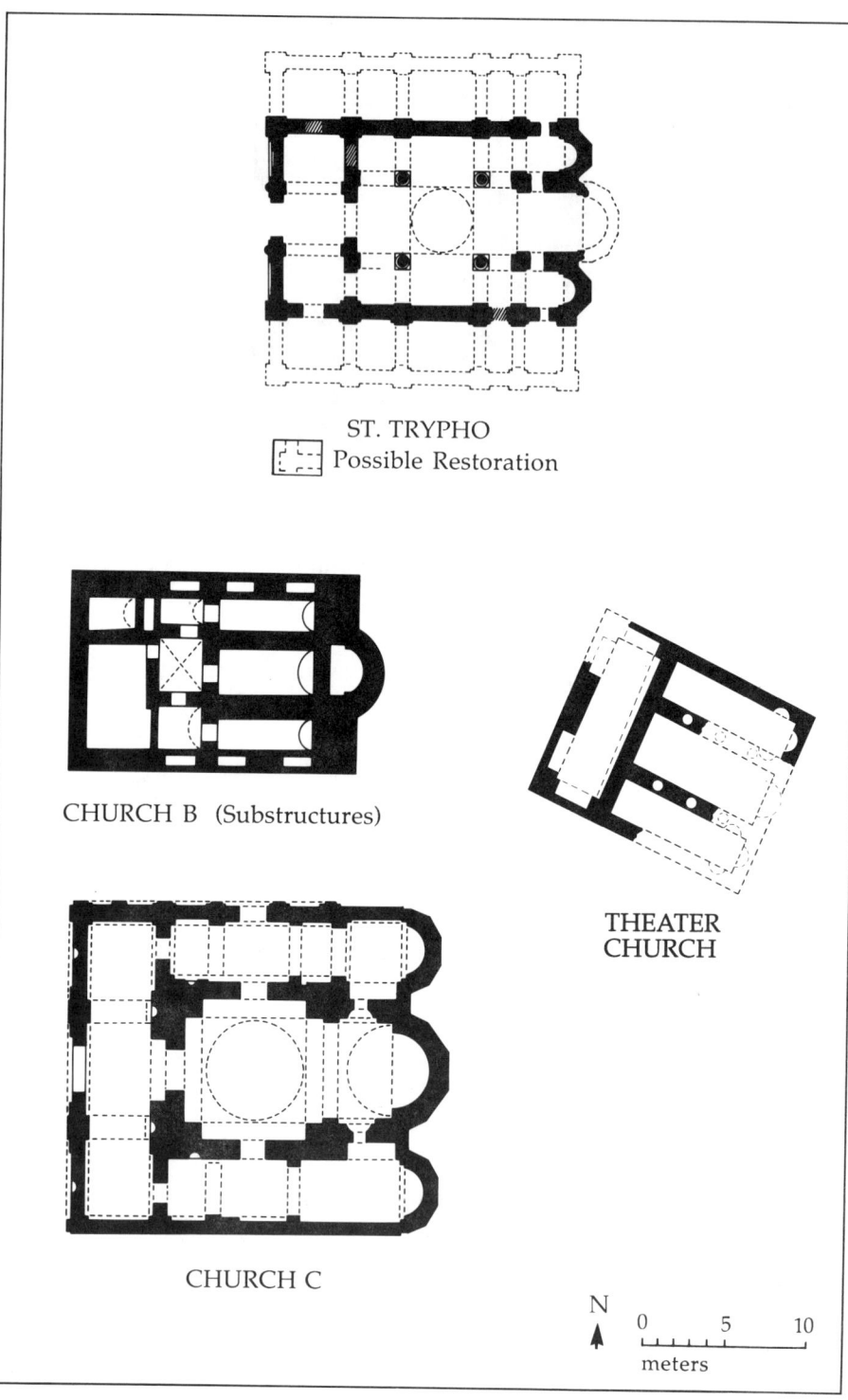

Fig. 16. Plan of surviving churches of Nicaea.

Fig. 17. Marble plaque of Hyacinth, founder of the monastery.

Fig. 18. Monastery of Hyacinth (Church of the Dormition) from the southeast, in 1912. Photo from A. Kingsley Porter collection Harvard University.

Fig. 19. Porch of the monastery of Hyacinth, work of the late eleventh century, as visible in 1912. Photo from A. Kingsley Porter collection, Harvard.

Fig. 20. Interior of monastery of Hyacinth, in 1912. Photo from A. Kingsley Porter collection, Harvard.

Fig. 21. Ambo, fifth or sixth century.

Fig. 22. Middle Byzantine capital, imitating a late antique type.

Fig. 23. Carved marble plaque, sixth century.

Fig. 24. Carved marble plaque, eighth-ninth century.